COMPROMISE
AND
POLITICAL ACTION

*Political Morality in Liberal and
Democratic Life*

J. PATRICK DOBEL

Rowman & Littlefield Publishers, Inc.

ROWMAN & LITTLEFIELD PUBLISHERS, INC.

Published in the United States of America
by Rowman & Littlefield Publishers, Inc.
8705 Bollman Place, Savage, MD 20763

Library of Congress Cataloging-in-Publication Data

Dobel, J. Patrick.
Compromise and political action : political morality
in liberal and democratic life / J. Patrick Dobel.
p.   cm.
Bibliography: p.
Includes index.
1. Political ethics.   2. Compromise (Ethics).   I. Title.
JA79.D56   1989   172—dc19   88–25953 CIP

ISBN 0–8476–7604–8

Printed in the United States of America

For Lea

"The limits of the possible in moral matters are less narrow than we think."

Jean-Jacques Rousseau

ACKNOWLEDGMENTS

This book was drafted while on a National Endowment of the Humanities Fellowship for College Teachers. I would like to thank the Endowment for the freedom to reflect and to create this work. It is a noble endeavor for one's country to give harried college teachers the chance to recover their intellectual wind.

The book began as a chapter in a study of justification in government. But the topic of compromise seemed to entangle every other justification and it gradually grew into a book of its own accord. While growing it received nurturance from many sources, and it is one of my pleasures to thank those who helped me in the project. Writing this book has once again reminded me that dialogue is the lifeblood of our quest for clear and plausible defenses of moral practice.

So with great pleasure and gratitude, I thank my friends and colleagues for their help. Joe Carens, Jane Mansbridge, John Chamberlin, John Nelson, David Reznick, and Walt Williams read various chapters and helped greatly with their comments. Don Herzog and Don Anderson read a very early draft and gave me immensely helpful comments which saved the manuscript from several dead-ends. I owe a special debt of thanks to Richard Dagger and Stephen L. Newman. They both read the manuscript in its entirety and gave me excellent criticism and help in recasting the final form. They exemplified for me what we all so often seek and seldom find, a true critic. They meticulously read the manuscript with sympathy and acuity. The book owes much of its final coherence to their help.

I would also like to thank Hubert Locke, John Tryneski and John Ackerman for their support and encouragement along the way. I would like to thank New York University Press for their kind permission to use sections of my article "The Ends of Ethics—The Beginnings of Politics" which appeared in *Nomos XXVIII. Justification*. The book owes much to Mary D. Simmons for her editing.

v

While writing the book, I have enjoyed the companionship and love of my wife and best friend, Lea Vaughn. The book is dedicated to her, and I thank her for first teaching me that compromise and integrity can complement each other. Our daughter Hilary arrived while the book was being completed, and I thank her for always giving me perspective when I needed it.

Contents

Introduction 1

1. Moral Claims in Political Life 7

2. Justifying Political Action 35

3. The Nature of Political Compromise 59

4. Principled Compromise 79

5. The Fundamental Political Code 101

6. Prudence, Politics, and Compromise 119

7. The Trouble with Compromise 139

8. A Good Compromise is Hard to Find 163

   Epilogue 191

   Bibliography 195

   Index 205

Introduction

*"You are permitted in time of great danger
to walk
with the devil until you have crossed
the bridge."—Proverb*

No one likes to compromise, but everyone does. People associate firmness of principle with integrity and weakness with compromise. Individuals are discovered in "compromising positions," manufacturers "compromise quality," or a person "compromises himself." At the same time, people are urged to tolerate others and try to recognize the other side's point of view. Democratic politics and associations are built upon negotiation, respect for diversity, bargaining and elections. Compromise is an awkward stepchild of morality, and even dictionaries reflect its moral ambiguity. Most first definitions suggest that compromise involves "mutual concessions," "negotiations," or "arbitration." But the second tier of definitions invariably points out that a compromise often concedes something "prejudicial" or "shameful."[1]

American history reeks with ambiguity about compromise. The national founding was made possible by a series of constitutional compromises over states' rights, slavery, and congressional power. Most constitutional liberties depend upon practices of tolerance and learning to "live with," "tolerate," "deal with," and even compromise with those with whom one strongly disagrees. During the first fifty years, great compromises, like the "Missouri Compromise," kept the country together. Ultimately, however, Americans tore themselves apart in the bloodiest war of the nineteenth century when the founding

1

compromise on slavery failed. On the other hand, almost every major political change arose from strident crusades that swept the landscape like prairie fires. Each cause boasted its own uncompromising prophets and crusaders. Moral crusaders for causes ranging from civil rights to temperance were often the only way to challenge ossified institutions and hardened or comfortable consciences, and they clamored into political life with strident calls for action and unbending hostility to compromise.

Today moral rhetoric and stridency engulf ever larger segments of political life. Politicians usually scramble for the high ground, and claiming moral righteousness remains a time-honored tactic. Viable political systems can absorb considerable amounts of moralized rhetoric and some deep moral disagreements as long as an abiding consensus exists about the framework within which these claims should be addressed and each side understands that they address fellow citizens, not "enemies," to be ostracized from the political community. But today extremism, especially on the right, is increasingly effective and well financed. When most issues are recklessly moralized and rhetoric viciously deprecates opponents, the civil resources to resolve issues peacefully, while respecting basic liberties, are threatened. Each moralized claim engenders a counterclaim from the other side and creates a dynamic of stridency with little room for civil and free accommodation of legitimacy, truth, and diversity.

Coalitions, best illustrated by the Leninist appellation "Moral Majority," make compromise a point of sin, dishonor, or betrayal. The list of moralized issues goes on, but the radical and vicious politics of abortion, gun control, homosexual rights or school prayer all reflect the same pattern. Each side demands complete victory and refuses to address the other side's concerns with any good faith; most groups would not mind the other side's banishment. At the same time, this increasing polarization coexists with a remarkable degree of apathy and nonparticipation inspired by lackluster politicians compromised by special interests and power. The center is being torn asunder and extremism is rewarded. The extremist rhetoric equates morality with absolute and unwavering commitment to concrete positions and sees only one outcome as consistent with principles or ideals. It assaults the integrity and freedom of others who differ with the ordained position—opposition is reduced to immorality or treason when moral majorities spawn immoral minorities. Yet a humane, democratic, and liberal politics depends upon compromise as the practice whereby the claims of free individuals in a complex and obstinate world can be reconciled with some respect, good faith, and a minimum of violence.

Even crusaders must compromise to give concrete content to their moral ideals and maintain their power base. Too often, morally inspired leaders deceive themselves as to the nature of their political morality while not acknowledging the integrity of others or of the rule of law. Crusaders and moral polarization make a dangerous combination when zealots take over the symbolic, financial, and coercive power of government. They answer to causes "higher than the written law." Stances of moral absolutism, which might have some validity outside of government, can wreak havoc on mutual respect, misunderstand the role of civility and minimizing coercion in politics, and ignore the need to engender consensual loyalty to political institutions. Self-righteous denouncers of moral compromise can too easily subvert law, due process, and legitimate politics in the name of "higher causes." Zealots seldom understand their own self-deceiving claims that they are somehow "above politics" even as they assiduously compromise.

This type of politics makes it necessary to apprehend and defend the proper role and limits of compromise in politics because it rests at the heart of action in a democratic and humane politics. Every so often liberal and democratic theorists must rediscover compromise to address resurgent sectarianism or quiet conformity (Morley 1893; Smith 1956; Crick 1972). John Morley cursed both absolutists and cynical conformists when he essayed to explain the role of compromise (Morley 1893, pp. 4, 23, 56 passim). In contemporary society, immense moral squalor in high places coexists with Morley's "disciples of the absolute." These zealots pose a far more serious problem today than does conformity, as they seek to take the "politics out of politics," as Thomas Corcoran lamented, and compromise needs to be defended against them. Compromise especially needs to be defended against their claim that morally inspired politics rejects compromise.

Responsible political actors are always compromising in liberal and democratic life. This essay, written from their perspective and not from some external or transcendent set of claims about the nature of moral goodness or right, is about how individuals should hold moral beliefs in political life. The essay seeks to avoid both the overheated moralism of the new right or left and the antimoralism which pervades *realpolitik* and some more conservative theories. I seek to explain, justify, and defend the central moral practice of democratic politics— compromise—and demonstrate how it is both compatible with the personal integrity of political actors and central to the success of liberal and democratic political life.

This essay, then, examines the nature of political morality and the role of compromise in the life of a liberal and democratic society, but it is not meant as a how-to book. Rather, it seeks to map the nature of moral-political justification by free and responsible individuals through charting the nature of political compromise and defending compromise as the central moral practice of a humane and free politics.

Chapter 1 explains what I mean by political compromise and shows how it illustrates the tensions of making moral claims in political life. It distinguishes different ways in which moral claims can enter politics and the consequences of each particular style of political morality. Chapter 2 explores the nature of personal integrity and how it is central to the notion of making compromises in public life. It shows how integrity and the search for good reasons to direct action should be grounded in the peculiar nature of justification in politics. Chapter 3 distinguishes political compromises from simple exchange relations, game theoretic calculations, and utilitarian ethical justifications. It argues that serious political compromises involve morally imperfect or questionable outcomes that exact moral commitments and actions to achieve them.

Chapters 4 through 6 examine the major principled, political, and prudential justifications to compromise in political life. Chapter 4 articulates the principles and ideals, especially equal respect for individuals, that justify compromise. Focusing on the fundamental choice about how to treat opposition in politics, Chapter 5 argues that many of the best justifications for compromise stem from the desire to minimize the role of manipulation and coercion in politics. Chapter 6 examines how prudence supplies the most far-ranging justifications for compromise and extends the penumbra of moral justification to areas such as shaping the concrete action, acquiring power, and effecting durable and minimally abusive solutions. The moral concern people feel about compromising is often justified; thus Chapter 7 examines the many problems of compromise, especially the ways in which the very process of compromise can undermine the political and moral assumptions needed to make a good compromise. Finally, Chapter 8 summarizes the role of compromise in moral and political life and, building upon the positions advanced in the rest of the book, develops a framework of maxims from which to evaluate compromises. These maxims synthesize the principled, political, and prudential concerns while accommodating the limits of compromise.

The essay seeks to establish the political morality of compromise against two tendencies. First, the essay addresses those who unwaveringly subject all political life to strident moral and unidimensional judgments, and second it disagrees with those who would make political life either an amoral or separate moral realm that eludes normal moral claims. On the other hand, most nonauthoritarian politicians are not noted as anguished moralists—they cannot afford to be—and compromise may come too easily. They are experienced in compromise and take pride in their ability to build agreement. But I explore compromises where people agree to accept less than they morally seek or when they participate in methods or outcomes that they find morally wrong or problematic in order to achieve imperfect but warranted goals. Thus, a moral tension lives in the heart of all serious moral compromises, and politicians should be reminded not only of compromise's virtues but also of its vices.

The tension between the aspirations of politicians and citizens and their accomplishments, and the tension between aspirations and the methods and trade-offs necessary to attain them makes compromise a problem worthy of serious study. These tensions can destabilize political relations, undermine promises to abide by solutions, haunt activist citizens, and invite excessive moralization of rhetoric and policy. An understanding and defense of compromise may enable political actors to compromise better.

At a more theoretical level, many studies of morality and politics seek a degree of analytic rigor and clarity that I do not believe politics can sustain. An endeavor such as compromise cannot guarantee neat or tidy results congruent to absolute standards. Reflective attempts to seek disinterested objectivity and impartiality to discover ideals and principles to govern actions toward fellow human beings constitutes one of the most important moral activities individuals can undertake. Such reflective discipline can lead to ideals and principles that challenge prejudices and institutional injustices and direct or motivate in political life. To discover a principle or absolute rule is one thing, but to discover exactly what it requires in a concrete situation is another. Political life is characterized by immense moral and real complexity: the dignity of autonomous persons with different moral beliefs deserves respect; other moral principles might also apply; resource constraints might limit what can be done; opponents might block efforts; and concerns over the level of coercion, or the abusive possibility of policy might blight practical methods of realizing goals. Consequently, any attempts to make sense of the shape of morality in political life must give adequate consideration to the diversity, obstinacy or serendipity of context.

Contextual justifications derive from prudence and politics and shape poltical justifications with considerable power and validity. A good reason often given in politics is, "I got the best I could, given our power." In such a world, principles and ideals perform vital critical and directive functions, but they only begin the political dialogue and orient the journey since one's ability to develop neat and clean rules or principles to govern all situations or determine outcomes is quite limited and often useless. Many compromises end up as bad compromises due to political and prudential concerns. Instead, I suggest a map of *prima facie* justifications that should frame our discussions and justifications. At best, they can provide the initial framework to justify and criticize particular compromises, but they exist as *prima facie* maxims. Good reasons culled from any of the families of political justification can direct individuals to other courses of action. To this end, I acknowledge Aristotle's warning to seek only the precision from a subject matter that it can legitimately yield (Aristotle, *Ethics*, I).

Given the contextual focus of judgments, my essay will utilize historical examples to illustrate the various types of justification. Most of the examples will be short, and many will focus upon the areas of civil rights where the moral stakes are so evident. In some cases, I will present more extended examples to illuminate the variety of moral, political, and prudential judgments. These examples will demonstrate that compromise is a most imperfect instrument in a most imperfect world. Compromise retains its edge of moral ambiguity because it culminates in morally incomplete or problematic solutions. Historical compromises illustrate this as much as they illustrate the power of justifications being used. The allusive quality of the examples points beyond themselves and will not provide neat analytic closure to my discussions. This goes with the territory, for compromises emerge from moral and political complexity as well as the obstinacy of reality. They embody controversial and debatable decisions, otherwise they would not be compromises. I hope to map out the grounds to understand and appreciate the role and limits of compromise.

Note

1. Webster's *New Collegiate Dictionary*, 1979, p. 230

1

Moral Claims in Political Life

"I seem to sense a difference between a man's convictions and what he believes to be politically feasible."—Dwight D. Eisenhower

"Our aim is to establish an order of things which will in turn establish a universal bent toward the good; which will bring faction swiftly to the scaffold."—Saint Just

Moralists seldom like politicians and the feeling is mutual. But individuals pursue moral purposes in political life. Today, abortion, environmental protection, the rights of women and minorities, and issues of poverty, among other issues, are fought over with resounding moral cadences. More than one proponent invokes Charles Sumner's undying creed in his fight to end slavery, "Moral principles cannot be compromised."[1] But harried contemporary politicians echo the disdain of Sumner's ally and opponent, William Pitt Fessenden, the Republican leader in the Senate in the fight over the post-Civil War Reconstruction, "My constituents did not send me here to philosophize. They sent me to act" (Les Benedict 1974, 38). The same tension separates Plato's ambiguous claim that philosophers must become kings before justice can rule from Machiavelli's sardonic yet passionate claim: "The gulf between how one should live and how one does live is so wide that a man who neglects what is actually done for what should be done learns the way to self-destruction rather than self-preservation'' (Machiavelli, 1961, Chap. 15).

The ill-fitted worlds of politics and morality, however, are locked together in any ongoing attempt to build and sustain a just and viable political order. Compromise poses a central problem for political life when moral convictions inspire actions. Behind this problem lies the abiding sense that moral convictions about right and wrong possess a powerful and compelling imperative and drive individuals to act upon them. Personal integrity is intimately linked to such convictions, and a person of integrity with moral commitments will be moved to act on them. Individuals will and should balk at actions that violate or fall short of these commitments. Compromises etch this problem with peculiar clarity and force since they involve morally problematic or imperfect agreements. The process of compromising can undermine these commitments. Simple bargains or trade-offs of interests or morally neutral concerns may upset people, but they have no necessary moral significance and do not affect integrity. But the important and interesting political compromises that I wish to study are partially suggested by the etymology of the practice. They involve situations where political actors must co-promise—make a binding commitment, which possesses its own moral and obligatory weight—to abide by a solution they find morally problematic.

I shall use compromise to describe a complex set of political actions, but they all hinge upon the individual political actors having responsibility for the moral dimensions of the means, trade-offs or end results of a political outcome. This responsibility depends upon the notion that the individuals possess sufficient power or interest to make a difference in the political outcome. It might involve active cooperation in forging the agreement or coalitions behind the agreement or just supporting an agreement when it arises. Such responsibility can also involve nondecisions, such as agreeing to stay on the sideline or not actively oppose an outcome when an individual's opposition could have nullified or prevented the agreement. Compromises do not simply involve the end states; they often involve achieving desired ends by agreeing to methods or using methods that individuals find morally wrong or problematic in order to attain a goal. Side trades might be necessary to attain a compromise where individuals give up something of moral worth in one area to attain important results in another. In the most complex dimensions, where compromise moves into collaboration, individuals may find themselves acting to implement policies they see as profoundly morally flawed in order to attain other desirable policies or attain some possible moral good within the flawed policy, or avoid some greater evil.

I am concerned with political compromises that involve both elements of responsibility and moral import. Without the moral significance, compromises become sophisticated calculations of trading off relative advantages, but the compromises that cause the most trouble and are so central to healthy political life are fraught with moral import. Generally as stakes go up in political life, moral concerns such as basic rights become more central. Individual participants see the means, trade-offs, support, and collaboration as having moral significance, because the issues involve moral commitments and assessments based upon those commitments. Many common-sense and even sophisticated understandings of morality set compromise against moral integrity. Compromising morally inspired goals brings on guilt, remorse, and a challenge to act in the future, all of which challenge the moral weight of the "promise" to abide by the agreement. It exposes the agreements and political actors to rhetorical attack by their own supporters as "sell outs."

In one of its greatest accomplishments, liberal democracy enables many individuals to satisfy this moral ambivalence by providing the opportunity to compromise and yet continue to oppose or fight for changes demanded by one's moral vision. It does this by focusing upon the moral and civil importance of respecting the dignity and freedom of other individuals as counterpoints to other moral commitments. Political conflict occurs then through procedures designed to respect rights and allow resolution, but also to provide opportunities to continue debate. But this requires an agreement to accept the rules of conflict resolution. Such rules, themselves, may have significant moral flaws. But the possibilities of compromise hinge upon the role of moral claims in politics.

Political compromises illustrate the tension between moral and political claims. Icons of an individualistic culture, like the sheriff in the movie *High Noon*, generally represent steadfast devotion to a cause and purity of heart in face of adversity; they sternly frown upon compromise. Language abounds with condemnations of "sell-outs." Strident allies or opponents of a compromise express their disquiet and work to destabilize its success. Yet liberal and democratic life depends upon tolerance, negotiation, cooperation, and respect for the freedom and dignity of others. Once individuals are committed to respect autonomy or surrender the tools of domination, compromise should become the central practice of political life.

The story of the radical Republicans, the passage of the bills of Reconstruction, and the antislavery amendments to the United States Constitution illuminate the various ways one can hold moral claims and compromise in politics. The long and bitter battle to end slavery in the United States reached crescendos of moral and prophetic attack with the emergence of a strong abolitionist movement in the Northeast in 1830s and 1840s. The abolitionist rhetoric was strident and utterly uncompromising in its attack upon the institution of slavery. The abolitionists grew increasingly frustrated at the failure of the federal government to move against slavery because Unionists worked a number of compromises to save the union with slavery within it. A number of radical abolitionists exemplified by William Lloyd Garrison argued for the dissolution of the Union. They demanded an end to the "devil's bargain," which tied the northern states to responsibility to sustain and enforce the hated sin of slavery in the southern states (Kraditor 1967).

A number of other abolitionists entered political life and made antislavery rhetoric a constant issue within American politics. Their insistence helped precipitate several crises and compromises such as the Compromise of 1850 (Potter 1976). The Republican party was founded upon the tenet of rhetorical opposition to slavery and its expansion. Within the party the radical Republicans represented passionate opposition to slavery and sought means to use the federal government to undermine slavery where it existed, and not just oppose its expansion into the territories (Foner 1971). This faction remained the most active and persistent in supporting the Civil War and demanding the elimination of slavery during the war's prosecution. By the end of the war, the radical Republicans had significant but not majority representation in the Republican Party in the House and Senate. Due to the radicals' influence, the Republicans were committed in principle to freeing black slaves, guaranteeing their civil and political liberties, and restoring the shattered union by readmitting "reformed" southern states.

The radical Republicans, symbolized best by the intense devotion of their two greatest spokesmen, Thaddeus Stevens, a Congressman from Pennsylvania, and Charles Sumner, Senator from Massachusetts, possessed an ambitious plan to implement these goals. They proposed the enfranchisement of black voters and wanted to guarantee full political and civil liberties by national Constitutional amendments. A Freedmen's Bureau supported by confiscated land and missionary efforts would provide land, money, and education to "create a black yeomanry independent and capable of self-defense and political initiative.'' Since the southern states were now ''conquered provinces'' as a result of the ''grasp-of-war,'' they could be ruled by the federal government and ''reformed.'' The southern states would be allowed back in the union only after they ratified the national amendments and built up a base of integrated local democracy that would replace rule by slave barons. The radical Republicans fought tenaciously for five years, and in the end, prudence and politics lead them to settle for a bare national guarantee of Negro suffrage and a skeletal Freedmen's Bureau. Southern states were precipitously readmitted to the union, old rebels dominated state governments and when the federal government withdrew its troops from the South in 1877, the rights of Negroes would be ultimately curtailed by law and terror.

During the course of this struggle, several major political changes occurred that caused prudence and politics to erode the idealistic goals. When Andrew Johnson became president, he consistently fought most planks of the radical program. He vetoed their bills and undermined Reconstruction's intent with his own pardons and appointments. Popular opinion remained lukewarm to the entire project of Reconstruction, and Democrats increasingly scored gains in off-year elections. Benjamin Wade, a prominent and defeated radical senator from Ohio, said candidly, ''We went in on principle, and got whipped'' (Les Benedict 1974, 273). Tired of the issues of Reconstruction, the electorate wanted the union restored quickly. By 1869 the major impetus for change had been lost and the looming election of the conservative Republican Ulysses S. Grant made it imperative to get any serious changes in place before he took office. At the same time, new issues such as the tariff, hard money, and railroads increasingly dominated elections and further split Republican ranks.

The basic radical response to such shifts in support and power was best summed up by Charles Sumner. ''Ample experience shows that [compromise] . . . is the least practical mode of settling questions involving moral principles. A moral principle cannot be compromised'' (Les Benedict 1974, 58). The radicals provided the consistent rhetorical and emotional impetus behind the efforts to get Reconstruction in place, but left on their own, they would have been doomed to defeat, since they proved unable to get around Johnson's veto or build the coalitions necessary to override it.

A larger group of Republicans shared the same principles but were determined to get concrete and acceptable legislation through the gauntlet and not settle for noble defeat. Others were interested in keeping the party together and not destroying it over the Reconstruction issues. Still a fourth group of Republicans were committed to states's rights and some idea of "voluntary" reconstruction in the south. They distrusted large concentrations of governmental power and detested the military occupation of the south. Only the "grasp-of-war" theory could justify their support of treating the southern states like conquered provinces. As peace came, the grasp-of-war theory looked more like a convenient sham, and their opposition to the radical program increased. Additionally, men like Sumner and Stevens tended to be righteous and rigid, and often seemed motivated by a desire to punish the south as much as to establish the rights of slaves. They demonstrated little success in building coalitions, while the moderates spent immense time building coalitions among the various factions and getting through passable bills.

At times the radicals seemed as dangerous as Johnson and the Democrats with their intransigence and threat to bolt as Senators like Fessenden tried to craft wording that would build the necessary coalitions to make viable gains. In anger, the moderates heaped disdain upon the "impracticals." The bitter enemy of Sumner and the architect of the Republican "successes" in the Senate, William Pitt Fessenden of Maine summarized this approach. "I have been taught since I have been in public life to consider it a matter of proper statesmanship, when we aim at an object which we think is valuable and important, if that object is . . . unattainable, to get as much of it and come as near it as we may be able to do" (Les Benedict 1974, 58, 39).

Time and again, the moderate coalition trimmed their demands to the requirements of Johnson's veto and the fears of the state's rights advocates. By the end, many moderates tragically believed that their dual commitment to federalism and antislavery would mean that southern states could undo all their measures, but they felt powerless because of their conflicting principles and constitutionalism. Time and time again, most of the radicals acquiesced as they became increasingly isolated from the population and party but desperately sought some legislative or constitutional protection. Sometimes they won significant victories only to be frustrated by Johnson's vetoes.

At such moments, principles may stand alone, uncompromising and independent, or adapt politically and prudentially. Neither position is without its costs. Thaddeus Stevens, the relentless abolitionist congressman from Pennsylvania, distilled his anguish when he defended the Great Reconstruction Bill of 1866, which was later vetoed. "This proposition is not all the committee desired. It falls far short of my wishes . . . I believe it is all that can be obtained in the present state of public opinion . . . I shall not be driven by clamor or denunciation to throw away a great good because it is not perfect. I will take all I can get in the cause of humanity and leave it to be perfected by better men in better times" (Les Benedict 1974, 182).

With the election of Grant looming and their political power waning, the radicals supported a drastically weakened Fifteenth Amendment. At this bittersweet moment and knowing this was its last chance, Henry Wilson sadly remarked, "I have acted upon the idea that one step taken in the right direction made the next step easier to be taken." Perhaps sensing that the next step would take ninety painful and unjust years, he concluded, "I suppose, sir, I must act upon that idea now; and I do so with more sincere regret than ever and with some degree of mortification" (Les Benedict 1974, 335).

The compromises made by the radicals were bitter, timely and informed by intense efforts to gain every alternative possible. They bowed to the realities of power and timing that they tried to change and could not. Their vision was only enacted in part, and by 1877 most of their dreams had been smashed. But in the 1960s, as Wilson and Stevens hoped, their amendments and legislation, so bitterly compromised, became the legal and constitutional prongs of the last great attack upon American oppression of Negroes.

Few issues illustrate the central importance of moral claims in political life more than slavery. Yet within the debate, many different notions of political morality and compromise surfaced. Many individuals argued that the debate should occur only within the bounds of the Constitution and supported acceptance of slavery extant while preserving the union. Others preferred to keep the moral dimensions of slavery out of politics entirely. Stephen A. Douglas's famous disclaimer, "don't care," when asked about the adoption of slavery in California was designed to show his disdain for excessive moralism in politics and reject its disruptive potential. Douglas argued that "popular sovereignty," another foundation of the American political system, was compatible with local communities' enforcement of slavery. The abolitionists reached outside the normal American political lexicon to transform the terms of the debate with their insistence upon abolitionism and Negro social and political equality; ultimately many abolitionists abandoned politics altogether for prophecy.

The compromises on Reconstruction illustrated three different ways of carrying moral claims in politics. The traditional conservatives finesse the problem by trying to banish absolute moral imperatives and rhetoric from political life. This makes compromise the norm and rests most justification firmly within the well-understood byways of the existing political culture. On the other hand, prophets and agitators challenge this narrowed conception of politics and justification. By rejecting compromise and "politics as usual," they work to transform the culture of justification and make moral protest central to politics. A last group like Fessenden and Lincoln see political morality as driven by principles but informed by vital considerations of prudence and politics. This makes compromise a hard but necessary practice central to a principled politics.

Compromise obviously appeals to traditional conservatives. Reactionaries, on the other hand, are obsessed with lost visions of a golden age, which they struggle to restore. Their strident opposition to further decline, and their relentless drive to restore the lost age matches the uncompromising militancy of radicals of any stripe. But a genuine conservative embraces the power of Burke's claims: "All government, indeed every human benefit and enjoyment, every virtue, and every prudent act, is founded on compromise and barter" (Burke 1970, Chap. 6). Michael Oakeshott, in his classic modern formulation, sees a conservative as centered by "a propensity to use and to enjoy what is available rather than to wish for or look for something else; to delight in what is present rather than what was or what may be" (Oakeshott 1981, 169–96). This leads persons to distrust the "unknown" and to be acutely sensitive to the customs, practices, and tradition of cultures. These encumbered norms represent accumulated experience and adaptations to social and political problems. Flexible, local, adaptive and unreflective, practices and customs possess great power because people believe them and accept them. All authority remains an exceptional accomplishment and should not be squandered heedlessly. The need for coercion and great central power is mitigated because customs are internalized. The density and localism of practices protect human freedom and diversity because they enable people to handle their affairs without heavy-handed commands enforced by coercion.[2]

Conservatism distrusts all overt coercion, especially coercion unbound by rules and expectations. This stand leads conservatives to defend compromise when individuals must eschew gains through violent imposition of their will. Political compromise accounts for fear of excessive violence, the complexity of a situation, and already existing beliefs and institutions as well as resource limits and the limits of human nature and obedience. Alexander Bickel points out that any time violence flares from a minority, it all but nullifies significant action in a liberal state. This violence signals the limits of acceptable state coercion and threatens all the state's other accomplishments. Conservatives generally stop concerted state action at this point (Bickel 1975, 100–14). In this world, political action, especially governmental action, needs to be circumscribed. Politics should resemble a "conversation" among members of a community who share understandings, practices, and civility.[3]

This political morality arose from Burke's own awe at and fear of the violence and revolution that he believed were spawned by the moralized claims on behalf of humanity, which the French revolutionaries made. These universal claims were addressed to no one in particular and carried no emotional or historical content or grounding. When the revolutionaries gained power, their contentless morality was subverted by the passions of the moment and the requirements of keeping power—a dictatorship was the predictable result of an overly moralized authority.

Burkean politics postulates an all-pervasive enemy—"rationalism." Oakeshott sees rationalism as based upon the attempt of individuals, usually democrats or "self-made men," to impose an order upon the world regardless of consequences. "The morality of the Rationalist is the morality of the self-conscious pursuit of moral ideals" (Oakeshott 1981, 35). Rationalists discover principles from which they judge all institutions and empower most citizens with moral judgments because principles and precepts democratize morality. These rationalists seek to wipe clean tradition and custom and create a new world from scratch. Textbooks and cookbooks of morality and politics replace training and experience. This rote moralism can unleash "armies of conscience" who practice a politics of "moral attack" that polarizes the system and delegitimizes all law and authority. Some historians see the polarizing dialectic of moral claims between the abolitionists in the north and the fire-eaters in the south as central to whipping up a war hysteria that made avoiding the Civil War all but impossible (Randall 1945). Civility and common understandings are undercut and violence becomes the only serious motive for obeying the law. Moral simplifiers seduce the population and countries seek moral and rational perfection by the most imperfect of means—politics (Bickel 1975, 11–25, 89–143; Oakeshott 1981, 1–36, 111–36).

Conservatism seeks to defuse strident moralism in politics. Prudence and compromise should dominate participation in the conversation of politics. Conservatives believe, rightly, that "we cannot survive a politics of moral attack." Political relations and agreements should be informed by process, tolerance, adjustment, and respect. People should "fix our eye on that middle distance where values are provisionally held, are tested and evolve within the legal order—derived from the morality of process, which is the morality of consent . . . The computing principles Burke urged upon us can lead us then to an imperfect justice, for there is no other kind" (Bickel 1975, 123–42). Politicians need to be disciplined and trained "to rein in one's own beliefs, to acknowledge the current shape of things, to feel the balance of things in one's hand, to tolerate what is abominable, to distinguish between crime and sin" (Oakeshott 1981, 195).

The traditional conservative conception of politics is certainly right in its plea that viable and peaceful politics should connect its moral claims to the customs and practices of people. But despite its truth, eloquence, and power, this conception of politics and compromise has profound flaws. As Burke remarked, "Custom reconciles us to everything," including suffering and injustice (Burke 1900, 250). Customs and traditions can easily hide injustice and suffering by the very terms with which they legitimize it. The whole approach demonstrates too casual a tolerance of injustice. It assumes people and their common language acknowledge injustices exist. Yet too often, the dominant terms of a culture deny the urgency of sufferers' pain, while the elite have no serious intercourse with the oppressed. The whole approach discourages serious efforts to rectify fundamental injustice. Active and consistent efforts to lead and reform are easily subverted. In the name of "moderation" and respect for the practices of the south, Dwight Eisenhower consistently refused to command the full power of the federal government in support of civil rights. This both undermined *Brown v. Board of Education* and emboldened extreme segregationists in their intransigent response (Ambrose 1984, Chaps. 8,14,17,18). His passive and careful response permitted southern segregationists to obstruct and outwit federal litigation and undermined federal court victories.

Harry McPherson, an aide to Senator Lyndon Johnson, chronicled his own anguish as he tried to come to terms with his southern heritage and the *Brown* decision. He brandished William Fulbright's brief to convince friends. The brief insisted that when we violate "ancient social convictions" or "principles deeply imbedded within them by inheritance, tradition or environment," we can expect violent resistance. Yet a friend of McPherson's cut through the obfuscation and brought McPherson up short. "Hell, I didn't think anybody was trying to destroy the Republic. I just thought some colored kids were trying to go to a white school down there" (McPherson 1972, 149–50).[4]

This insistence upon slow incrementalism and deference to established practices practically disbars the government from serious efforts to rectify the structural disadvantages of class or cultural discrimination. Since enduring customs justify themselves on their own terms, the political culture can cancel the most serious criticism of unjust or oppressive practices. Most societies develop elaborate fictions to justify the status of the oppressed. Often those in the lowest levels of society internalize a self-image of sanctioned inferiority. Consequently, this notion of politics simply reinforces present class distributions of power. It corrodes any efforts to use government as a tool to democratize power and permits local pockets of oppression to flourish.

Even more problematically, traditional conservatism desiccates politics as an activity and denies effective activity to citizens suffering from injustice and oppression. The unwashed and untutored are discouraged from using politics as a method to air their grievances and rectify their situation. By denying people moral voice and passion, the conservative conception presents a stark choice between a halting and unresponsive politics or rebellion. Ironically, this approach weakens the very concept it wishes to defend—compromise. Compromise defended solely in these terms possesses no independent moral power to respond to the angry pain and moral claims of citizens. Counseling patience before suffering and injustice only undermines the credibility of the political order.

The conversation metaphor demonstrates the same flaws. Many individuals are not included in political conversation. Some are denied the tools to articulate their positions well; others are denied the basic tools to be heard. Often the very terms of a debate disparage groups trying to be heard. A woman seeking to make a political point can be dismissed as a "girl"; a black demanding voice has no standing as a "boy" or "nigger." McPherson deplored the end of the easy intimacy among whites and blacks in much of the south when everyone knew their place. "But the relationship did not admit of maturity on the part of the Negroes, or of their standing to insist upon their rights . . . Such an association would have been intolerable to me if I had been a black man" (McPherson 1972, 152).

In such a conversation, people must raise their voices, sometimes yell, even scream. Advocates of civility might have to be grabbed and shaken to get their attention. People must struggle not only to be heard but to change the terms of discourse so that they can be considered citizens. Moral claims, sometimes loud and angry, make politics responsive. Crusaders, agitators, and uppity people who will not shut up and be genteel inject the political process with possibilities. Great pain or repressed silence clamors for politics to come alive. A robust political life must be able to encounter these demands and accommodate a multitude of voices, whether couth or not.

Such moral claims do not reduce to a rationalist demand to reorder all society. Moral claims can be made and principles demanded without sterile rationalism. Other moral principles can be acknowledged and people can ask that moral claims "make sense" by connecting them with common moral understandings. Morally inspired claims can be suffused with prudence without being reduced to moral absolutism. Some moral claims can even introduce new terms into the common vocabulary and transform the practices of justification in a society.

The conservatives make a straw man of moral claims and rule out the kind of claims that successful reform movements often must make. Principled claims can expand the moral agenda, reinterpret moral experience, and question clusters of practices hoary with injustice and inequity. Oakeshott's aristocratic nostalgia would be far more credible if it ever evinced any sense that the injustice of suffering, inequality, or exclusion debilitated his conversation in ways that vitiate the entire power of his metaphor. Similarly, Oakeshott might persuade if he demonstrated any sense that power, vigilance, and harsh and consistent action will sometimes be necessary to engage certain forms of perduring injustice that discredit or destabilize a political order. A preference for reform over rebellion requires a muscular government and a politics capable of assimilating loud and moral claims. The "legitimist reformer" must be able to demonstrate the moral viability of the political order and the moral and realistic superiority of compromise to angry and committed citizens (McPherson 1972, 443–49). A conservative may thrive on the enjoyment of what is, but that presumes that persons possess something to enjoy or have a sense of self that enables them to enjoy what is.[5]

"Prophets are a scandal in democracies. They are not 'representative.' They cannot be controlled . . . They create their audience, and compel it. They do not follow or submit to it. They make a claim because it is right, not because it is wanted . . . normally it is not wanted" (Wills 1980, 165–66). Prophets, saints, agitators, and martyrs bear witness to a politics without compromise. Antithetical but ultimately not incompatible with a conserving political order, this style rhetorically moralizes politics with a vengeance.

Politics without compromise usually flows from the discovery of an overriding moral imperative or goal. This imperative then dictates specific and univocal outcomes. For the radical abolitionists it was that the equality of all humans or fellowship before God demand that slavery be immediately ended and that Negroes be given the vote and full legal rights. These witness-bearers to moral truth refuse to modify their commitments to fit the diverse audiences of political life. They take symbols or traditions and reinterpret them. By force of example and power, new symbols can erupt into a political order. Their actions and words can simultaneously challenge one order and create a new one from within.

Such prophetic and uncompromising moralism repudiates politics, even as it seeks to transform it. Conscience-bound actions serve as an example and call others to a way of life that defies the incessant demand for compromises (Dobel 1977). Saints bring this message through personal action and witness-bearing communities such as those of Mother Theresa or Francis of Assisi. The power of example and purity of commitment inspires others to take their views seriously and reform their personal lives. Public action and even suffering demonstrate the power of the cause.

Prophets and agitators openly call a people to reform. They discomfort quiet consciences and jolt people to attention. People are reminded of the moral substratum of life and of hidden injustices they would rather forget or deny responsibility for. When political leaders isolate themselves from the pain and leadership of oppressed groups, witness-bearers force them to take notice by taking to the streets. The freedom riders and marchers forced the cautious Kennedy brothers to take civil rights demands seriously. Sojourner Truth and Frederick Douglass bore witness to the reality of slavery in the north when most people wanted only to deny its reality and injustice.

Prophets call for active reform of personal lives, but their calls can spill over into political and social life, especially if they address leaders as the Old Testament prophets did. Once great sins or wrongs have been identified, personal actions against them lead quite naturally to political efforts to end them. The zeal and courage of prophets and agitators can both scare and inspire. Nonetheless, prophets can change political agendas and force issues onto the society, especially when people want to ignore the issue and rely upon civility and cooption to mitigate serious moral demands. The dialectic of liberal and democratic politics, and prophetic and agitational politics, can prove extremely fruitful for society. Great wrongs and harms can be identified and brought onto the agenda where political actors can build the consensus and actions necessary to forge durable and successful efforts to address them. Every major extension of civil, political, and social rights has involved zealous prophets and "direct action."[6]

Because they change the boundaries of society and force the confrontation of issues, prophets and agitators often suffer persecution, sometimes even martyrdom. Neither Thomas More nor Martin Luther King sought to become martyrs. But they reached points beyond which they could not tolerate the pervasive compromises necessary to keep a political order working. Martyrs' deaths present unanswerable arguments for the power of principles and the failure of the political order to encompass them. These deaths challenge the ethical foundations of the existing political orders. Dying for a cause torments citizens with the question of whether or not the system has broken down because of the failure of an individual or the failure of a system. Martyrs haunt the conscience of a political order like Shakespearean ghosts. Political change does not come easily; it begins with "individual risk and heroism" (Wills 1980, Chap. 14).

Prophets may or may not be explicitly political in their aspirations and demands, they usually function best outside official power. But some prophets, their followers, and other passionately principled persons can crusade more directly as agitators. Moral rhetoric and direct action agitate outside government and the normal electoral channels to identify a problem, educate citizens, and keep the issue on the political agenda. These actors see their moralism as an adjunct to successful political action and negotiation. "Action comes from keeping the heat on" (Alinsky 1971, xxiii).

William Lloyd Garrison and the abolitionists constantly assaulted "politics as usual." They demanded an immediate end to slavery and advocated disunion if this failed, even as they knew the immediate hopelessness of the task. These "reveilles to conscience" reminded complacent northerners of their complicity in a proslavery Constitution. The abolitionists refused to water down their visionary demands and courted visibility and persecution much to the consternation of their "moderate" allies who worked inside the system and sought what was "attainable." But the agitators shifted the boundaries of the attainable for those in office. "The abolitionist, while criticizing such compromises, would insist that his own intransigence made favorable compromises possible. He might have stated his position thus: If politics is the art of the possible, agitation is the art of the desirable" (Kraditor 1967, 28, 207). The moderates and those in office often depend upon the energy and outlandishness of the agitators to give them leverage in negotiations. They cast themselves as "reasonable" alternatives to the "crazies." Good politicians know this. Franklin Roosevelt told a reform convention delegation, "Okay, you've convinced me. Now go out and bring pressure on me!" (Alinsky, 1971, xxiii).

Prophecy and politics balance very delicately in liberal and democratic life. Alinsky points out that agitation in a free country requires a "political schizoid." A person must whip up people with vitriolic speech and imaginative tactics for days on end, then sit down with the loathed "enemy" and negotiate hard and carefully. Finally, agitators and leaders must sell their "compromises" to their followers despite the expectations they have raised (Alinsky 1971, 78–79).[7] Any individual can be easily seduced by the "glamor of good ends" that purify consciences and easily justify violence (Shklar 1984, 64–69; Weber 1969). For "Moral certainty is satisfying to the soul" (McPherson 1972, 85–86), and its dynamic can push people beyond prophetic stance and agitation to coercive control of lives. Oliver Wendell Holmes underlines this in a defense of free speech. "Persecution for the expression of opinion seems to me perfectly logical. If you have no doubt of your premises or power and want a certain result with all your heart you naturally express your wishes in law and sweep away all opposition" (Bickel 1975, 76).[8]

Moralized power undisciplined by commitment to liberal democracy, autonomy, or compromises simply destroys basic freedoms and human dignity. When moral zealots gain political power, their unyielding stance and zeal can unleash purifying conflagrations, while their absolutist and univocal style can lead to either tyranny or tragedy. As political leaders, they possess absolute surety of their purity, the rightness of their cause, and the perfidy of their enemies. With little regard for moral or practical complexity, they will unbendingly enforce their will to attain their ends. Autonomy is seen as an opportunity for apostasy rather than a value to be respected. The Ayatollah Khomeini in Iran, Stalin in Russia, or Cromwell in England unite their unbending absolutism to political power and militantly enforce orthodoxy. While ruling, however, they must compromise and lose the very sources of zeal and legitimacy that propelled them to power. Increasingly, force will replace charisma. They end as martyrs or tyrants.[9]

Paradoxically, uncompromising commitment to principle can also breed incompetence. Machiavelli jeers at those who act, untempered by political or prudential sensibilities. "The fact is that a man who wants to act virtuously in every way necessarily comes to grief among so many who are not virtuous" (Machiavelli 1961, Chap. 15); the fate of the disarmed prophet Savonarola haunted all his reflections. Unbending or naive moralism not only comes to naught but betrays its goals by its own ineptitude. When the United States Social Security System was rescued from its near demise in 1983, a bipartisan commission was appointed by President Reagan to work out a rescue proposal. The final negotiations took place among a small group of leading actors. Senator William Armstrong of Colorado, an archconservative opponent of Social Security, muscled himself into the group. But he so alienated the group by his intransigence and leaks to the press that the group spent considerable time working to steer him outside the real negotiations. He had no serious input into the final proposal drafted by the group (Light 1985, Chap. 15).

Most prophets and agitators do not seek to rule, but many moral absolutists seek to gain control of government. The structure of justification for an absolutist remains the same, although the guise may change and is characterized by three major attributes that reject compromise. First, they possess moral certainty about the absolute moral priority of their goals. These might be requirements to follow a law or to achieve an end state. The warrants might come from God, science, or history, but the goals and required behavior possess absolute moral priority over all other considerations. This priority means any "moral" considerations must be assessed solely in terms of their one dimension of evaluation or translated into their moral sources of justifications. No other "moral" considerations deriving from other sources carry any serious weight.

Second, the goals or norms sanctify all methods to achieve them. Any harmful consequences drop out of the moral equation. The inviolate norms or goals demand obedience to their dictates regardless of consequences and exonerate actors of all personal responsibility for actions. Any moral "wrongs" committed or flowing from their actions have no standing in their scheme of justification. Any counterclaims must be justified in their own terms. Third, opponents are morally reclassified as reprobate or inferior in some way. A commitment to respect others' freedom or dignity could undermine the absolutist demands, so the autonomy of opponents must be undermined. This can be accomplished by making opponents malevolent and unredeemable "enemies" or by undermining their moral status by challenging their competence or knowledge. Heretics, victims of false conscious-ness, heathens or enemies of history may then have to be saved, reeducated, or eliminated, depending upon their persistence in oppos-ing the absolutist goals. Variations abound on how to dehumanize opponents, but once this had been done, no compromise with them has any binding moral status. President Ronald Reagan summed up this rejection when he asked of fundamentalist Christians facing com-munists, "How can you compromise with evil" (Ball 1984, 5)?[10]

Once opponents possess lower moral status as enemies or dupes, the absolutist needs give no moral weight to "promises" with enemies or deluded individuals, so compromises or agreements exist as mere tactical stops with no moral power and can be violated when conven-ient or required. Zealots need have no respect for the institutions and procedures built up, even with consent, of a society. Laws and repre-sentative institutions can be subverted for "higher causes," because the consent is based upon ignorance or malevolence. Alexander Berk-man, an anarchist who tried to assassinate Henry Clay Frick, inimita-bly sums up the advantage of such moral superiority. "It is to be a man, a complete MAN. A being who has neither personal interests nor desires above the necessity of the cause; one who has emancipated himself from being merely human, and has risen above that, even to the height of conviction which excludes all doubt, all regret; in short, one who in the very inmost of his soul feels himself a revolutionist first, human second" (Berkman 1970, 8–9).

Zealots can submerge their personality under Max Weber's "ethic of ultimate ends" and find their joy and proof of their integrity in their purity of intention regardless of the consequences (Weber 1969, 119–23). These zealots cannot even compromise to help the success of their project and would prefer martyrdom or noble failure as proof of their purity to victory. Other absolutists might well know the consequences but see compromises as necessary to attain a larger set of ends. In his masterful "Left-wing Communism—An Infantile Disorder," Lenin brutally assaults those purists who want to "attain our goals without stopping at intermediate stations, without any compromises which only postpone the day of victory and prolong the period of slavery" (Lenin 1975, 550–617). Lenin offers one of history's most astute accounts of conditions for a good compromise while seeking broader goals. He focuses upon relative power available, the role of coalitions and the conversion or overthrow of allies and systems once you compromise with them. Lenin's arguments are driven by a relentless absolutism, which describes compromise as a tactical stop. He assigns no moral weight to promises made in compromises, so feels no moral anguish in compromising or violating them. He assigns even less weight to minimizing violence, keeping an open system, or respecting individual's autonomy and participation.

As Thomas Hart Benton ruefully said of John Calhoun, "So it is that extremes meet, that all fanaticism, for or against any dogma, terminates at the same point of intolerance and defiance" (Potter 1976, 44). For many absolutists compromises can actually pose a danger because compromises can create a tradition of negotiation and mutual gain, they can build a community among enemies. Many absolutists would argue that it might be necessary to kill moderates or compromisers to eliminate the possibility of an emerging, coopting middle. It might be important to discourage compromise and cooption and try to provoke a counterterror to undermine the legitimacy of the political order.[11] In the end, the absolutist resorts to the one supreme, incisive argument—bullets.

From the beginning, western civilization has understood political life and authority to involve words, discussion, justification, and free assent. Society struggled to separate free politics from violence and coercion. In the *Iliad,* Patroklos makes the point, "War is the use of arms, words are for council."[12] Aristotle makes explicit these assumptions when he suggests that humans use their unique "faculty of language" to discover among themselves the nature of justice. This justice then becomes the end of the political community, a community that transcends their economic, familial, and clan interests (Aristotle, *The Politics,* I, 2).

When individuals seek to do the right thing in political life, they search for good reasons to direct and justify their actions. Personal integrity assumes that a person can, in fact, be persuaded by reasons and is not driven by internal or external forces for which words are simply rationalizations. Persuasive and plausible reasons need to connect to the reality that political actors are leading and the goals they seek. From this perspective, I think a far more pluralistic understanding of the role of moral claims in politics makes sense. Individuals can and should recur to their own ideals and principles derived from some "moral point of view." Such moral principles perform vital functions in personal and political life. Those principles can connect with the public principles that undergird liberal and democratic life as well as the "regime values" exemplified in the constitutional order, where court decisions and existing laws deserve considerable moral weight (Rohr 1978). Personal moral commitments make the most sense not just when they motivate and direct an individual, but when they ultimately connect to or transform the existing moral and political rhetorical claims of the country.

Political actors should introduce and hold to moral principles and ideals in liberal and democratic political life. At one level, the institutions of society need to have moral foundations to answer the clamor of moral claims brought against them. To the extent the constitutional processes can be defended by their grounding in respect for human dignity, protection of human freedom, and security, these principles should be referred to and direct action. Compromise should be the preferred moral strategy in engaging autonomous humans. At another level, politics is inextricably linked with morals. Issues of security, basic rights, the common good, and welfare all need to be discussed in moral terms. When governments draft individuals, send people to jail, even kill people, confiscate wealth, redistribute and regulate property, claims of ethically neutral self-interest cannot encompass the goods and harms to fellow humans. This becomes especially true when harms transcend evident material interests and affect dignity or subvert autonomy. Likewise, calls to include others in the fellowship of citizenry and extend positive civil rights appeal not simply to interests but to obligations to other persons. Environmental claims on behalf of future generations extend the same realm. Other forms of justification figure prominently in political life, but justifications of obligation, sacrifice for others, and distributional policies are best buttressed by moral terms.

Whether the principles be deontological or consequentialist, their force remains the same once they have been articulated. They spell out what individuals ought and ought not do towards fellow human beings and serve as very special stops in debates and potent final reasons for action (Weldon 1970). An individual's ethical obligations and basic humanity is framed by principles and ideals. They give individuals powerful independent moral reasons to act. Principles introduce a set of discriminations and valuations into lives with their own logic, and direct and motivate persons to act out of duty. Most principles find their reality in moral practices and common-sense rules like "killing is wrong" or "fairness is right." These are internalized and taken as "right as a matter of course" (Phillips and Mounce 1970, 20, 39, 54).

Several characteristics of principles or ideals, which I view as their equivalent, are relevant to this consideration of how they should shape political justification.[13] First, ethical principles generally derive from the "moral point of view." This is a form of disciplined moral reflection where individuals ask how they should treat humans by virtue of their humanness. It seeks to transcend for a moment the welter of immediate communal or emotional ties that can lead persons to habitually judge or exclude humans by virtue of perceived "differences." From a moral point of view, many of these differences and habitual prejudgments are held up to critical scrutiny as based upon standards over which persons have no control or make little consistent sense when individuals apply them nonhypocritically to themselves and other humans they know.[14] This angle of vision militantly drives towards impartiality and universality since all persons must be considered equal. A moral view initially disallows idiosyncratic preference for oneself or friends and requires that individuals extend the same moral considerations to all. It disallows hypocrisy, for if a principle applies to one, it applies to all.

Second, principles are public and freely chosen or accepted. Unreflected beliefs count only insofar as they can be defended in moral terms to other free and rational creatures. Prejudice does not supersede principle. This view reinforces impartiality and universality because all reasonable beings who possess principles should be admitted to the fellowship of obligation. It focuses moral justification in a public arena where reasons can be given, refuted, and discussed. Moral justification is not confined to a small sect possessing privileged information and superior status.

Third, principles are right and moral. This means that they answer only to other principles or the "requirements of other dimensions of morality such as fairness or justice." Rightness gives principles special status in decisions towards others. Principles serve as trumps in these discussions and supersede most other claims of nonmoral interests, idiosyncratic desire, or personal prejudice. To invoke a principle shifts the burden of justification and demands that opponents provide moral reasons of their own or give much better and weightier political or prudential reasons.

Fourth, the principles are also clean in the sense that they are clear and indubitable within their realm. They cut through ambiguity and weigh in with decisive positions and sharp conclusions on rightness or wrongness. Fifth, because principles are right and clean, because they fit a person's world, characterize it and give it coherence, they demand authenticity. They define duty, and if individuals have integrity, they then hold to them with the keenness and tenacity that basic moral commitments demand. For principles and ideals anchor one's moral self and give it substance against the welter of individual and socially created desires that inhabit a person.[15] Finally, principles are imperious. They demand acknowledgment once a person holds them; they motivate an individual to act upon them. Imperiousness suffers little contingency or even complexity within its own logic and answers only to other ethical considerations. The imperative power of principles demands positive fulfillment, even when they require that an individual refrain from action. The logic of imperiousness discounts sacrifice or obstacles and generates urgency to act and impatience with lack of action or progress.[16] Principles might tolerate expediency, but only in the terms of William Lloyd Garrison. Garrison chided Charles C. Burleigh for his unkempt appearance, "Where there is no moral principle involved, it is sometimes wise to sacrifice what is convenient or agreeable to us, that no unnecessary obstacle be thrown in the way of a great or good cause" (Kraditor 1967, 223–24).

Principles and ideals, then, provide strong and independent reasons to act; the strongest principles may warrant immediate and clear actions towards others. This gives principles a decided political role. They obligate people to use them to assess the rightness and wrongness of actions; as such they define terms to constitute the ends of politics. Principles can warrant people to direct government to attain these ends. Paradoxically, the limits of legitimate government action can also be defined by principles that set limits beyond which political power should not be exercised. Not all principles necessarily warrant political action. The principle that individuals should be grateful to those who benefit them, for instance, does not necessarily require that government should mandate that children take care of their parents. But since principles deeply influence how individuals characterize good and harm and how to defend choice, they constantly generate political concern.

Principles resolve into judgments and give critical perspective from which to see, analyze, and judge. As such, they push individuals to a common humanity and shift the burden of proof onto those persons and practices who would degrade or unequally treat fellow humans. "Reflective equilibrium" or the discipline of impartiality and consistency can subvert pieties and muddled intuitions that support prejudice, hypocrisy, apathy, self-serving elitism or rationalized self-interest. Reference to principles and the moral point of view opens background conditions of inequality, covert oppression, and casual exclusion to standards of humanity and equal dignity. The natural tendency of all human communities to stereotype and exclude is subjected to the counterpoint of common humanity and obligations that discipline comfortable exclusionary impulses. All claims of power can be interrogated and required to defend themselves with reference to their effects upon humans. Old orders can be subverted, but also deepened, reaffirmed or reformed; new ones can be directed.

Principled rhetoric and idealistic calls can challenge superior force and discipline power and discourse. The invocation of shared principles can reveal the hypocrisy of governors and citizens and strip the patina of moral legitimacy from rule and obedience. Conscientious or even self-interested rulers might limit themselves to comport more carefully with the sources of their integrity and legitimacy. These claims can galvanize the consciences and actions of other citizens, and change the terms of political discourse and justification.

However, moral principles alone suffer from severe limits in politics. First, as discussed above, the univocal and absolutist style they engender can unleash tyranny or tragedy when conjoined with state power. Second, principles generally do not stipulate the exact shape of concrete actions or outcomes required by them. While a rule like "never lie" stipulates exact behavior in all situations, a principle like "lying is wrong" makes a *prima facie* case against lying, but does not preclude its justification under certain conditions that can address the moral reasons behind the principle. The principle's general form militates against exact specification except in rare circumstances, and leaves open the exact nature of charged value terms like equality, freedom, or respect. Principles function better as justifications that direct or influence a concrete outcome rather than as determiners of an act. This indeterminacy of outcomes means that the exact concrete shape of an outcome must be agreed upon. Even agreement upon the exact solution leaves open the means to be used.

Third, other moral principles might have to be taken into account. Even if people could find higher-order principles that break deadlocks among principles, the autonomy of other persons who resist that action still limits the dictatorial powers of any higher principle. Additionally, the higher order the principles, the more vague they tend to be and the more acute the problem of shape and means becomes.

Fourth, principles gain power by reference to shared understandings of moral practice just as the conservative case suggests. They refer to justice, respect, fairness, freedom, or equality as opposed to terms of aesthetic or scientific justification. Yet these terms prove slippery. When understood they point to established practices and usage. But as moral concepts, they retain an open cutting-edge that yields a critical stance. Individuals reflecting from a practice can generate principles to challenge existing norms by the norm's own terms or discover a new and innovative understanding. The perennial debate over whether justice refers to promulgated laws or to principles that enable us to pronounce a law unjust reflects this problem (Pitkin 1972, Chap. 8). Moral claims must ultimately link to or transform established understandings in order to make sense and persuade citizens.

Finally, principles do not stand by themselves or even in a closed world of mutually referential terms. Their own justification is implicated in other terms of judgment and practice that are relatively open-ended. Most ethical terms possess a complex internal structure of characterization and application. The meaning of the terms may be relatively closed, like bribery, but still depend upon other principles such as "government power should not be used for personal gain," or "government contracts should be awarded on competence, reliability and price." New problems might arise, as when individuals take jobs in industries they have regulated or purchased from. This introduces subtle and new possibilities of bribery. Should this be characterized as bribery and should government then regulate it? People could even disagree over the application of relatively closed principles, like the debate over whether abandoning severely deformed or retarded children constitutes murder. Closure remains conventional and subject to extension or reopening, given the elasticity of language, the unpredictability of reality, and the creativity of humans (Connolly 1983, Chaps. 1,2,5).

Principles and ideals justify action, but they need not dictate it. They should weigh in heavily in political discourse with powerful and independent reasons while performing vital functions. Imperious, they demand authenticity and generate urgency, but persons holding them confront the problems of accomplishment in a public life where power must be massed and used. Principles and ideals should comport with political and prudential justifications that possess great power and validity in their own right.

Notes

1. See Les Benedict (1974), p. 58. I will draw extensively upon Les Benedict's painstaking and powerful study of the failure of radical Reconstruction in Congress in the late 1860s. The book abounds with examples of justifications as the participants were called upon to defend compromises of principle when confronted with political and prudential limits.

2. This summary distills the position offered by Oakeshott (1981) in "Rationalism in Politics," "Rational Conduct," "Political Education," and "On being Conservative." For a less sophisticated but rhetorically effective conservative defense of compromise see Smith (1956). See Hallowell (1944) for a response to Smith, that converges with some of the points I will make.

3. See Oakeshott (1981), "The Voice of Poetry in the Conversation of Mankind." See Rorty (1979, Chap. 7) for an overt extension of the metaphor to political life. The model underlies almost all of Oakeshott's comments about politics. See Beiner (1983) for an overt extension of the model from a democratic point of view. Barber (1984, pp. 178–98) expands the metaphor in a manner compatible with my critique.

4. Alexander Bickel is no simple conservative by Oakeshottian terms and supported *Brown v. Board of Education* and the sending of troops to Little Rock to enforce a court-ordered desegregation decision. The school desegregation decisions settled an issue of principle in a reasonable way and justified serious government intervention (Bickel 1962).

5. Too many modern conservatives succumb to Oakeshott's aristocratic nostalgia and pretensions. For them, politics requires great virtue and self-discipline as well as correct apprehension of the goals and practices of society. This requires study and training and is hardly available to most citizens who have neither the talent nor the time to become Oakeshott's "connoisseurs." Too many would-be aristocrats subvert their own acute historical recall of the uniqueness of politics with a circular justification of their own privileged superiority in governance and political apprehension.

Bickel again demonstrates the power and originality of his vision where he accepts a much more robust and aggressive political life. He is especially sensitive to the need for free, open, and even vitriolic speech and the role of citizen self-help. Ultimately, he argues that society must change first under the impact of speech and self-help before government should finalize a moral consensus. Even then, the legislature should do this, carefully, since it is imbedded in the active political life of change. Courts especially should be extremely cautious before they impose value judgments before a consensus emerges.

This separates open political life from the responsibility of governors. It represents a far more plausible claim about minimizing moral pretensions and claims in government but allowing them to flourish in political life at large. This theory, however, undercuts Bickel's own concern that the moral tone of the new left outside of politics infected and helped justify crimes of the Nixon administration and its self-righteous aggrandizement of power. Government politicians should be more committed to compromise and procedure because of their greater responsibility and power, but the open political life needs to ventilate moral claims of the population and meld them into a workable legitimacy (Bickel 1962; Bickel 1975, 55–88, 90–105).

6. Wills (1980) presents a provocative defense of nonviolent and sometimes

violent prophets and moral agitators in the life of liberal democracy. See especially the chapters entitled "Do-Gooders" and "Good Doers." These incisive essays demonstrate that one can be conservative in a profound sense and still appreciate the limits of official politics and the need for moral advocacy.

7. Alinsky refers to a "well integrated political schizoid," who avoids becoming a "true believer." Such a task takes immense self-knowledge and discipline, and Alinsky finds it very difficult to find and train good organizers. On the other hand, the problem is simplified if agitators generally stay outside of official politics and leave the negotiating to the "moderates" and insiders. It is worth noting Alinsky's own changed attitudes towards compromise. In his earliest writings, he denounces it incessantly while, during the sixties and seventies, he praises it as central to the resolution of problems in an open society. Compare Alinsky (1969), pp. 134–35 with pp. 224–35.

8. In both theory and practice, strongly held moral beliefs do not necessarily lead to the politics of moral absolutism. Individuals can hold "exceptionless moral norms" but also be committed to human autonomy and equal dignity. Autonomy and equal dignity can lead people to respect moral diversity even as they struggle to give shape to their ideals in politics and reject moral imposition.

9. Savonarola offers a remarkable case of a prophet who demonstrated immense political acumen upon coming to power. Beneath the umbrella of the remarkable histrionics of his regime, he established a republic in Florence. Ultimately his own legitimacy declined when his prophecies failed and enemies amassed against Florence (Weinstein 1970). Most prophets blessed with political acumen seldom try to establish republics. They eradicate or ostracize opposition. Constant wars against omnipresent enemies help maintain their legitimacy and justify their internal violence against "traitors." Ultimately, if they cannot regularize their rule, they must rely more on force and repression as reality and time eat away at the moral fervor that raised them up. The fate of Cromwell's "Protectorate" presents an interesting lesson. His "revolutionary" army sold out Cromwell's son and heir to the hated Stuart heir Charles II in exchange for arrears pay. In general, armed prophets represent a subset of Max Weber's problem of how a charismatic ruler transforms charismatic rule into enduring legitimate government (Weber 1969).

10. Managers, experts, or professionals can sometimes fall into a less metaphysical version of the same trap. Armed with their expertise and good intentions, they may too easily dismiss the autonomy of their clients, market, or opposition as based on "ignorance." Therapy or public relations can handle opposition.

11. This breakdown draws heavily upon the the provocative work of David Rapoport (1984).

12. (*The Iliad* Bk. 16, 396). *The Iliad* teems with references to the vital importance of words and council to create order in a chaotic world. Violence

is needed to sustain the order but hovers around it as its most dangerous enemy. See also the example on the Trojan side where Hector and his friend Polydamas were born "on the same night; one excelled in handling weapons, one with words" (Bk. 18, 443). Polydamas, unlike the warrior Hector, saw "what lay ahead" and spoke for "the good of all." Adkins (1975) argues that all Greek thought and politics hinged around a battle between cooperative virtues, council, and speech, and warrior excellences and the imperatives of survival in a brutal world.

13. Ideals can obviously inform and direct actions in most of these same ways. In most cases, ideals, especially more abstract ones, can be transposed into principles. The principles will be far more help in applications, especially across different dimensions of life. On the other hand, personalized ideals or exemplars can have great persuasive and educational power, but they should not be immune to the more general considerations of principled reflection.

14. While my work moves in a very different vein, I believe in the fundamental importance of rigorous and impartial ethical reflection and theory-based defenses of beliefs in equal human dignity and freedom. I find such theorizing and judgments extremely important for the functions they perform in political life. These can range from the austerely analytic (Gewirth 1978) to neo-Aristotelian reflections of equal human nature (Galston 1980). Among them I find the approach of John Rawls and the notion of "wide reflective equilibrium" an extremely important and forceful way to pursue moral reflection on political life. The approach and insights are extremely powerful because Rawls provides a way to examine the implications of commitments to equal dignity and freedom, but also because he possesses an often overlooked, sometimes willfully ignored, but extremely vital political dimension.

From the beginning, Rawls presumes the reality of conflict and moderate scarcity and deliberately addresses individuals who are seeking to cooperate within a community. He is concerned with assessing structural dimensions of political, social, and economic life. His arguments are influenced by a sharp awareness of the need to generate principles that do not strain the commitment capacities of citizens and can earn public loyalty over time, as well as withstand and encourage severe public scrutiny and debate. He is attuned to the need to constrain coercion and demands that all rigorous reflection also engage existing practices and commonly-held intuitions. The procedure of going behind a veil of ignorance as well as his minimal demands on altruism invite the widest possible number of individuals to enter into reflection and community building. The theory recognizes that the creation of a workable policy embodying principles depends upon the inhabitants ultimately developing their own "sense of justice" built upon practice, reflection and loyalty to the practices. His various formulations and recommendations almost always acknowledge the considerable and vital role for prudence in determining concrete policy (Rawls 1971). For instance, see Rawls (1986) for an explicit discussion of the political dimensions of his theory of the self.

On the other hand, in the moral sphere, I assume the existence of far more diverse principles and ideals that both exist and might emerge from rational reflection. This makes the job of ordering and weighting far more difficult and less satisfactory than Rawls would want. It is entirely plausible to me that people could decide upon a lexical ordering or protection of certain moral principles in writing a political constitution, although the reasons might be as compellingly prudential and political as they are moral. But attempting some definite ordering or even Rawls's own lexical ordering of principles does not necessarily solve the problem. In reality, for instance, Rawls's own first principle of the priority of equal basic liberties really grants priority to a clustering of principles or liberties. Even if one accepts that clustering as deserving some lexical protection—and people might well choose to do so—within that first clustering individuals will have considerable problems with weighting and directing the compromises among principles when they conflict with each other.

15. This does not always hold for utilitarians. Here the weight of total utility for an immediate gain always threatens to wash out the underpinnings of any principles the utilitarian may arrive at.

16. This discussion draws heavily upon Dworkin (1978),"The Model of Rules I," "The Model of Rules II," and "Justice and Rights," pp. 14–80, 150–83; and Griffiths (1972), "Ultimate Moral Principles: Their Justification," pp. 177–82.

2

Justifying Political Action

"Magistracy does not oblige him to put off either humanity or Christianity; but it is one thing to persuade, another to command; one thing to press with argument, another with penalties."—John Locke A Letter Concerning Toleration

"Would that be justice, ladies?" asked the just man. "It would be success, Mr. Low— which is a great deal the better of the two."—Anthony Trollope, Phineas Redux

Compromise is a serious moral and political problem for individuals who possess integrity and act as responsible agents in political life. As the derivation of the word suggests, compromisers perform an act unique to responsible and reflective individuals—they co-promise to abide by agreements. This means they agree on their own behalf to accept and act upon certain directives and trust that other individuals will similarly commit to their side of the bargain. Both sides assume of themselves and others that they have reflected upon the agreement, judged it according to their lights, and will discipline their other desires or motives to act against it. In other words, real promising begins with the assumption of free individuals of integrity who can reflect, judge, and act.

The tensions and interest of compromise arise both from the co-responsibility and the gain. Individuals are implicated in responsibility by actually crafting the compromise either in formulation or implementation or by making it possible through their support or acquiescence. But additionally, within a defensible compromise the individuals are not just tolerating or ignoring, but accepting gains for themselves or their cause in return for their efforts. This gain deepens the complicity and obligation to live up to the made promises. Yet for individuals of integrity and commitment, the problematic moral nature will also generate resentment, guilt, and frustration given both their gains and responsibility.

Making such political compromises takes for granted that politics represents a nonmanipulated and minimally coerced activity by individuals. For both coercion and manipulation undermine the assumptions of promising. Free and democratic politics is aimed at both creating and sustaining an order capable of defending itself and enabling individuals within it to flourish according to their lights. The notion of a responsible citizen, unique to this conception of politics, differs profoundly from subjects or slaves, in that citizens demand and judge reasons for actions from themselves and others.

For practical purposes, autonomy means that individuals have the noble capacity to reflect upon their beliefs and goals, make decisions about the content of them and seek their destiny in light of them. In liberal and democratic politics, this dimension of life forms the basic matrix for compromise. Autonomous persons of integrity are capable of giving reasons for what they have done and what they choose to do. They are also capable of being persuaded by other reasons and example and acting upon their own reasons. As citizens and political actors, they determine the range of acceptable and good reasons that justify actions. Much of political morality and action consists in searching for good and powerful reasons to justify actions to oneself and others.

The major moral task of this politics becomes the search for good reasons to direct and justify actions. This search for reasons involves a cooperative and social dimension, for politics requires not just that individuals persuade themselves of the rightness of an act, but that they persuade others, including allies, opponents, and indifferents. The reasons discovered are grounded in the nature of political life and successful political action. To this extent they provide powerful political and prudential reasons that complement moral claims in justifying action.

Personal integrity in liberal and democratic politics builds upon the notion that each person possesses a dignity worthy of respect. Integrity, the sense that individual lives possess a coherence and vitality, is linked intimately to this sense of equal dignity. The dignity of individuals is manifest when they act ethically upon the bases of their lives.[1] In a further way, the integrity of free persons depends upon the notion that they can reflect upon their lives and beliefs and relate these beliefs to one another under questioning. Personal integrity does not presume that all the beliefs and intuitions must be deductively reducible or encompassed under one overarching judgment, nor does it assume harmony among them. But individuals of integrity can defend actions with reasons and relate the reasons to one another in plausible ways. They can show a coherence or make sense of their actions—their life and judgments possess a plausible wholeness. In this sense, integrity assumes that individuals align their inner judgments with their outer statements and actions and that they can align their different selves and roles in some cohering manner. Such an understanding of coherence is critical for political morality. First, individuals promise and the inner commitment and outer commitments should cohere to take promises seriously. Second, such a centering and direction is vital because in political life many individual actions may seem contradictory, while in fact they have the same moral purpose and thrust but respond to different conditions. The classic political metaphor about a captain who must shift weight from side to side in order to maintain an even keel when the wind changes captures this dynamic.

Moral responsibility and integrity mean persons can achieve a critical perspective from which to judge and give coherence to their various personae or roles.[2] From this perspective, they can assess the quality of reasons they or others give to justify actions, and no one role or station can ever completely fill this reflective moment without a conscious act of will. This reflective capacity and psychological space makes one historical self possible and prevents persons from dividing into autonomous "selves" unconnected to any broader moral responsibility to their humanity or integral self. Unless the person of integrity has the reflective and willed capacity to align them, these "selves" become uncontrolled and irresponsible, subject only to the demands of competency within a role or achievement as defined by one persona. Without this sense of integrity, people can claim immunity for actions done within the role from any claims made on behalf of broader humanity or standards of justice or dignity because these come from standards outside any roles. Personhood and coherent moral responsibility have no meaning, since individuals' actions have no consistent pattern or moral coherence, and a person cannot be identified as having overall responsibility for the actions of each persona.

Individuals then become responsible as persons for actions that could not have taken place without their conscious acquiescence, support, or participation. This responsibility traverses roles and personal history. In this sense, all participation in office or roles in independent spheres of life is based upon a continuum of moral judgments. Even the vaunted claims of national security flow from the analogue of self-defense and the rights of individuals to defend themselves and their delegation of this to their governors.[3]

No role or persona, whether political, artistic, or professional, should exonerate individuals completely from the requirements of broader human responsibility and judgment. As long as an action needs conscious personal participation or acquiescence to occur and as long as individuals are not forced to act or act out of nonculpable ignorance, they retain individual responsibility for participation. The action may ultimately be justified or excused, but not because the "role" excuses. It is rather because persons can give good and plausible reasons to justify or excuse the action in broad moral terms that any responsible and autonomous person of dignity can answer to. All actions and decisions remain legitimately open to questions and judgment by such standards of humanity and community values, not just the role's criteria. For the special permissions and obligations inherent in the role depend upon one's ability to defend the role in the basic moral and constitutional terms of the society.[4]

Political agents like surgeons or military officers may have to harden themselves to the suffering around them as they struggle to accomplish vital goals, but this hardening should be a psychological device, not a moral escape. Roles and office do not become Nietzschean warrants for a higher morality unconnected to basic moral commitments and humanity. Individuals should still answer for the rightness of their role and its consequences as well as their competence within the role. Without this ideal of human integrity and responsibility, individuals can become the banal purveyors of evil that characterize the functionaries of any vicious system. As Hannah Arendt demonstrated, the horror of Adolph Eichmann's quiet conscience as he helped exterminate millions of Jews was not the the spectacle of *Ubermensch* morality unleashed. Rather all "good" people have the capacity to insulate themselves from human moral responsibility by denying the integrity of their lives (Arendt 1965).

Granted that roles and offices in politics may give special dispensations, the permissions are invariably linked to special responsibilities especially given the means of coercion and law and the stakes of the success. These responsibilities are based in more basic moral, political, and prudential justifications. Still, individuals are answerable to the reasons that justify the role itself before they are permitted the excuses and justifications denied individuals without the authorized role, competence, or responsibilities. This occurs constantly in government where officials can confiscate property via taxes or use violence and even deceit to further the public weal. Given the assumption that political actors will seek goals of right sanctioned by the community, individuals still should judge and evaluate the roles and the goals because they are persons possessing integrity, and no role is reified and independent of the matrix of human life from which it emerges.

This is doubly true since within almost all offices and roles, individuals always possess considerable discretion to negotiate meanings and influence the actions required by them. Even direct orders and clear rules can be subject to renegotiation and interpretation as well as to indirect actions. In carrying out responsibilities or orders, the situations invariably call for discretion and offer opportunities for interpretation and even subversion (Harmon 1981; Warwick 1981). Consequently, the reality of most social actions comports with the moral responsibility I am arguing frames our actions. This moral perspective utterly rejects positions such as Alexander Berkman's in his defense of his anarchism and shooting of Henry Clay Frick: "My own individuality is entirely in the background; aye, I am not conscious of any personality in matters pertaining to the Cause. I am simply a revolutionist, a terrorist by conviction, an instrument for furthering the cause of humanity" (Berkman 1970, 7–10).

This claim amounts to moral suicide. It eliminates the individual as the focus of responsible decision. The costs or harms of the consequences become irrelevant to the person making a decision since the individual ceases to exist as an independent moral agent. But the claim rests upon delusion. Either the "cause" remains vacuous and individuals still continue to decide and act giving it substance. Or the "cause" is determined by someone else and persons will have abdicated their selfhood to another person, a mortal, not a "cause." In both cases, individuals deceive themselves as to basic responsibility.[5]

There is a tendency to argue, especially in the Machiavellian tradition, that political office and concerns have their own moral logic and concerns that free political actors from most normal moral constraints. Machiavelli emphasizes this when he argues that being too personally moral can actually produce immoral results by betraying one's own cause and responsibility. But an office or role, whether as citizen, politician, or government official, is assumed by individuals as autonomous persons. My approach assumes that responsible integrity means that personal moral beliefs and commitments should matter very much in evaluations of justifications. I think political power and justifications, to the extent they differ from "personal" powers and justifications, should be viewed as a delegating of special powers, responsibilities, and permissions to individuals. These special powers and responsibilities are grounded, at least by analogy, in basic moral convictions and practices. Reflective assessments then exist on a continuum with personal convictions and assessments of governmental limits and goals. Responsible moral agency means that individuals possess a continuity across roles and through their personal history. Persons can address and justify roles and their ability to fulfill them by standards they hold independent of any particular role. Persons can be called to account for the history of their performance in the past to justify their actions (Thompson 1980).

Compromise becomes a real moral option and problem only when persons recognize that personal integrity entails responsibility for all the means and consequences of actions. The fact that individuals co-promise makes moral responsibility central to political compromises. Promising requires the notion of responsible individuals to be comprehensible. When persons promise to abide by the terms of a compromise, they take on obligations in a very powerful and special way and others rely upon those obligations. Promising lies at the heart of integrity and makes no moral sense without it. It presumes individuals can bind themselves in the present for future actions or be bound now by past promises. These promises then actually direct actions. Thus, promising puts the existence of selfhood as a morally coherent entity on the line. Thomas More sums it up in *Man For All Seasons*. "When a man takes an oath, Meg, he's holding his own self in his own hands. Like water. And if he opens his fingers then—he needn't hope to find himself again" (Bolt 1960, 81). The very act of promising adds a moral dimension to endeavors that actual context or even consequences may not invoke.

To the extent individuals benefit from the reliability of the practice of promising, fairness obligates them to respect a promise. To the extent that others rely upon a co-promise and build their welfare around these expectations (albeit sometimes highly qualified expectations), people are obligated to live up to it in order to avoid harms.

When individuals successfully compromise, they build trust in a society and minimize the need for resorts to violence. If they help to undermine promising in the political order, they unleash tremendous potential for harm and coercion as well as the loss of innumerable social benefits.[6]

The moral dimensions of promising can oblige individuals to respond with good reasons to questions addressed to why they acted as they did. This also means that people need to be able to defend actions to others and themselves in terms of basic convictions about the right and good, if pushed that far. People may often invoke the special permissions and responsibilities required by a role they have assumed, but these permissions and responsibilities assume people have delegated or permitted persons the power given certain goals the people value. These goals themselves, as well as the means used, should be defensible. Nothing in politics really frees individuals from the responsibilities imposed by human autonomy and the integrity that gives it life.

On the other hand, many people intuitively set integrity against compromise, as the dictionary definition hints. I would suggest that such a notion of integrity makes it a passive and protective endeavor, rather like virginity, something one protects which, once violated, can never be recovered. I think real personal integrity in political life more resembles love, an active engagement of care and concern for the world that takes risks and actions. To see integrity as inviolate conceives of integrity as predominantly a state of the soul, a state of intention and innerness. Morality becomes predominantly a self-referential concern.

Political morality and actions involve trust obligations that affect the welfare of other human beings. People who enter political life, lead others, and hold office act in ways that directly affect the basic rights and welfare of other human beings. Political life involves building a community of meanings and beliefs that make moral suasion possible. For example, persuasive argument, even from disinterested viewpoints, needs some extant commitments to consistency, humanity, and equal dignity to give the act of reflection much sense in one's life. The whole structure of justification for political power and the notion of political legitimacy depend upon a connection with the consequences on people's lives. The stakes, ranging from self-defense to basic freedoms, are too high to permit a form of moral narcissism.

Serious political morality flows from what I call the effectiveness imperative. Individuals of integrity enter politics to accomplish good.

Their moral convictions and commitments define the nature of the good. For a conscientious person, these commitments generate imperatives to act and bring about enduring good as defined by their conceptions of right and to engage obstacles to achieve these results. Arm-chair moralists and "contentedly otiose" consciences never need compromise (Smith 1956). But once persons begin to act to achieve purposes derived from integrity, if they fail by ineptitude, negligence, laziness, or inattention to results, they violate the effectiveness imperative.

The effectiveness imperative also means a willingness to take risks and work in nonlinear ways. Just as morality is not a deductive science, effective moral action in politics moves in roundabout ways. Such action may require side trades to get power to do something else, it may mean waiting for the proper timing or working to change opinions before one can change laws. The imperative to "do something" means that no extraordinary impediments block a person. Moral responsibility obviously presumes one has the capacity to act. If impediments block action, the effectiveness imperative moves individuals to use imagination and effort to remove the obstacles, including gaining enough power to remove them. It also means that individuals should act despite the inherent imperfections and limits of life. To rest content with moral purity and impotence violates the imperative thrust of political morality. If integrity is not seen in this light, individuals face a stark choice between comfortable if ineffective "morality" or a brutal realism that exempts politics from most moral direction and constraint. People "should act, even when motives were impure and results certain to be disappointing" (McPherson 1972, 95–98, 159–64).[7]

The connection between political action and integrity should never be lost. Politics can drive individuals mad. The obstinacy of reality constantly frustrates best efforts and mocks deepest aspirations. The intensity of deepest beliefs or interests can be all too easily violated by the slow drudgery of politics. People are tempted to justifications and excuses that exonerate or sanctify their anger and violence. But a centered focus upon personal integrity and responsibility for all actions as well as others' dignity can usually prevent individuals from becoming "people who are merely hiding psychosis behind a political mask" (Alinsky 1971, xxii). This way of understanding political morality and compromise enables persons to connect principled, political, and prudential concerns and see politics as an arena where people shape these concerns into understandable and cooperative justifications for political life. It also means that political actors always remain responsible individuals subject to questioning on moral grounds by those with whom they live. No one possesses privileged immunity from responsibility and justification for their actions.

Individuals search for good reasons to justify compromises. These reasons are critical because they need to possess the weight and persuasive power to offset the moral unease, which a compromise might entail. In liberal and democratic political life, a plethora of reasons arise both from the moral foundations of the state and from the nature of political life itself. Each of these dimensions provides another set of reasons to which political actors can justly recur to justify compromises in complex situations. In particular, each of the domains that arise from the complexity and obstinacy of political reality and the nature of political success provides good reasons for actions.

Justifications begin with an individual's own strengths, as well as limits and weaknesses. This is compounded by the existence of other individuals who possess interests, convictions, dignity, and power. Many of the other individuals are powerful and ambitious, and they may agree or not agree with a political actor. Institutions and persons of great and unequal power exist and must be confronted if anything durable is to be accomplished. This engagement with other humans also occurs within a bounded cultural and historical setting. This places severe limits on the resources available and confronts a person with existing rituals and symbols that enable conflict and resolution to occur without civil breakdown (Geertz 1973, 193–325).

At the most general level when individuals justify an action, they give "good" reasons for what they did or believe. These reasons should demonstrate that a person did the "right" thing or show that an act or belief "makes sense." The goodness of the reasons depends upon the appropriateness of the setting and the people who must be convinced. To vote for a bill because an individual liked the looks of the sponsor would be dismissed as ethically, politically, and prudentially bad reasoning. Accepting scientific results from colleagues because they were physically stronger is not acceptable. Political justifications involve reasons that identify a situation as suitable for political action and connect to the realities of achievement. Once an issue is "identified," this justifies individual action, the mobilization of people, resources, law, government institutions, and ultimately coercion to do something about the situation. Very often, morality leads politics in the sense that, if individuals can demonstrate "harm" or "wrong," then they can motivate people to political action.[8]

Justification is an inherently social activity. Even when persons justify themselves before their consciences, they may engage in a raging internal debate across their "selves." Most of the time people justify to others. Generally speaking, justification defends against questions, doubts, or charges. Successful justification involves reference to what people accept as good reasons appropriate to a sphere of action, or it convinces people to accept new standards or reasons as equally legitimate or better than ones they presently hold. These may refer to moral reasons—I respected his right; or practical reasons—I cannot accomplish it; or legitimate procedures—I won the election; or symbolic orderings of authority—I possess the office to issue this order.

As a political activity, justification presumes open and free discussions of reasons. This makes it the heart of liberal and democratic life because citizens of integrity are addressed as free and competent. The claim that I am bigger or have more power, untempered by legitimate procedures, does not justify—it dominates. No discussion or free assessment has occurred, individuals have no reasons other than coercion to consider the assertion "good." In a similar vein, if beliefs have been manipulated by a closed educational and information system, then justification becomes a vicious circle. If someone deceives, then their reasons do not justify because acceptance presumes both accuracy and candor. Justification is neither coerced nor manipulated.

On the other hand, "because I said so" can possess considerable justificatory power. When a person possesses recognized skill, proven leadership, or legitimately gained office, his or her word or pronouncement can serve as a contextually acceptable justification. The skill or authority, however, cannot be closed and should be subject to further appeal, discussion, or modification. A person's word still constitutes a "reason," not a command or dogma, and reasons must always be open to further questioning and refinement to remain "reasons" and justifications.

Political justification involves uncoerced and unmanipulated persuasion by reasons people accept as valid to warrant action or belief. However, in political life, justification is not simply defensive or *ex post facto*. Politicians do not just answer the question "why did you do that?" but "why do you want to do that?" or "why do you want us to support you when you do that?" Consequently, political justification becomes an active form of persuasion to convince free individuals not just to accept but to cooperate. Successful political action mobilizes citizens to devote time, energy, and money for a cause, and individuals must convince others to accept their proposals. Such justification will depend upon rhetoric that builds a community of belief, explains positions and educates, persuades or convinces citizens.

Conflict inheres in the diversity and heat of political life. The size, classes, diversity, and multiple poles of authority of the modern state guarantee that conflict will remain a central aspect of political and social life. Any endeavors to mobilize citizens, change policy, law, behavior, or attitude runs against the obstinacy of reality. A welter of reasons must be proffered to justify a political position and to answer a flurry of questions or charges. The multiple audiences and the standard forms of reasons available set the constraints that shape political justification.

Successful justification means acceptance. The people who accept also determine what constitutes a good reason. This acceptance and ability to set the terms implicates all citizens in co-responsibility for the legitimacy of actions. In technical endeavors, individuals may share a narrow and widely accepted set of premises and methods. This enables them to pursue "normal" science where they can narrow the range of justifications and increase the precision of what counts as a good reason or evidence. The emotional or self-interested content of justification can be minimized and more weight given to impersonal rules of procedure and verification.[9] But politics, even "normal" politics, possesses no such paradigmatic stability. Political justification is a multifaceted, open, even Janus-faced endeavor because of the multiple audiences.

Politicians must mobilize allies. Since a political leader seeks concrete results, two different problems present themselves. First, a politician must often yoke together people who want similar outcomes, but for different reasons. Antiabortion leaders must simultaneously satisfy Southern Baptists who trace their opposition to biblical references to life in the womb, and Roman Catholics who base theirs upon a natural law claim about the moral status of the potentiality of the fetus. Neither side necessarily accepts the reasoning of the other. Second, allies may hold similar premises but differ about the shape of the solution or the methods of attaining the goal. Many environmentalists are committed to preserving resources for the future, but differ profoundly over whether society should use regulations, mediation, or incentives.

Many other potential allies may have to be roused out of their indifference and educated to the reality of the problem. Martin Luther King used his marches to demonstrate to northern moderates the reality of the race problem and provide good reasons to support the movement. Many successful movements organize themselves, and often politicians must not only rouse the indifferent, but also choose between vigorous pursuit of a goal and maintaining an institutional base, which makes long-term success possible.

If persuading squabbling allies were not enough, justifications must be addressed to many indifferent citizens. Here again, individuals share different attitudes and premises. Even when they hold common ones, they are "imperfectly shared" terms of an open-ended discussion.[10] An environmentalist might have to awaken latent ethical and religious attitudes toward "stewardship" of resources and then connect this to activists who may believe that even trees have "rights." An antiabortion activist would invoke the term "murder" to arouse individuals, while proabortion advocates would emphasize widely shared beliefs in "free choice." Both sides must address those who feel abortion is "wrong," but are reluctant to legislate coercive bans or those who would limit abortions but make exceptions for rape, incest, or threats to a mother's life. Unlike the early apostles who could speak one language and be heard by many different audiences in the audience's own language, politicians must sometimes speak different languages to different groups and weave a fabric of justification from different strands.

Finally, political justifications must be accepted by those who oppose one's positions, goals, or organizations. This poses the central paradox of liberal democracy and accounts for the nondeductive or nonlinear nature of political morality. For individuals must be persuaded to stay within the fellowship of law and community even as they disagree over profoundly important issues. The reasons given to opponents will differ profoundly from those conveyed to allies, the indifferent, or the ignorant. Very often, politicians need to overtly recognize their opponents' integrity even in opposition and acknowledge their continuing right to think, feel, and believe. The openness and fairness of a political order might be emphasized and reaffirmed to remind opponents that they had their say and will have future opportunities. People may invoke shared loyalty to symbols, rituals, and territorial integrity to reaffirm fellowship even in conflict. In some cases, individuals might compromise and accept some of their opponents' positions either because they were right or out of respect for their autonomy or power. Ultimately, losing opponents must be persuaded to accept the law or policy, obey it and give financial and human support. They must also be persuaded not to take up arms despite their defeat, but to fight by established rules. To gain acquiescence from opponents for ethically inspired policies remains the central problem and constraint upon political justification and action. Given this problem as well as the diversity among allies and the indifferent, there is no simple and neat model of political justification.

Cultural tools shape political justification as much as diversity of audience. These include common-sense criteria by which citizens judge, the symbols and rituals of political legitimacy, the methods of power acquisition and conflict resolution, and characterizations of citizens' experience and interests. In political life people imperfectly share many judgmental terms of discourse. Some, like murder, are relatively closed in terms of meaning and application. Some, like discrimination, are agreed to be wrong but are still very open as to the extent of the term and its exact application.[11] When individuals apply established terms, they characterize actions and imbed them in a web of considered judgments and moral practices that most share. Actions can be justified by appealing to commonly shared and understood moral practices (Phillips and Mounce 1970). Here moral terms are at their strongest and most obvious. But often the issue does not involve the morality of the practice, but whether or not actions are subsumed under it. The question of whether abortion counts as murder or free choice does not debate the evil of murder or the desirability of free choice. Rather, it concerns the correct characterization of aborting a fetus.[12]

Citizens possess foundational or symbolic rhetoric and shared moral aspirations embodied in basic political symbols. "Liberty, equality, and fraternity," or "We the people" establish powerful and enduring terms of shared political heritage and reference. These symbols are deepened by shared history, territorial unity, and education. The creation of symbols and agreement upon them enables people to disagree, debate, and adopt meanings within a broad historical and cultural continuum. This creation represents a great historical accomplishment for a viable political order.[13] Such symbols enable multiple audiences to proclaim their loyalty while holding different but related conceptions of public good and interest. It may behoove political actors to keep the symbols flexible and manifold for just such reasons,. Seeking tighter closure can often engender as much alienation as good. These symbols shape and limit the range of acceptable options while making legitimation of solutions possible for the entire population.

These foundational terms are the most widespread and hence the most imperfectly shared of symbols and carry multiple historical

interpretations. Additionally, most foundings involve their own compromises, like the American tension between federal supremacy and
states' rights. So, principles embodied in the symbols may not mesh
neatly or have a clear-cut priority or consensual meanings. Each side
of the compromise may have its own interpretation. Liberty and
equality, although theoretically compatible, remain poles of competitive discourse and justification in "liberal" "democracies." But to the
extent that politicians strive to justify their aspirations under the rubric
of common terms, these terms domesticate opposition and justification.

Shared moral practices and symbolic rhetoric provide no determi-
native outcomes for politics and, consequently, politicians must utilize
or create accepted methods of exercising power and resolving disputes.
These methods legitimize conflict resolution and are strongest when
they take on symbolic and ritual power. In a liberal democracy,
participation, elections, courts, law-making, representative bodies,
and administrative decisions legitimize patterns of conflict and elicit
public support while shaping the form of conflict. Justifications cluster
around the requirements of gaining power, creating coalitions, passing
or implementing laws, and gaining peaceful acquiescence.

These conflict resolution procedures can also be defended by refer-
ring to the common benefits all sides achieve by agreeing not to
eliminate their opponents. But procedures that replace violent and
coercive conflict should possess integrity and fairness if they are to
carry weight. Individuals may choose to mute their political indict-
ments and rhetoric or pull back from demands in the interests of
maintaining civility and trust. Such reasoning is often necessary to
satisfy the opposition of shared loyalties and fellowship, and to reassure opponents of further chances for discussion and change. The
claims of ritual, law, and civility may well channel the urgency of
moral justification of the reformers. The very power of these reasons
informs the justifications of those who might use civil disobedience to
call attention to unjust laws and motivate others to support the cause.
Civil disobedience simultaneously affirms loyalty to order, civility, and
the rule of law, while powerfully criticizing the moral failures of an
order.

If law and governance are to generate loyalty and obligations, they
need to link symbols and ritual to moral practices and beliefs of most
citizens. To be successful across a wide range, justification must work
at different levels and for different audiences. Individual consciences,
group loyalties, and normal practices need to be touched. Most justifi-

cations will possess a patina of coherence but ultimately remain open, contextual and shifting, always reinterpreting to accommodate change, serendipity, and various publics.

Finally, justification must link human experience to political goals. Laws, politics, movements, and institutions must earn their legitimacy over time by providing experienced benefits in the lives of citizens. In this, politicians rely upon symbols, rituals, and moral practices because these enable a citizen to characterize an experience as a benefit. To a great extent, symbolic understanding shapes experience. But justification requires not just giving good reasons but the characterization of a situation as one that warrants political action. Here political actors can actively demonstrate what harms or wrongs are being done, or what good is being frustrated, that sustained political action could rectify. Attention might be called to a new or hidden experience, and this may be characterized as harm or wrong. Politicians might recharacterize an old experience and transform it into a political matter subject to action.

At one level, this is most commonly accomplished by linking political action with interests. While not all interests have the same moral standing, some interests may be morally grounded, others neutral, or derivative of autonomy, but they possess immense durability and power in personal lives. Interests matter because people experience them as their own and as vital to material and spiritual welfare.[14] Political actions materially affect these concrete concerns. But people may experience interests as harmed in ways that seem beyond governmental action. A job layoff or cancer from exposure to toxic wastes may not seem to connect with normal understandings of harm done to us by responsible agents whom government can address. Many justifications will link to interests in order to make the human connection between individual lives and political action.

The core work of liberal democracy focuses on the effort to distill or create from common experience terms of common reference so that people can accept meanings and act upon them. Often, individuals need only point to a disaster or wrongs, that once recognized, motivate and implicate people in responsibility. At other times, people must work to redefine an experience. Individuals might well believe that bad luck or God's will gave them cancer or deformed children. But a leader changes their experience by calling attention to the toxic waste that has poisoned their water. This connection reinterprets a situation as one justifiably subject to political and legal actions. In a similar sense, individuals of an exploited group may internalize a low self-image and feel impotent at their oppressed plight. But politicians can identify this low self-image as a social creation sustained by social institutions. Courageous individuals can demonstrate its falseness by their success, and the group can recover its identify and harness its energy by assertive political action.

Justification usually conserves. It relies upon established moral and political practices as well as shared symbols and rituals. But political life, especially in complex societies, seldom sits still. When justifications use symbols with open texture and complex historical genealogies, these justifications can be extended and transformed. To the extent that justifications can touch or articulate old and new experiences, people enter the borderland between "normal" and "revolutionary" politics.[15] Political violence and terrorism represent the failure of justification. Justification presumes giving and accepting uncoerced and unmanipulated reasons. Terrorism and civil war mean that citizens no longer accept symbolic and ritual reasons to acquiesce in the political order. These groups believe that their own experiences of harm or injustice are powerfully and morally compelling. But their own experiences are characterized differently or dismissed by the dominant order, as when victims are blamed for their victimization. On the other hand, the voices of the disenfranchised might not be heard simply because they lack the tools of amplification or language of the dominant order.

Revolutionary activity represents a breakdown and basic change in the quality but not the kind of political action. Political justification must always innovate, extend, and reinterpret. It always speaks to several audiences and weaves a fabric of many threads. It uses imperfectly shared understandings in an open-textured world. Reform proceeds in any viable society, and justification must expand to encompass new harms, new names for hidden dangers, and injured silences now alive with voice.

People should never lose moral control of politics. Basic human interests in safety, defense, shelter, freedom, education, and earnings are affected for good or bad by politics and government. Government concentrates immense power to accomplish its purposes while exerting enormous cultural, legal, and practical influence on the beliefs and actions of citizens. It affects their freedom and life chances; it defends their security and rights, and takes large chunks of their earnings. It both prohibits and enables many actions. The stakes of politics require powerful and persuasive reasons, and citizens who determine the range of acceptable justifications rightly turn to moral language to assess both the foundations and daily consequences of such activity. The existence of principles and ideals in political life reminds individuals that institutions and practices remain trustees of aspirations and not their ultimate embodiment.

But the ends of politics and moral claims are pursued in a community. This community needs to be defended and peace needs to be maintained for moral aspirations to have any reality. To accomplish these ends, government needs legitimacy in the use of force and education denied to other individuals or groups. In moments of crisis, governors need immense flexibility to succeed in their appointed purposes. The viability and justice of an order, as Hobbes underlines, depend upon the exercise of power and its domestication. The reality of power and the problem of enemies accounts for the success of projects like Machiavelli's puncturing of piety in politics. It also explains the tactic of realists to debunk "morals," when they use extreme examples to argue, for instance, that torturing innocent persons might be "justified" in order of discover the whereabouts of a nuclear bomb about to blow up Cleveland. It should be no surprise that moral claims break down in a world where moral reciprocity does not exist or when incredible danger confronts people. But it should constantly worry citizens that the drive to success can override normal moral constraints.

Political authority sustains itself by success. Politicians exist in dialogue with citizens' consciences and exercise power with the responsibility to achieve results consonant with the interests and consciences of the citizens. Political ethics, then, is consequentialist and is judged and justified by the quality of humanity, peace, and justice experienced in lives. Neither purity of intention, autonomy of will, nor consistency of commitment matter as much in this dialogue as success in sustaining safety, and humane and just social practices. At the same time, because of the dialogue and accountability, citizens actively share in the setting of the terms of justification and confirm their validity. The ability of a liberal and democratic order to keep a humane and viable life and to keep compromises just and workable depends upon all citizens actively offering, judging, and acting upon the public justifications. This responsibility is doubly important because the nature of compromises can lead individuals to self-deception or to forget their moral limits. Only the questioning and justifying of all citizens enables compromises to be justified well and to avoid their myriad dangers.

The dimensions of successful political action provide good reasons for compromise that complement the moral reasons. Political success involves changing the behavior and, often, the beliefs of people, and this change should be durable and have minimal necessity for coercion or manipulation to attain it. More specifically, good and successful political outcomes have multiple dimensions. The external dimensions include any goals beyond the immediate priorities of the actors, while the internal assessments are made in terms of the political actors' goals.

Liberal democracy bounds the justifications in two ways. First, the political outcome should respect or enhance the basic constitutional processes and rights as well as the dignity and freedom of citizens while remaining accountable to the requirements of the rule of law in society. Second, a successful political change is one whose outcome will comport with the basic ethical and political goals of the supporters of the policy. It has passed through and been legitimized by the accepted rituals of conflict resolution and governance. Once formally legitimized, the policy is adequately funded and institutionalized. It endures by fending off political and institutional challenges. A true political success gains acceptance and obedience and is internalized by the normal institutional and personal actions of citizens. This means obedience is gained without resort to great manipulation, and solutions succeed without generating massive and polarizing backlash or undermining perceptions of legitimacy in the political order. For purposes of this essay, I will refer to the classes of reasons generated by these concerns as political and prudential and will discuss them at length in Chapters 5 and 6.

Political reasons refer to the fundamental political choice not to eliminate but to treat with opponents. This family of reasons clusters around claims to establish methods of conflict, cooperation, and conflict resolution that minimize coercion, keep peace, and maintain civility. They justify tailoring political actions and claims both to cohere with symbols of legitimacy and to abide by accepted processes and rituals of resolution. Each institution of power and coercion may be designed as much with an eye to possible abuses of power as to its immediate workability. During political discussion and conflict, citizens may go out of their way to recognize the right of opponents to speak and even to acknowledge the legitimacy of their opponents' position and power. These can reinforce both sides' commitments to peaceful resolutions of controversy in ways consistent with civility. Above all, politicians may invoke reasons derived from the desire to minimize the coercion necessary to gain compliance. Actions and rhetoric to avoid driving other citizens to civil war or terrorism fall under these rubrics as well as those to bring enemies into a circle of trust.

Political justifications converge around maintaining an order that enables people to deliberate and seek goals with minimum coercion. They invoke system-sustaining concerns and difficult-to-measure trade-offs. When politicians struggle to maintain civility and common terms of debate even as they battle over deeply divisive issues, they are motivated by political concerns. A principled abhorrence of violence or a respect for human autonomy sometimes tracks these concerns, but they possess a perduring independent dimension. Many political acts can also be defended in terms limited to self-interested defenses of freedom or the desire to avoid tyranny while maintaining peace (Crick 1972; Biddle 1957).

What I call prudential justifications flow from a broader concern with the logic of implementation. The effectiveness imperative captures its thrust—if individuals have principled or interest-derived goals worth pursuing, then they should discover outcomes required by the commitments, seek the means to attain them, and seek solutions consonant with the goals within the sphere of life in which they are pursued. This places a great emphasis upon finding concrete solutions that take into account the truth and complexity of a situation. Accomplishments should be durable, minimally coercive, and open to change and adaptation. Obviously, this family of concerns overlaps with political justifications, but its range of options and concerns goes far beyond the domestication of force.

Prudent judgments first shape political goals. Because political morality focuses upon consequences and not intentions, it demands a concrete shape to the principle and ideals given the historical and cultural possibilities. Second, prudent concern leads individuals to find the necessary power to attain goals. Third, to seek durable and right solutions, citizens should seek truthful assessments of the real world and its moral and physical complexity. Limitations on resources and knowledge, uncertainty of all sorts, and other legitimate claims can be invoked to change the shape or a plan or action. The rhetoric of a struggle and public terms of justification might have to be adapted to comport with commonly shared moral beliefs and practices. Additionally, prudent policies dictate openness to future change that can rectify mistakes and accommodate unforeseen consequences or new knowledge. In this way, the good accomplished will not be offset by unanticipated harm. In an open politics, opponents can abide changes and defeats since they will have a chance to reform the reforms in the future.

But neither politics nor prudence necessarily gains justice or humanity. They are limited by concerns to maintain peace, order, and effectiveness within bounds set by cultures and distributions of power—not inconsiderable achievements and intimately necessary to attain any moral goals in political life. But coupled with principled and ideal claims, these three families can provide the matrix of justifications within which individuals can forge a viable and humane political order.

Politics does not guarantee happy endings. No serious student of political life has claimed that politics in the raw presents a neat and tidy moral world—that remains largely for those "who would make a desert and call it peace." Since political justifications must make sense of this world while constituting and sustaining it, the welter of reasons and tensions should be expected. The welter focuses upon the responsibility of individuals within the political order. Citizens provide the justifications and also determine the range of acceptable ones. Only the efforts of citizens to raise principled, prudential, and political concerns can guarantee adequate justification for policies and ensure that good compromises are struck.

Justification, however, makes no sense unless reasons are accepted. Acceptance depends upon reasons being intelligible and linked to interests and experience. Accordingly, the pursuit of durable and stable ethical goals in political life cannot be reduced to analytic reflection on the implications of intuitions and principles, neither for that matter can it be dictated to by the same endeavor. These austere moral reflections limit the audience, possess no motivational power, dictate without regard to prudence or politics, and seldom connect with widespread modes of justification and understanding. They do not give the tools to recharacterize experience in coherent and motivating ways. Yet the requirements of political acceptance have profound limits. Audiences begin with very conservative assumptions imbedded with prejudice for institutions of problematic justice or humanity.

The relations among the principled, political, and prudential families of justification suggest several conclusions. First, no one realm of reasons does sufficient justice to the demands and complexity of political life. Second, each realm of reasons limits and enriches the others by forcing each set of reasons to expand and address vital issues missed in its own purvey. Third, moral claims possess a constitutive priority and do shift burdens of proof and powerfully call forth better reasons. Fourth, the actual justificatory power and persuasiveness of a course of action rises as the three families converge. Fifth, only an open, accountable, and participatory politics can do justice to the three realms because citizens determine the range and validity of the reasons. This means that the rightness of most justifications will remain inherently contextual and fine-graded. While this suggests that political justification is ineluctably unsatisfying from a philosophical point of view, it shifts the burden and responsibility for creating good compromises squarely upon the shoulders of the individuals who give and accept those justifications.

Notes

1. Although the words "ethics" and "morality" tend to slide together in the essay, I generally use the word "morality" because I seek to emphasize the reflective dimension of decision and judgment. For purposes of the essay, moral reflection usually involves disciplined attempts to discover impartial, disinterested, or human-based directives for action. I accept Aristotle's own preference for speaking about ethics as a more habituated and less reflective form of discrimination and judgment and also believe that individuals judge this way most of the time. To the extent that reflections occur within accepted practices, moral reflection and ethical decision support and enrich. To the extent that moral reflection seeks to be more rigorous and wide-ranging in its questioning of practices through what Rawls would call a wide reflective equilibrium, such reflection can conflict with practice and lead to significant revision of practice upon the basis of reflective moral judgment.

2. Autonomy and dignity need not support the claims I make about integrity here. Autonomy can be used to offer a theory of radically free and alienated individuals capable of totally reconstructing their life with infinite leaps of faith and commitment. Autonomy can also be interpreted to mean radical individuals without integrity, such as Hobbes or some versions of free market economics would postulate. These individuals simply act from seething and morally inchoate desires and needs. They express preferences, they do not deliberate and judge and make decision. I do not find either conception of individuality morally attractive or plausible.

Dignity, on the other hand, can often become an excuse to assert willful, privileged, or closed conceptions of selfhood. Very often, persons who declare "here I stand, I can do no other," privilege their own commitments and declare themselves immune to all further questions and judgment. While all human commitments deserve a *prima facie* respect, some commitments may, in fact, be manipulated or totally unreflected distillations of closed socialization, peer pressure, charismatic leadership, or ignorance. In some sense, unexamined commitments hardly represent individuality at all and can barely be said to be claimed as "mine," since the persons have made no honest effort to reflect upon them, look at their foundations, and judge them. Some "selves" exist as smug gridlocks unanswerable to anything but privileged authorities embedded in the gridlock. To the extent such claims of the dignity of a way of life entail claims of the life's superiority over others and imply a justification to dominate or limit other ways of life, any respect for such dignity becomes even more suspect. Commitment should not be valued for commitment's sake. Individuals should always ask if the commitments assault or deny the dignity or integrity of other human beings and whether they exist in willful ignorance or by manipulation.

3. See Feinberg (1970) and Nagel (1978) for the analytic foundations of the notions of moral evaluation and responsibility used in this chapter. This essay depends upon the expansion of this conception of responsibility developed in the work of Dennis Thompson (1980, 1981, 1983). See Dobel (1982) for an example of how to analyze a political justification in light of this notion of responsibility. Sabini and Silver (1982), pp. 55–88, provide a sobering reminder of the limits of this conception.

4. This approach denies any radical discontinuity between basic moral justifications while admitting that political actions often involve actions and justifications that are not permitted to ordinary citizens in their daily lives. See Nagel (1978) and French (1983), Chaps. 1–4, for more technical discussions of this position.

5. The chapter "On Destroying the Innocent with a Clear Conscience: A Sociopsychology of the Holocaust," in Sabini and Silver (1982), provides a terrifying analysis of the personal consequences of individuals under political stress severing their personal responsibility and integrity from the their actions after assuming political roles. The pressures of political life always tempt individuals to adopt such strategies as do certain ethical theories like utilitarianism.

6. This account of promising builds upon that given in Rawls (1971), pp. 342–50. Wertheimer (1972) makes some helpful clarifications about promising in politics, but also points out that obligations can certainly arise in other ways besides promising.

7. McPherson (1972) also points out quite rightly that postulates of a higher morality lead to the same problems of brutal realism. Either approach exempts officials and political actors from normal moral constraints or questioning. They end with the same blank check as the realist.

8. Even if a subject is characterized as suitable for political concern, people might argue that it is not serious enough to warrant government power. Others might also argue that the task cannot be performed well by government or that government would do more harm than good in trying to accomplish the task.

9. Kuhn (1970). Rorty (1979), Chap. 7, suggests that even such densely specified communities of discourse as science resemble politics, because

science has no definitive method to adjudicate among various incommensurable paradigms.

10. The idea of "imperfectly shared" terms of discourse draws upon Connolly (1983), Chaps. 1 and 2.

11. The rest of this section draws heavily upon the Connolly (1983) and Pitkin (1972).

12. Moral practices do not form either neat hierarchies or one seamless web. Discussion of an issue might involve reference to many practices that impinge on an issue or characterize aspects of an activity.

13. Geertz (1973), see especially "The Integrative Revolution: Primordial Sentiments and Civil Politics in New States," and "The Politics of Meaning."

14. Connolly (1983) refers to interests as a "cluster concept" that links vital areas of life with broader political and moral realms.

15. I use these terms from Rorty (1979) with some trepidation since Rorty seems very naive about the difference between intellectual discourse and political change. Several times, he hints that the "deliberative process" involved in intellectual paradigm shifts in science does not differ significantly from the shift from the *"ancien regime"* to bourgeoise democracy, or from Augustans to the Romantics" (Rorty, 327). He questions whether there is really a difference "in kind" between Bellarmine—Gallileo and "Kerensky and Lenin, or that between the Royal Academy (*circa* 1910) and Bloomsbury" (Rorty, 331).

The obvious answer is, of course there is! The political changes used power and violence to silence or eliminate their opponents. Such social beliefs are supported by power and domination and defended with legal violence; their overthrow does not signal a shift in sensibility, gestalt, canons of proof or theoretical acceptability. Their triumph entails power, persecution, elimination of opponents, and hegemonic education undergirded by self-censorship influenced by power. Rorty's book suffers from a serious unwillingness to take the role and danger of power and coercion seriously, certainly in politics, but even in his own concerns with scientific shifts.

3

The Nature of Political Compromise

"Only the dead need not compromise."—Anon.

Liberal and democratic politics depends upon people to transform moral aspirations and interests into workable law, policy, and consensus. Anyone who enters political life to seek goals becomes a politician and participates in the common life of making claims and accommodating the obstinacy of reality. Political actors are ensnared with coresponsibility for the community in which they act and the consequences of the goals they achieve. These political actors, even when they deny it to themselves, use compromise to hold together the variety of purposes pursued in political life.

Many compromises more resemble simple bargains or capitulations. The most troubling compromises possess an intractable dimension of wrong or harm that does not drop out in the final evaluation, unlike a straightforward "trade-off." Capitulation defines one boundary set of cases and emphasizes how political compromise depends upon reciprocity. The other boundary cases delineate the rarified agreement among persons solely on the basis of mutual respect for each other's autonomy and dignity. These last cases illustrate the strongest moral reasons to compromise, but purify compromise so much that the whole ambiguous activity is not encompassed. Within these ranges, individuals struggle to justify compromise in a manner consistent with responsible integrity.

The compromises I am concerned with differ from a bargain, deal, or simple exchange relation. While these words are used interchangeably, bargains and their ilk represent interesting technical problems of how to gain the maximum amount of a good in an exchange or negotiation. Bargains usually lack the moral tension and problem suggested by the two of *Webster's* definitions: "a concession to something derogatory or prejudicial" and "to make a shameful or disreputable concession."[1] More bargains probably involve this unsavory aspect than is ever admitted, and many politicians underplay or forget the moral tension in many "deals." But consciences need not "make cowards of us all," however, to become more sensitive to this dimension of compromise. When the moral costs are recognized, gains are calibrated more honestly. This awareness will help make better compromises and defend them more successfully against the absolutists.

Political compromises that pose moral problems might be viewed as a broad subset of bargains, but they are hardly encompassed by the normal intellectual tools to understand and evaluate bargains—game theory or economic rationality. In a simplified bargain or game, individuals negotiate to exchange goods for another person's goods. Both sides place values upon the goods possessed and the goods sought. No symmetry need exist in the valuation of the goods; all that matters is that people can reach an agreement to exchange them. The other side of the exchange coin from gain is loss. Individuals give up something valued such as time, support, money, or opportunity for the good received. If individuals get something they value highly for something they value less, then they get a "real bargain." The goodness of the bargain is tied to the spread between the good obtained and the cost, or between the good obtained and the situation without any bargain. Bargains can also be struck because harm is threatened either by denial of needed goods or by imposing sanctions, if one side does not deal.

These assessments focus exclusively upon the seemingly *prima facie* evaluations expressed in the actual willingness to deal. The significant moral dimension of compromise and its problems, however, arise at the second-order level where individuals assess the criteria by which trade-offs are evaluated. A game theorist, a microeconomist or related moral theorists like act-utilitarians can reduce the bargain to a sum that lets individuals know whether the total utility gained exceeds that given up or whether people have moved closer to a more optimal aggregate sum of gains compared to the situation before the bargain. Accordingly, utilitarian political ethicists and their surrogates in economics and game theory evaluate compromises as if they were all simple bargains and transform principled assessments into expressions of preference or interest denuded of moral significance.

In this world view, bad compromises are distinguished from good ones by unambiguous sums of total good gained versus good lost, or by comparing one outcome with the relative outcomes of rejected bargains or no bargain. While individuals may have wanted more or be pained by loss or even cooperated in wrongs or harms to achieve the goal, these are subsumed and banished from the final calculation. Utilitarian political ethics leaves no room for internal moral tension or anguish after the calculation and decision. Any wrong or harm done drops out or is canceled by the good attained, and individuals should need feel no responsibility or remorse for the means or differentials. In other words, no moral wrong accrues in accomplishing purposes unless individuals should somehow bring about more harm than good in the final summing up or less than the original starting point. Only then does the issue of responsibility for wrong or harm done arise. Moral questions focus on the accuracy of accounting and adequacy of resources.

Paradoxically, while making compromise too easy by masking internal effects, the strictest forms of utilitarianism destabilize all compromise externally by relentlessly obligating individuals to maximize all possible good in any situation. Harm, wrong, and moral complexity still fall out in internal evaluations, but ineffable guilt accrues to all outcomes short of solutions that maximize total good given a set of resources and constraints. Such strict utility demands pervade all dimensions of a solution, creating never-ending remorse and undermining acceptance. Internal purity exists when moral remainders drop out, but externally, strict utilitarianism undercuts compromises by a demoralizing demand to push to Pareto limits of maximum gain for all sides given resource constraints. At the same time, utilitarians seldom ask about starting points in negotiations and relative power, nor do they question the distributional consequences of outcomes. Yet all these concerns are relevant if individuals ask about the compromise's fairness or acceptability.

Many seemingly simple calculations of utility and right are far more complex. Politics drives individuals to decisions and actions. Its modalities simplify complex judgments and make them seem more unitary than they are. Budgets reduce moral concerns to line items and single appropriations. Voting, especially, simplifies complex equations into stark and seemingly unidimensional actions (Luce and Raiffa 1957, 360).[2] At the same time politics allows decisions involving multiple dimensions and trade-offs across incommensurable areas in compromises. It involves commitments to process, procedural values, and symbol and community as well as to specific issues and interests at hand. Decisions might involve different time dimensions as well as multiple decisions in formulation, passage, and implementation. All these dimensions might be assessed in a complex compromise even though the compromise decision looks discrete.

But individual integrity and responsibility are built around convictions and commitments. These involve commitments to ideals, principles of order or human relations or consistent attempts to take the good of others into account. Exemplary ideals of behavior or concrete norms can give life to these moral commitments and guide behavior and judgment. In any case, these commitments and convictions do not lend themselves to easy commensurability; they cannot be simply folded into one unitary judgment with no moral remainders (Schick 1984, 84–95, 120–24; Sen 1977). They may be foundational for all other assessments or the conditions for giving individual assessments any weight at all. For instance, it makes little sense beyond some grounds of efficiency to give weight to individual preferences without some serious principled concern for the equal dignity of persons. The tendency of microeconomists, game theorists, and some utilitarians to reduce such foundational assessments to weighted sums in an equation summing up one's preference misses entirely the nature of integrity and the nature of moral and ethical assessment in personal life (Goodin 1982).

Often individuals may hold convictions or commitments that conflict. Basic rights may conflict, ideal images of oneself as a person may confront assumed images tied to a policy role, or loyalty to family might clash with official responsibility. The covert moral dimension may enter into a seemingly straightforward trade-off. But the final action expresses a complex "decision" made, not the emergence of an opaque preference (Lindblom 1977). Both models of moral conviction—principled or ideal—do not reduce to simple unidimensional outcomes (A. Rapoport 1964, 50–95). For such a person giving up a moral good, acquiescing in a moral wrong, or collaborating with a morally imperfect goal entails the moral pain of knowing one has both succeeded and failed. Individuals may balance convictions, ideals, and rights, but they should not sum them.

This essay focuses upon compromise which involves an inescapable moral dimension. It involves a promise to live with a solution that is informed by: an urgency to attain a goal that involves moral stakes as defined by the politician's integrity; some realistic room for maneuvering so that the compromise is chosen, not forced; a commitment to pursue goals within accepted limits in preference to terrorist or revolutionary activity; a willingness to "live with" an agreed-upon solution, which could mean anything from collaborating in its establishment, to accepting it, to grudgingly accepting it and working to change it but under the publicly accepted guidelines; a minimal level of trust that the other side will abide by the terms of a settlement and also carry on conflict under agreed-upon methods.

This way of understanding compromise does not drop out or abolish moral remainders and tension as does absolutism or utilitarianism. Responsible agents and politicians should acknowledge the wrong or harm of a solution, accept responsibility for it and still be able to say they did the right thing. To do the right thing does not violate integrity, but to deny wrong or harm when individuals are responsible does.

This essay is not designed to explore the casuistry of committing moral wrongs to gain moral goods.[3] Rather, it seeks to map out the "good" reasons available to compromise in politics even when moral dimensions exist. While it often makes good sense to try to transform issues into ones of interest to diffuse political polarization and make debate more civil, this tactic should not allow people to purify the moral equations to help their consciences. Individuals are inextricably responsible for the moral remainders as well as the good. When persons judge a wrong or harm to be "justified," they mean that they can give good and persuasive reasons to justify the "wrong." When one's conscience or others challenge what was done as morally wrong or problematic, this increases the demand for very good reasons to justify what individuals did. People need reasons that can comparably answer moral claims; not all reasons can, and the more severe the moral harm or wrong, the better the reasons must be (Phillips and Mounce 1970, 20–40, 110ff.).

Political compromises can be tainted in a number of ways. Individuals seek goals in politics. They may be vague like empowering people, changing attitudes or symbols, or explicit like changing law or budget allocations, but they have a concrete shape and observable effects. The goals may involve rectifying immediate harms or injustices, or they may be more optimistic and seek to expand the rights or opportunities of citizens and increase the human flourishing in a society. Compromise comes first, then, when people must accept less than they sought. Individuals compromise the shape of the goal.

To achieve a goal in politics, people need power. To gain a stable and minimally coercive solution, they should use or change the rituals and procedures of the society and legitimate the law in terms people accept. Short of coercing people, individuals must persuade and use the methods of the system. The classic recent defenses of compromise focus upon the needs to avoid violence and maintain a civil order for future politics (Smith 1956; Crick 1972). Allies, voice, and visibility are all needed. To get them, individuals may trade off acquiescence or even support for policies they object to but regard as less important than overall objectives. If the system is biased to operate in one particular way, individuals might use methods that they despise, short of violence, in order to garner gains. Finally, they might strike a devil's bargain with abiding enemies on an issue and risk being influenced by them while exchanging support or acquiescence for a project of theirs. Individuals compromise in the means to attain the good.

Lastly, political compromises become solutions only if they are accepted. When people compromise, they promise to abide by the negotiated result, both the good and the bad, and related trade-offs. In some cases, if persons have official power, despised laws might have to be enforced in order to keep the other laws viable and working. Compromises represent imperfect solutions and both sides know this. One or all sides will continue to work to further their goals and all agree to work by the general rules and accepted practices.[4] But because people co-promise this cooperation, the agreement has a robust and durable quality about it. Compromises hold despite temptations, otherwise they fail as effective political solutions. Individuals compromise in collaborating in the solution.

Compromise has built-in instability because it entails personal responsibility for states of affairs involving moral wrongs as well as gains. They may be the right result given the circumstances, but the wrongs persist. Acknowledging these left-over harms and wrongs matters profoundly. Many politicians will know this, others will try to hide them or subsume them as they become committed to the compromise they helped forge. Sometimes the stability of the solution is helped by minimizing the moral import. But in an open and free politics, others will remind leaders of the moral stakes and costs of an issue, even if the makers would like to forget. Most political compromises, even those made in secret, take on a life of their own as they endure and prove their worth. As official solutions or practices, compromises become authoritative and gain symbolic and ritual legitimacy in people's eyes. Once settled, politicians prefer not to renegotiate painful issues. Compromise solutions become embodied in the practices, laws, and expenditures of the government and even in the expectations of the those who live with them. Sunk costs and political and social inertia support them (Downs 1967, Chap. 20).

But continuing responsibility exists because individuals actively form and express values when they act; they know the imperfections and choose to act anyway. Political actions are seldom dictated by preferences welling up from within or from circumstances. A person can actively use one's "own brains and be able to find one's bearings in each particular instance" (Lenin 1975, 588). To remain passive in one's own beliefs and before the unpredictability and obstinacy of political life means that one's "conscience either compromises or gets compromised" (Smith 1956, 55). When politicians act, they shape their preferences and the world around them. They judge and modify desires, decide their preferences, and pursue actions to gain them. The expression of a preference only masks the complicated judgments that precede the act. These judgments entail actions in a web of responsibility. Compromise flows from the active and responsible element of personal life, not from passive expression of determined preferences. (Lindblom 1977, Chaps. 1, 2, 3, 9)

The Missouri Compromise demonstrates the multiple dimensions of an imperfect but successful compromise. When Missouri petitioned for admission to the United States as a slave state in 1818, a number of forces and issues converged. Northerners and southerners were anxious to maintain parity in the senate for their respective sides even as they jostled for superiority. This became increasingly vital for southerners as they lost representation in the House of Representatives. At the same time, northern antislavery sentiment increased both as northern politicians appealed to Negro voters and were influenced by the wave of humanitarian reformism sweeping the country. Abolitionists first began to sound their calls. Additionally, a number of Federalist politicians were antislavery and saw this as an opportunity to break the hegemony of the Democratic party by splitting its northern and southern branches on the issue of slavery. The various antislavery politicians proposed "memorials" and amendments that sought to prohibit the expansion of slavery into new territories when the issue of Missouri's statehood arose.

The battles over statehood and the limitation of slavery exposed profound violence and cleavage within the country and incited a virulent southern reaction. The first self-conscious defenses of slavery as a positive good in the south were precipitated by this crisis. Battle lines hardened on the edges as abolitionists and fire eaters gained strength and self-consciousness. Amid threats of violence and secession, Henry Clay, the Speaker of the House, sought to fashion a compromise to avoid the violence and increasing sectional polarization. He played upon the desires of northern Democrats anxious to save the unity of the party and moderate and border state Democrats, ambivalent about slavery but committed to saving the union over other substantive issues. Using his ample powers of appointment, persuasion, and bluster to build the coalition necessary, he pulled the compromise together.

In reality, he got three separate bills, each mutually reinforcing one another, passed. The bills passed because a moderate center provided the margin of success and voted alternatively with the slaveholders and the antislavery forces to gain the necessary compromise. The adamant opponents and proponents of slavery remained unmoved. Eventually, the bills melded into one historical compromise. Missouri was admitted as a slave state; Maine became a free state; slavery was abolished in the rest of the Northwest Territory, but permitted in Arkansas and Oklahoma. Despite its unstable and awkward pedigree, the compromise took hold. It served the self-interest of Democrats and Whigs; it avoided violence and war—a war the North was in no position to fight or win—and maintained the precarious balance of power. The south still had some maneuvering room while slavery was prohibited in the vast majority of the free territory in the country. The compromise brilliantly addressed the prudential, political, and moral motives of each group while achieving a remarkable victory for the as yet weak antislavery forces who were clearly unable to dislodge slavery in place. The union also remained intact making it possible to continue a long crusade to eliminate slavery within one constitutional order. Eventually the compromise's success at defusing issues and preventing expansion made it a legitimate and durable settlement. It established the framework for sectional conflict for the next thirty years. Its demise in 1854 spelled the beginning of the end of the intersectional peace (Moore 1953). Thus, a workable compromise can gain political and moral effectiveness despite mixtures of motives, opposition at the limits, and great imperfection.

Individuals usually compromise because they cannot get their way given the reality of a situation. This means there are at least two sides to a compromise. The compromise presumes reciprocity for its validity. Not all promises require reciprocity, but political solutions require all sides to agree to abide by the stipulated performance. When individuals live in the same community and continue to interact and live together, this united future can alone guarantee a tremendous degree of cooperation (Axelrod 1984, Chaps. 1, 8, 9). Such political and moral obligations and responsibility hinge upon promises to abide by the compromise, but individuals are not bound if the conditions of promising are violated. On one hand, promises made under direct threat of totally unacceptable harm have no moral standing. If the other sides feel no obligation to abide by the compromise and will violate it at will, then one's promise is vitiated. If others cheat on the terms or if they radically violate the practices of conflict to get their way, especially if they resort regularly to violent coercion, then promises do not bind. Yet even here, promises presume performance, not intention. If the other side feels no real obligations but lives up to the bargain for self-interested or other reasons, the promise holds. To the extent self-interest and obligation converge, compromise gains strength. As they diverge, problems can be anticipated and individuals may give wary assent and have qualified obligations.

Promises and their attendant obligations assume other politicians can be trusted to live up to the compromise. What matters in the final analysis, though, is that performance, and true performance, even for self-interested reasons, can increase trust and obligations to the compromise. If compromises possess no moral authority other than coercion and individuals cannot trust the other side to abide, then compromise becomes a far riskier but still viable enterprise, but far more contingent on one's ability to enforce sanctions if violations occur.[5]

Compromises occur with opponents, adversaries, antagonists, rivals, and even friends or allies. All agree to accept solutions and abide by rules, however broad and flexible. Both sides give and accept good faith promises, that have authority with each other. They do not depend just on coercion, but authoritative force or threats of retaliation may reinforce the agreement. Individuals agree to continue the struggle but to forgo violence and "play by the rules." Consistent threats backing up promises can help build trust that later becomes self-reinforcing and makes compromise seem a safer and more viable practice for parties.

Enemies, as I intimated above, radically change politics. The term enemy sometimes merges with opponents, especially in the exaggerated rhetoric of politics and sports. But enemies change the moral character of conflict and introduce much deeper levels of hatred, hostility, and desire to injure or destroy.[6] When people target someone as an enemy, they reserve the right to use any means necessary to get their way. An enemy rules others out of the normal moral community and its obligations. Enemies are in a state of war and are not bound by the "rules of the game." To the extent an enemy denies that opponents possess human dignity and autonomy, this further frees them from any obligations to live up to promises. This warrants the use of violence and undercuts any moral commitment to promising.

Individuals may compromise with enemies, but their moral responsibility is considerably lessened and the latitude of good reasons to break the compromise considerably broadened. Enemies narrow options by their warrant of force or their denial of the full humanity of the other side. Individuals react in self-defense and realize that real compromise may be impossible. Any agreements need to be undergirded by threats of violence. No communal authority or mutual respect for each other's autonomy or dignity bind the participants. In these cases individuals may act as much out of necessity determined by the power of both sides as anything else. On the other hand, agreements based upon threats of retaliation can have startling durability as long as both sides have sufficient power and will to respond when provoked (Axelrod 1984, Chaps. 1, 8, 9). Individuals may start with agreements with enemies and, slowly, through successful agreements and compromises, build up trust. Many good compromises can be justified as attempts to build attenuated community with enemies or even transform them into opponents.

If given a chance, enemies would force individuals into a capitulation, not a compromise. A capitulation defines an end boundary on the continuum of compromises. People capitulate when the weight of another's power so overwhelms them that a solution is enforced upon them. They accede only from fear of adverse consequences, not because of any positive gains. The threat is so great to individuals and what they value that they go along because they are neither saints nor martyrs. The agreement has no moral or cooperative aspect.

Even capitulations to violence can sometimes evolve into compromise. The complexity and serendipity of politics make it impossible to rule out any possibilities. The imposed settlements at the end of World War II demanded "unconditional surrender." The "masters" of West Germany and Japan avoided the harsh extractions of World War I and rehabilitated the countries even as they imposed new governmental orders upon them. The allies' interests as well as their historical experience lead them to respect their enemies enough that the vanquished came to accept and even embrace many of the imposed conditions when they regained their autonomy.

What appears to be a capitulation, may also be a livable compromise if it lays foundations for future gains. If a seeming capitulation in reality keeps a strong power base alive rather than risk it in a suicidal confrontation, the compromise can be defended as Lenin defended his grossly unequal treaties with Germany during World War I:

> Imagine that your car is held up by bandits. You hand them over your money, passport, revolver and car. In return you are rid of the pleasant company of the bandits. This is unquestionably a compromise . . . (I "give" you money, fire-arms and a car "so that you give me" the opportunity to get away with a whole skin). It would be difficult, however, to find a sane man who would declare such a compromise "inadmissible on principle," or who would call the compromiser an accomplice of the bandits (Lenin 1975, 563).

As long as individuals can reasonably conclude that actions will enable them to "survive" and continue to "fight" for goals in the future, they can defend it as a tattered compromise. These preserve openness for real future gains and might even qualify as a first step in a longer road. If it ends in permanent enslavement, eviscerates a people's will or power to continue, or ends in obliteration, a capitulation remains just that.

If capitulation stands as one boundary of compromise, "integrated solutions" stand at the other end. An integrated solution occurs when all sides cooperate in a political accomplishment where everyone gains the greatest possible gain they think possible with the least amount of moral qualms. In fact, all sides believe it to be not just the best or most utilitarian but also the "right" solution. These solutions endure the longest and possess the least inherent instability because of the very little perceived moral harm (Carens 1979, 127–29; Follett 1949).

The persons who negotiate integrated compromises respect the other persons and their interests, they also presume a high degree of trust in the other side's honesty and promises (Raiffa 1982). People enter negotiations seeking gains for all and try to minimize any sense of zero-sum bargaining where one side's gain must mean the other side's losses. Such solutions arise best where a community of belief and interests are already shared and where enough trust has been developed by past encounters. Such conditions probably exist on a more widespread scale than is generally recognized. One of the great skills of political life is the ability to characterize situations in ways in which integrated compromises can occur. By adopting that approach, everyone's interests in many areas might be more justly served (Fisher and Ury 1981). These negotiations seek to meticulously unpack all the issues for each side and either move solutions to the outermost boundaries of mutually satisfactory gains, or enlarge the potential gains for each side (Raiffa 1982).

Although more widespread than normally thought, even integrated solutions cannot eliminate all moral tension. First, they do not take into account power. If participants still believe not enough has been accomplished or agree because they do not have enough power, then the solutions can still be questioned and pursued later. Second, participants might have to make side deals that involve moral compromises to get enough power to negotiate an integrated solution. Consequently, the solution itself looks good but the methods taint it. Finally, even good will and respect for the other side do not completely cancel out moral evaluations of desired goals. To the extent the solution does not comport with basic commitments, individuals can still feel the gnawing dissatisfaction. This is probably a pretty good reason to defuse moral terms in political debate or use autonomy to trump other moral concerns. To quiet moral complaint makes integrated compromises easier to attain, assuming people negotiate from relative equality, but it also places autonomy at the center of the moral stage.

Compromise is purified and has its strongest ethical defense by focusing upon compromise out of respect for autonomy.[7] In such a defense, reasons associated with power, inequality, and reality constraints are dropped out because they have no "moral" status. Compromise has its greatest moral strength as an act motivated by respect for the autonomy and dignity of other persons.[8] True and morally autonomous compromises derive from a "certain sort of respect for his opponent" and according the other side's interests "some degree of moral legitimacy" (Golding 1979, 15–17; Benditt 1979, 27–28). As a moral strategy, individuals should not regard opponents as less worthy and at least approach the problem in a "spirit of mutual accommodation" seeking "genuine, long-term reconciliation"(Kuflik 1979, 44, 53–54).

These claims provide the best reasons to compromise and highlight that compromise lies at the heart of liberal and democratic politics. They do not, however, do full justice to the practice of political compromise. Politicians seek concrete solutions in a world of power and resource inequality. Political officials are charged with a range of other responsibilities such as maintaining security and the legitimacy of law. Many persons hold radically different moral views, and the moral stakes may differ. Individuals might have good reason not to respect the "interests" of an enemy whose interests consist in denying people their own humanity. Many opponents shade towards enemies in the heat of political struggles, and individuals who compromise should be as sensitive to that as to their autonomy.

In this world, politicians compromise for many good prudential and political reasons as well as moral reasons. Anti-slavery forces in 1820, 1833, and 1850 did not compromise because they recognized the moral legitimacy of slavery or the dignity of the way of life of the slave owners. They recognized the other side's power or they valued the continuation of the union. To limit valid compromise to equal respect confuses some good reasons to compromise with the actual structure of the activity. This purified compromise, by definition, rules out the really hard cases where both dictionary senses hold—individuals settle something by consent or mutual consensus, but it involves "something derogatory, hazardous or objectionable" (Carens 1979, 123).[9]

The moral purity of compromise might be kept intact by a slight variation. This would argue that principles direct action but interests are what should be compromised. If interests can be separated from integrity and principles or ideals, then they can be negotiated and traded off with minimal moral tension and few moral remainders (Benditt 1979). Unfortunately, the two cannot easily be distinguished. Interests stand as tangible and seemingly fungible items such as food, jobs, opportunities, a vote, or lawyer in trial. Many interests, however, also express the basic preconditions of living or the day-to-day expression of selfhood, and the self is imbedded in integrity. Most interests are grounded and defensible, even if sometimes remotely, in moral principles or ideals. As interests conflict, they draw in a complex web of moral conflicts. For instance people "earn" their salaries, yet money is taxed away. Citizens pay taxes for police to protect their possessions; but they also pay for legal aid lawyers to guarantee fairness to the people who threaten those possessions. These distinctions are undercut even more as individuals and groups gloss their interests with rights claims. Compromises then become inexorably drawn into moral quagmires unless people make specific attempts to hide or forgo the moral dimension. Calling something an interest, however, does not insulate compromises of interest from moral justifications.

One last attempt to make compromise a morally consistent endeavor separates the process of compromise from the actual end state (Golding 1979, 7, 8). Yet neither distinction particularly helps in understanding or judging political compromise. Political processes, especially formal ones, are linked with basic moral concerns like fairness and self-expression. The process itself is negotiated and imaginatively used as seriously as any end state since any process advantages certain groups and determines many outcomes. Additionally, the resources individuals possess deeply affect their ability to use or manipulate seemingly fair procedures. Different processes have different resource thresholds to use as well. A democratic and liberal politics always opens and revises its processes as seriously as end states, sometimes more so, because the process legitimates so many political resolutions. Autonomy requires participation, so one "end" may be to open the process and the process becomes a major goal to defend and maintain. To accept or reject participation entails compromises as much as any end states. Even end states in politics open up onto the processes of financing, enforcing, and interpreting them. Finally, some end states may involve empowering the dispossessed that reopens not only the problem of process but also the outcomes determined before the group was empowered. While it might seem a nice heuristic distinction, the difference between end and process does little to clarify the moral dimensions of political compromise.[10]

Individuals seek to justify compromises because they are compromises and initially suspect. Justifications are strong arguments—they give reasons that persuade oneself and others that a compromise was the right thing to do given the circumstances. Justifications are not excuses. When individuals justify, they present strong claims that others not just "would" have but "should" do what they did in the same situation. Such justification presumes freedom to decide under constraints and responsibility for the action. Even if a *prima facie* "wrong" is committed, the justification does not seek to excuse the wrong and deny culpability for it. Rather when individuals justify an act in politics, they claim that even though the wrong or harm occurred, they did what should have been done and what anyone else of similar beliefs and responsibilities should have done. Justifications defend "right" actions, they do not seek forgiveness (Greenwalt 1984; Bok 1978, Chaps. 6, 7).

When individuals justify an action in these terms, unless they are an absolutist or utilitarian, they do not abolish the wrong or harm done. What does it mean to suggest that an act may be right given the circumstances but individuals are still responsible for the wrongs in it? It means that individuals can still acknowledge the harm, feel remorse or guilt for it, and apologize. Because the wrong is not abolished, they should take it very seriously when they make any decisions and seek to avoid it if at all possible. All other remedies should be exhausted to ensure that the wrongs are absolutely necessary to accomplish the right act. People might even be obligated to compensate for the wrong afterwards. Others have the legitimate moral right and maybe even obligation to challenge and accuse persons for the wrongs and require that people defend themselves with good reasons. Opponents might legitimately seek to change the actions for these reasons. If the actions transgress the criminal codes, despite the special permissions of political life, it means wrongs can be punished by society. Wrong and harm exist but do not vanish and should weigh heavily and shape decisions. Actions might legitimately be praised and blamed for these reasons. In private life or later public life, individuals might seek to expiate these wrongs or make up for them. This awareness should lead persons to remind the public and themselves of the costs of successful action. Ends may justify but they do not exonerate.

This approach sometimes can lead individuals to overdramatize the tragic aspect of political life.[11] Max Weber presents a famous dichotomy between the "ethic of ultimate ends" and the "ethic of responsibility." While famous and often quoted, these categories are not all that clear (Weber 1969, 106–28). As discussed in chapter one, those committed to the ethic of ultimate ends really represent two kinds of persons. One takes joy in his own purity and finds his fulfillment in devotion to an end. He or she refuses to compromise even when it might help attain the end. The second kind is committed to an ultimate, even utopian, end, and discounts all other consequences in the march to gain that goal. The two categories do not represent the same phenomenon. A Red Brigade terrorist fits under the first, a committed Leninist under the second. But both deny any personal responsibility for complex or plural consequences.

In response, many commentators, especially conservative ones, leap on Weber's dichotomy to rule out all passion and commitment from political life. The "ethic of responsibility" recognizes that, by nature, political action involves morally dubious means at times and unanticipated evil ramifications. To the point, all good politicians are inextricably bound to the violence that must enforce any stable political gains (Weber 1969, 120–22). This can easily become a cover to deny the power of strong moral claims and criticisms in society. Moral claims are consigned to fanaticism or the grotesque utilitarianism of the "ethic of ultimate ends." This critique reduces responsible politics to accommodation with what is and denigrates serious moral aspirations. Responsibility and prudence become handmaidens of existing inequality and injustice.

But Weber's approach is far more complex, and I have adapted many of his insights in this book. For him, the ethic of ends supplements the ethic of responsibility. For without the passion and power of ends, politics is reduced to actions of political machines merely maintaining those in power, or to sterile exercises in power. Weber suggests that politicians must have "warm passion and a cool sense of proportion" to do justice to the "vocation of politics." A good politician should be capable of assessing the facts, be aware of the pitfalls and temptations of power and sensitive to the full extent of consequences of actions. "Politics is a strong and slow boring of hard boards. It takes both passion and perspective" (Weber 1969, 128).

Weber's politician can act from passion and conviction and, hopefully, can respond to the aspirations of others when defending compromise. But Weber's pessimism and obsession with the demonic role of violence in all politics lead him to underestimate the potential open orders have to domesticate and respond to passionate crusades without destroying themselves. In viable liberal and democratic orders, open politics permits passion, commitment, and responsibility to flourish in a dialectic more effectively than Weber thought. These attributes may not adhere in the same person, as Weber asked, for them to work in the system. Politicians and citizens can exist in tension with agitators and prophets who push the system and give office-holding politicians the jolt and leverage they need to achieve passionate goals by moderate means. Even acknowledging this, Weber still saw an inextricably tragic dimension in the need to use the "decisive means of politics"— violence. "No ethics in the world can dodge the fact that in numerous instances the attainment of 'good' ends is bound to the fact that one must be willing to pay the price of using morally dubious means or at least dangerous ones—and facing the possibility or even the probability of evil ramifications" (Weber 1969, 121). This sobers the possibilities of political life and should humble practitioners.

The central moral tenet of this book is that individuals possess responsibility for their actions. But the tragic should not be trivialized. To see all politics as a guilt-ridden and tragic undertaking rings hollow for most politicians and misses both the optimistic and realistic dimension of moral action. Persons of integrity seek their interests and moral goals in politics. But all moral goals require concrete shapes. They are almost always underdetermined, and their shape will be influenced by the possibilities of an historical moment. Individuals of honesty and integrity will see limits and flaws in any solution. But they carry little initial responsibility for the practices, limitations and modes of politics within a society. People cannot control them, but must use them, influence them, and modify them to accomplish purposes.

But responsibility presumes the power to influence. Most of the time when individuals use the means available, they do not take on the cosmic guilt that Weber assigns to political actors. They do take on moral and prudential responsibility for the wrongs done and should acknowledge them and seek to change the most vicious of the practices. Even Weber's obsession with violence, while warranted, hardly does moral justice to the use of violence in self-defense or when constrained by open due process and accountability. All politicians take responsibility and risk contagion and corruption, especially those in office, but the risks differ from life only in quantity, not in kind.

Notes

1. In *Webster's New Collegiate Dictionary* (Springfield, Mass.: G. & C. Merriam Company, 1973), 230, the definitions for the noun and verb "compromise" have two aspects. The first emphasizes mutual accommodation; the second, which I quote, highlights the moral tension of compromise as an action and settlement.

2. Just as importantly, the paradoxes of voting and the ability to manipulate voting outcomes through strategic voting or agenda control make it extraordinarily difficult to garner a morally consistent outcome even if preferences are simple (Riker 1984). Miller (1983) addresses some of Riker's concerns in this area.

Game theory discussions of bargaining can aggravate this oversimplification of moral reality. Utility functions, whether ordinal or cardinal, demand an ordering and individuals must express a preference on which conditions are allowed to the ordering. Any moral concerns or tensions are simply summed in as variations on other forms of gain or loss. Psychological nuance or internalized conscience are not considered unless they show up indirectly in a game by "irrational" preferences. In these situations, players might try to break out of a typical prisoner's dilemma and deliberately lose for awhile to induce cooperation because it is "right." This psychological thinness of assumptions reduces power to threats and offensive bargaining. It misses entirely the role of symbolic and moral authority and demonstrates the blindness exemplified by Stalin's question, "How many divisions does the Vatican have?" (Sen 1977, 336–39; Walzer 1973; A. Rapoport 1964, 154–57; Schick 1984, 120–48).

Hardin (1984) describes how "conventions" to which individuals commit can be integrated with the model of decision-making. Interests then becomes a much wider, almost tautological, term and it is still not clear that conventions can capture the nature of integrity that is at stake for political actors.

3. McCormick and Ramsey (1978) explore in extensive detail the problem of "doing evil to achieve good." All the articles reject any utilitarian approach that drops out evil from the equation. But it is never exactly clear to me or the theorists exactly what it means to recognize that harm must often be involved in doing good. McCormick and Ramsey both argue that individuals do the "right" thing even when some evil consequences inhere in an action. However, they share the perspective of this book in that they insist that we cannot simply drop "ontic harm" out of moral equations or exonerate people of all responsibility for it, even in right actions.

4. The idea of accepted practices of politics leaves considerable room for openness and innovation. In a liberal and democratic order, as long as individuals avoid direct violence, imaginative politicians, especially with few resources, can extend the boundaries of practice even if violating sensibilities and taste. Sometimes civil disobedience and the expressed willingness to go to jail can become a practice that enables citizens to identify serious issues while not abdicating loyalty to the system.

5. Hobbes' *Leviathan* provides the unrivaled analysis of the fundamental importance of controlled coercion to make agreement possible amongst non-moral individuals. Axelrod (1984) provides a challenging alternative whereby cooperation can evolve with less centralized violence than Hobbes required.

6. *Scribner-Bantam English Dictionary* (New York: Charles Scribner's Sons, 1977, 299), suggests that all these words "agree in naming an opposing agent." But "enemies" clearly suggests the "strongest term, connoting not only one who hates, but one who desires to injure the object of his hatred." Raiffa (1982) Chap. 1, focuses upon "cooperative antagonists" who have interests but are neither malevolent nor altruistic. These negotiators commonly are slightly distrustful and expect each side to make a good case and indulge in some strategic posturing. He acknowledges most negotiating techniques reach their limits at "strident antagonists" who are totally malevolent and untrustworthy and do not keep promises while exploiting power advantages to the fullest.

7. Pennock and Chapman (1979) has essays by Golding, Benditt and especially fine ones by Carens and Kuflik that present this case. The Carens essay covers political compromise and corrects many of the limitations of the more exclusively moral essays.

8. Kuflik 1979, 40, 53, 54; Benditt 1979, 29; Golding 1979, 15, 16.

9. See Carens (1979) for a more technical discussion of a number of these points about moral compromise in politics.

10. Because process and outcome are so linked in politics, it is not clear that separate criteria by which to evaluate them can be found. The fairness or justice of a process might be judged differently from the outcomes it produces, but in a liberal democracy or from the point of view of autonomy or equal dignity, the two converge. The two dimensions would be the distribution both at the end and in the process. Autonomy demands distributions in each.

Additionally, in a theory like Rawls (1971), the end state may be defined as minimal conditions to guarantee an open process for all in the state. Many outcomes are allowed as long as the basic conditions are satisfied.

It might make more sense to speak of internal and external evaluation of a compromise. A compromise can be evaluated from the point of view of the goals sought and this generally focuses upon end states. But the compromise might also be judged by how it comports with political order, minimizing violence, or respects equal human dignity. Any of these apply to both the activity and the end result. Needless to say a politician can invoke any of these but must answer to all.

11. The approach of this chapter is deeply influenced by the eloquent treatment of these issues by Walzer (1973). At some point, however, Walzer seems to imply that most politics is existentially flawed and requires that individuals profoundly "dirty" integrity when they enter the arena. Politics seems to require an existential leap into the abyss. In his example, a reforming politician in a corrupt city must promise a dishonest ward boss influence in getting contracts in order to get elected and govern well. Walzer concedes that the reformer should do so rather than let others continue to corrupt the city, but the reformer contaminates himself and bears a great burden of guilt, that must be expiated. The politician becomes a scapegoat for necessary crimes on behalf of the common good.

This position ignores, as does Weber, one's lack of responsibility for what is and the demand to use the instrumentalities available to do good. I also think it underestimates the more positive moral dimensions of this position, which I enumerated above. A broader understanding minimizes the existential leap and guilt of Walzer's example without sacrificing his focus upon responsibility. Alan Donagan (1977, 186–87) provides an alternative account:

> Even in a society in which corruption is normal and lawful, it is wrong to initiate the corruption of others or to harden them in it; but it is not wrong to defend yourself by means of corruption against corruption already initiated by others.
>
> There is much that a reforming politician in the situation Walzer describes may do without dirtying his hands. He may not initiate the corruption of a previously honest ward boss. He may not promise to secure him a contract unless he can do so lawfully; and he may not make other wrong or unlawful promises, for example, to arrange to have work contracted for inadequately inspected. Moreover, the harm done in granting the contract—presumably that the public will pay more than it would with another contractor—must be outweighed by the good gained by means of it.

4

Principled Compromise

"In the world as it is, 'compromise' is not an ugly word but a noble word. If the whole free way of life could be summed up in one word, it would be 'compromise.' A free way of life is a constant conflict punctuated by compromises which then serve as a jumping-off point for further conflict, more compromises, more conflict, in a never-ending struggle toward achieving man's highest goals."—Saul Alinsky

"Compromise, as a self-sufficient principle divorced from all considerations of truth and justice, is simply, in the last analysis, the ancient Thrasymachian doctrine that makes it right."—John Hallowell

Compromise makes liberal and democratic life possible. Liberal democracy does not equal compromise, as T.V. Smith sometimes suggests, but without compromise, democracy and liberty could not flourish together (Smith 1956). On the other hand, majority coalitions can compromise among themselves and dominate minorities within a pluralist order. Unequal bargaining positions or ignorance can lead citizens to compromise away their autonomy or basic civil rights protections. These compromises can occur within what passes for a

79

formally liberal and democratic order (Kuflik 1979). But the connection is not fortuitous. The principles that justify liberal democracy also provide the strongest moral reasons to compromise.

Mutual respect for each individual's autonomy and dignity justifies a liberal and democratic political order and directs individuals to consider political compromises as the norm. Respect for the requirements of free individuals and the diversity they generate in political life provide a framework not only to justify compromise but also the strongest reasons to limit or disallow compromises. They can also direct people to ensure conditions which make compromises more fair and democratic.[1]

Consistent with his view that the purpose of compromise is predominantly to maintain civility and peace, T. V. Smith argued that one should never compromise unless forced to by necessity. Unforced compromises demonstrate bad faith (Smith 1956, 64,65). For Smith, as for Machiavelli, necessity refers to the obstinacy of another's power and point of view. But principled compromise can occur for good reasons separate from a sheer concern with another's power. Individuals can compromise because they respect the personal autonomy or dignity of other citizens, or because the compromise ethos extends and strengthens liberal and democratic life. Humility and conscientiousness can justify compromise. People also can compromise to protect a system of institutions and practices that give life to liberal and democratic ideals.

Individuals assume their own worth or the worth of their assessments of goals when they enter political life. This self-respect gives strength to their integrity and fuels their active participation. At the moral level, when they seek to be heard and taken seriously, they demand respect for themselves as persons and as purveyors of goals of worth. In this sense, the drive for accomplishment in politics is supported by claims of respect for one's freedom and dignity as well as by the worth of the goals or ideals pursued. This places self-limiting moral constraints upon the drive to action, since all other humans possess the same dignity and autonomy, which deserves *prima facie* respect. Short of the claims of absolutists, respect for oneself and one's right to pursue goals is self-limited by respect for other individuals who are in the political order. This is defined most clearly in the liberal and democratic constitutional limits placed upon the government when it engages individuals. The rights that constrain government action and prosecution all embody the respect that should be accorded all humans. This dual process gives reality to that respect and the freedom and dignity of individuals when they confront the massed powers of government.

These self-limiting moral claims about one's own integrity introduce the major initial compromise of liberal and democratic life. It pulls people up short in their drive to accomplishment by obligating them to respect the procedures that protect their and other's rights and dignity. This imposes constraints on means and time and effort that might frustrate or slow down their urgent efforts at arriving at their goals. It requires them to take other people and their interests or views seriously and to listen, talk, and even negotiate rather than dominate them on the basis of pure power. It also means that one should allow others to organize their own power and efforts to oppose or modify one's goals, assuming this is done within the range of liberal democratic means.

When individuals engage other people in political life, these moral assumptions do not permit them to assign others subhuman inferior status or exclude them from political power or community benefits just because they oppose a goal. For the operating assumptions are that, initially, all individuals, even if they hold differing positions, possess the right to speak and organize on behalf of their interests and commitments. The principles of respect for human autonomy and dignity justify one's own political pursuits as well as those of allies, opponents, and spectators. At the moral level, individuals engage each other not because they have equal power, talent, or wealth, but because they respect their personhood.

What does mutual respect for other individuals in politics actually require from humans? It begins with the self-limiting ordinance to not destroy the foundations of another's autonomy and dignity. When individuals engage each other in political conflict and cooperation, this self-denying ordinance means that individuals should not use coercion or manipulation against others to undermine their very capacity to reflect, judge, speak and act on behalf of their commitments. This involves pulling up short in political victories over opponents and while winning on issues, not destroying them. It, of course, does not preclude efforts to coopt or change the minds of opponents and their supporters.

At the most basic level of engagement, such moral respect involves a willingness to let the other persons speak their minds, present their positions, and work to get them accepted. Speaking and justifying is the essence of open democratic life and no free politics or promising is possible without it. This respect for speaking should be accorded each individual or group regardless of their initial power. To deny someone their opportunity to speak and work simply because they are not powerful in the process violates the core of liberal and democratic life.

The next dimension of moral-political respect accords people the respect of listening to them. Serious listening is an art; it is augmented when another has power and is needed for an alliance. All speaking and acting citizens are potential allies or opponents, all possess votes, manpower, and the potential for effort; so listening can be serious political and prudential as well as moral business. Listening to another can also introduce the underestimated possibility that the other side may have something of worth to say, that they may be right about an issue, have new facts, new perspectives. But most important, listening accords due respect to the people, their insights and life experience.

After pulling up to listen seriously to others, compromising involves taking other people's efforts and positions seriously—giving due to their right points and trying to integrate them into solutions. Respect for other persons does not entail agreeing with all they say or accepting it all—the others may be profoundly wrong or mistaken. But it entails the respectful attempt to discern the truth in what was said and to accept persuasive and good reasons to change the course of action. Individuals owe to other political actors reflection on their positions, not agreement. But if the others are not integrated into the compromise solution, the last dimension of political respect lets the other side continue to pursue their own causes within the political order. Individuals, even when they lose on an issue, do not lose their own autonomy or respect for their own ideas. They are free to pursue those ideas and reopen issues later.

This last point is crucial to the moral ecology of integrity. It offers the hope that one or even a series of defeats does not mean total defeat of moral goals and ideals. Individuals of integrity can console themselves and keep their commitments in some equilibrium by accepting the defeat or imperfect solution while having the option of expressing their commitments and fighting for them in the open political arena. Thus the urgency and imperative nature of moral integrity can be grounded in fair obedience and pursuit of issues at the same time.

Finally when individuals are included in a compromise, the act of negotiating with them, listening, asking them to listen to the other side, and trading with them, enhances respect for them. It marks them as citizens. When individuals make promises to one another, they treat each other with the greatest respect. They inform each other that they trust their integrity enough to rely upon the others' capacity to discipline themselves and the group, and live up to the agreement. Compromising with others invites and pulls the estranged and alien into the community of citizenship. It transforms alienation into effort and effort into recognition and accomplishment.

Such negotiating, promising, and taking seriously creates an ethos, a set of social and political expectations among citizens of a liberal and democratic political order. This ethos deserves defense and expansion. It encourages people to enter politics rather than sulk, sink into apathy or turn to terror or revolution. It offers even individuals of relatively little initial power the chance to be heard and imposes on them the responsibility to decide what they want and work on the issues. If the resource threshold is relatively low, the ethos invites people into politics and makes it the arena where serious conflict can be resolved rather than allowed to fester. Such patterns of negotiating and compromising can build up communities and traditions. It can knit a plural order of isolated and sometimes antagonistic groups and individuals into a more lasting community because individuals cross their boundaries and meet, talk, agree and keep faith with each other. Thus, society becomes more than a co-association of independent groups. It provides a powerful boost for individuals to empower themselves. For if others in the political order will compromise with people who possess power or positions and if individuals have at least an initial hearing, they will work harder to build power bases and alliances, since all have an initial chance to enter the fray.

The possibility of compromise encourages the acquisition and expansion of political skills by many individuals and groups and makes possible accomplishment without dominating power. It encourages the dynamic towards peaceful accretion of power, and funnels energy, anger, and hopes into construction of coalitions and community. It also gives people a way of seeing things in the long term. Many great issues in democratic life take a very long time to reach fruition. Defeats have marked every great political campaign, but the hope for change remains because no total closure has occurred and people do have the right to speak and the possibility of being heard.

Such a moral-political world encourages the values of cooperation, mutual respect, and peaceful, if at times rambunctious, accommodation within the political order. It can encourage respect for law because most people have had a chance to influence the law and because laws can, in fact, be changed by concerted effort. Law, therefore, becomes a potential ally, not a permanent enemy; it breeds familiarity across class and group lines, it throws opponents together and encourages civility and trust, if not agreement on positions. Compromising with other humans, then, need not be a tired or cynical activity; rather, it gives personal and political reality to the values of liberal and democratic life.

Respect for persons of autonomy and dignity can justify the compromise of one's goals for a wide variety of good reasons. Individuals might compromise to empower groups within a society. A profound weakness of liberal democracy is that it too often ignores the social and economic preconditions of exercising autonomy and political power. Individuals can justly compromise their other morally inspired goals to ensure the preconditions of the values that justify pursuing their goals. They might compromise to ensure that the primary goods of shelter, education, health care and institutional protections against government duress are in place. Compromises can be made to ensure that people or groups presently silenced can enter the arena and give voice to their aspirations. Short of empowering, individuals might compromise on their tactics to ensure that they listen to these voices or try to ferret out what silenced people would seek if they could speak. Liberal and democratic political actors should seek to respect the legitimate interests of their opponents, even if the opponents lack the power to give them substance.[2]

Persons and associations have strong ethical rights, derived from autonomy, to pursue their own interests and influence the public realm. Politicians should respect these rights and activities, even when politicians believe that their opponents are wrong. This involves the critical moral discipline and compromise with the imperative nature of many morally inspired goals. It compromises among the moral principles of autonomy, respect for dignity and the imperative goals one is pursuing. Political actions can seek to remedy a harm or achieve a good, but not to destroy the other's ability to pursue legitimate interests, unless the other side chooses to resort to coercion or violate others' basic rights and interests. This mutual respect can be reinforced by acknowledging the other side's sincerity. Individuals should shift efforts to persuade or change others' convictions or at least out-organize them, rather than cripple their freedom of action. A morally attuned ear would listen carefully to independent and sincere opponents and openly recognize that the other side might have plausible, if "mistaken," positions. On a critical or underrated point, politicians might even be persuaded that the other side is right or insightful.

These reasons generate obligations to treat with opponents on issues and compromise to avoid crippling their autonomous ability to judge or act. Respect for autonomy and dignity, however, does not generate an absolute requirement to accommodate an opponent's freedom to pursue any interests by any means. Some opponents may be enemies to others and inflict violence on persons or violate other persons' autonomy through coercion and manipulation. In some localities, a majority might even use law and official coercion to dominate local minorities or unpopular individuals. Nothing obligates individuals to compromise in such situations; such enemies or local tyrants may be overturned while avoiding a totalitarian or tyrannical regime. This respect for autonomy would not require compromise with a rising and violent party that actively subverted liberal and democratic government, for instance, the Nazi's in the late 1920s or the neo-Nazi Aryan Nation today.

The values of liberal and democratic regimes have always supported local autonomy and have been reinforced by prudential concerns with minimum abuse. But on the other hand, for over a century "states' rights" served as a code to defend legal and structural discrimination in the American south and, recently, to frustrate efforts at solving problems such as cross-state pollution. It does not follow that national efforts to eradicate state-supported abuses in civil rights or regional pollution by federal action means that all discretion and power of the state governments should be abolished. The autonomy of a state's citizens might be considerably enhanced by the higher quality of participation available at state and local government levels. Experiments in governance and greater responsiveness to decentralized government might also support independence in state governments, despite limitations in areas like civil rights or the environment. Full and vital national action can and probably should supersede states in the enforcement of civil rights and the provision of neglected basic human needs without undermining state authority in other areas (Dobel 1985). Respect for individual and associational autonomy may justify compromises even if individuals do not respect the position or interest of opponents.

Autonomy finds its reality in reflecting individuals who choose legitimate interests and claim inviolate realms of judgment and action for themselves. Politicians might justify compromise because they respect the legitimate interests of their opponents. When these interests are closely tied to the grounds of autonomy, this obligation increases. When other persons possess organizational power and leadership, however, unilateral obligations to discover interests and unilaterally pull short or compromise decline. People can generally accept the assumed competence of individuals or groups to determine their own positions and negotiate from their position of power. The self-denying compromise, out of respect for others' autonomy, becomes most severe when opponents do not possess power commensurate with their autonomy or dignity.

Individuals might rightly compromise because of the moral complexity of a situation. At any political nexus, several moral principles or issues might be involved, and usually there will be no clear lexical priority among the various principles. Even if an ordering exists, the ranking seldom overwhelms all the weight of other moral obligations and concerns. Most political battles over property and redistribution, for instance, begin with principled claims that autonomy or communal obligations requires that individuals ensure that all citizens of a community have the basic preconditions and tools to make decisions and pursue life plans while maintaining their civic integrity. These just claims put obligations upon society to redistribute funds to ensure that those—especially children—born without the basics of shelter, education, health care and legal protection, are provided with them. Oftentimes, these obligations raise questions concerning how seriously many individuals "deserve" all their own "wealth" because they gained their wealth based on many undeserved or relative advantages, since many relative advantages, such as intelligence, physical stamina, education or even motivation, come from conditions beyond an individual's control, such as the talent, parents, or social status.

These claims conflict with a series of intuitively plausible arguments to defend unequal wealth distribution. On one hand, individuals have "earned" their property by devoting time and effort to gain remuneration or by taking risks that others refused. All the while, these individuals sacrificed pleasures and gratifications and worked to develop and perfect their "lucky" attributes. Utilitarians would claim that unequal distributions create an incentive system that generates more wealth for the entire system. Property rights can encourage self-respect and self-empowerment. Unequal property distribution can encourage hard work, thrift, and risk taking as well as innovation. At the same time, widespread distribution of property can counteract the tendency of the state to aggrandize power while providing more opportunities to foster intellectual and cultural diversity. These arguments might be augmented by claims that if society has agreed to respect certain property arrangements and individuals have built their lives, made plans, and even risked their future on these promises, then opponents must proceed with great caution before they violate these past promises and wreak havoc on property owners. For instance, both the exercise of eminent domain and most expropriation in the name of self-determination require just compensation. Mutually legitimate, even if differently weighted claims, require that a prudent and principled morality compromise among moral positions.

Nowhere is this more evident than in the continuing conflict over abortion. I would not even attempt to suggest a compromise, but a cursory glance at the moral issues reveals the complexity. Concern for autonomy and equal dignity suggest that individuals should respect the wishes of the woman as paramount. As a norm, governments should avoid, if at all possible, all special claims of embodiment that make women particularly subject to state coercion. Few more intrusive claims can be imagined than to bring the full panoply of state coercive power against a woman and require her to carry in her womb a fetus she does not want and to obligate her to care for and raise that child for the rest of her life. To use the law and incarceration to control the body with its intimate connection with destiny violates almost all conceivable notions of autonomy. If women are required to carry the child to birth, other concerns arise, such as compensation for the mother who was forced to carry the child. If the state forces her to carry the child against her will then, at birth, the issue of state responsibility for the child's welfare increases. Special obligations would be imposed upon government to care for the children it forced to be born. This accrues whether the mother elects to keep the child or not. No one would have had the child, and no one would have had the burden of caring for the child, had not the state intervened.

The above description does not even touch the issue of whether the state can force mothers to have Caesarean sections to protect the life of the child or force medical procedures upon the mother in the name of the "child's" welfare. Nor does it address the basic asymmetry of forcing the mother to carry the dependent child, when no similar Samaritan obligations are imposed upon anyone else in society.

But, the other side gives little rest. Most people are disturbed by the fact that the status of a newborn or prematurely born infant is wholly dependent upon the will of the parent. Few people feel morally comfortable about aborting late second trimester fetuses that have brain activity and developed neural systems. Individuals' intuitions about miscarriages underline some of this. Few people experience the level of grief and sorrow at an early miscarriage than they do at the death of a premature infant or third trimester miscarriage. Western legal and religious traditions barely acknowledge the early miscarriage while treating later deaths of third trimester fetuses differently. By the second trimester, the fetus moves and interacts with the mother and have developed all characteristics of a new child. This becomes more problematic as technological ability to save such fetuses develops.

While the fetus is not a person, even at the blastocyte phase it possesses a biologically unique destiny if allowed the normal course of its development. It remains a human body in embryo, a potential person. At a certain point, no serious moral differences exist between it and a newborn child, except its presence in a womb. Any principles suggesting that life and potential for development should be respected lead to a concern for the fetus. The concern for life is augmented by obligations to protect the helpless and innocent which the fetus is in abundance. This concern is increased by the knowledge that the death of the fetus forecloses all options of development. All potential is terminated, while the mother's life still remains open, but perhaps more sober after an abortion. There exists a profound asymmetry in the level of harm done in the act of abortion. Mothers can be compensated, the aborted fetus cannot. When issues are in conflict, the respect for life and development, the concern for openness should in some way inform considerations.

No easy answers present themselves and I claim no prescience. What I do claim is that the moral dimensions of the problem expand far beyond what proponents and opponents admit. Any answer that does justice to the situation shall ultimately involve defensible compromises respecting the need for an autonomous time of decision for the mother as well as recognition of interests in protecting the potential person in the fetus. And even this must be tempered by recognition that in no other situation does the state impose such onerous burdens upon one person to carry forward the life of another person under threat of such a severe penalty. Further, no compromise can be defended unless people also reorder and finance the possibilities of life and growth for the children forced into the world by the mandate of the state.

The list of examples can be expanded indefinitely, but almost any issue of political life involves a nexus of multiple principles, usually with no neat lexical priority. While rankings and priorities might be determined, the conflict among principles in one person or situation underlines a number of moral reasons to compromise. Individuals might hold reasonable doubts about the absolute priority of their convictions over all other values. More importantly, they might wonder about the exact requirements of the principle when in conflict with moral diversity. One need not espouse relativism to suggest that people might acknowledge the Millian possibility of error in either the exact priority or requirements of their moral beliefs. Morally conscientious people would acknowledge their own humility and seek to do justice to the complexity of an issue. Individuals can compromise in these situations without compromising our integrity (Kuflik 1979, 48–52; Benditt 1979, 35ff.). Abortion only illustrates the problem that many political issues reflect difficult and sometimes tragic conflicts among vital moral principles and aspirations.[3] Conscientious politicians and citizens should do their best to balance the competing moral claims, for even weightings and priorities, unless explicitly lexical, do not determine outcomes. When rights and goods conflict, only compromise avoids tragedy.

Conscientiousness and humility can encompass the complexity of the problem. If problems extend to technical and complex issues that are open for resolution, individuals might rightly compromise to acknowledge this complexity (Benditt 1979, 34–36). Complexity is often accompanied by incomplete information, and a compromise might be made to allow for experiments and multiple tests before any clear and hard stands should be taken. Here, as is often the case in politics, procedures may be as much a matter of compromise as the substantive ends since they are so intertwined. Humility and conscientiousness lead not only to caution in finalizing an issue's requirements, but also to respect for diversity and experiment (Morley 1893, 202–5, 252–55).

Individuals might also rightly choose to compromise out of respect for the quality of persons in the political order. The virtues and beliefs that support liberal democracy do not arise naturally. They represent an historical accomplishment and are renewed by education, experience, and political participation. Citizens must learn to enjoy diversity and excellence without envy. It requires self-discipline and experience to rein in expansive consciences that seek to regulate others' personal sins. Much effort is required to learn to tolerate difference in politics and areas such as religious belief. If compromise is to become a powerful moral strategy individuals need to be taught to hate intolerance and bigotry. Public discourse and actions inspire and educate citizens so that individuals might choose to compromise their rhetoric and eschew moral domination and vituperation.

Public actions and ritual enactments by politicians often exemplify ideals. The rituals and actions literally educate citizens as to ideals and inspire loyalty for them. Politicians might rightly choose to subordinate their private feelings to preserve the power of public rituals and use a rhetoric that affirms, rather than divides, commonality and loyalty. People turn to leaders and rituals for guidance in their daily beliefs and reactions. Governments educate as much as they lead; compromise can emerge from these realities.

The last set of moral justifications flow from the defense of a liberal and democratic constitutional order. These justifications may resemble the more self-interested defenses of an open and compromise-based politics, but they differ in that they are grounded in more basic principles than achieving success or avoiding violence. A commitment to human autonomy and dignity combined with commitments to equal personal respect and social and political equality provide the basic justifications for a constitutional democratic order (Kuflik 1979, 41–48; Benditt 1979, 26–37; Carens 1979, 123–40). A commitment to such an order leads a person to compromise, but it presupposes that all is not compromised away. It differs from Bernard Crick's elaborate defense of politics based on avoiding tyranny, in that compromise serves to preserve a system that makes possible autonomy, dignity, and basic preconditions of freedom (Crick 1972). If these are systematically denied by the compromising order, then the institutional justification for compromise fails. It might be argued that individuals should pursue democratic methods even if this pursuit involves extremely slow and minute gains. (Violent or totalitarian methods might be initially more efficient, but they lay the groundwork to frustrate any future liberal or democratic gains.) Such a justification requires great forbearance and clear empirical claim that the political system actually does or can provide for autonomy and dignity for all its citizens by the means in place.

Politicians compromise for constitutionalism by defining what may not be compromised away. This imposes the self-limiting ethos discussed above. Compromises can be made to ensure some degree of fairness and predictability in methods of conflict that sublimate coercion. Compromise, nonetheless, does not equate with democracy. A maldistribution of power and resources can make compromise a mask for "friendly" domination. But a tradition of compromise might slowly subvert maldistributions of power by allowing groups to assert themselves and gain entry to the political arena. Over time, compromise might even extend benefits to groups, domesticate violence, and produce a constitutional democratic order (MacPherson 1968).

Compromises to defend the ethos and institutions of a constitutional order should not reify them outside of all moral context. In pre-Civil War conflicts, Democratic and Whig unionists were committed to the

"Union" as a separate and almost independent moral principle, which served as its own justification. Lincoln and many Republican unionists viewed the Union as overwhelmingly important but ultimately grounded in a commitment to "national freedom." In their minds, the great battles were over the ethos of society and the extension of the principles that justified the Union. A Democratic unionist like Stephen A. Douglas might personally regard slavery as wrong, but he viewed the union as the supreme and perhaps only embodiment of constitutional principles and would not threaten it. Douglas further believed that "popular sovereignty" underlay the Union and was quite compatible with local slavery.

Lincoln could never abide the manifest contradiction that principles of equality and liberty could justify enslavement of a minority of humans and that the Union should embody and extend these flawed principles. Armed with his belief that the Union embodied the principles and that the principles were compatible with slavery, Douglas would compromise far more than Lincoln, not because both allowed slavery in place, but because Douglas was convinced that the Union mattered more than slavery and should not be jeopardized over it. He was willing to defend the possibility of its extension into the free territory, even if he thought the possibility unlikely. Lincoln could accommodate almost anything, but refused in principle to allow slavery to expand into the free territories or allow the federal government legally and symbolically to abet its expansion. While Douglas did not believe that slavery would expand into the territories for economic reasons, he refused to limit it in principle. This defined their differences and ultimately helped precipitate the Civil War (Foner 1971, 138ff.; Potter 1976, 328ff.; Jaffa 1982).

It has become fashionable to criticize this reliance upon equal respect for autonomous persons as dangerous and dehumanizing. Critics of liberal and democratic principles argue that this view postulates an impossibly narrow moral psychology and reduces rich human fullness to abstract creatures who possess rights and duties prior to the goods they choose to seek.[4] The theorists making these claims also fear the imperialism of moral principles in political life. This concern has two dimensions. First, technical moral theory often strives for a small set of certain and dominant principles by which all other moral and life concerns should be judged. In particular, it devalues or assigns a much lower status to pluralistic and political or prudential concerns. While giving itself this privileged position, technical moral theory, with few exceptions, seldom ever addresses the very conditions necessary to its acceptance and motivational power, which are central to a non-totalitarian political life. Second, moral stridency and rhetoric too often damn opponents as immoral while ignoring consequences and prudential or political concerns. Such rhetoric often challenges any broader community loyalties and membership and tends to divide and polarize conflict rather than lead to resolution and stability. Both the technical and rhetorical tendencies of morality tend to engulf reality and miss its complexity or undervalue other weighty considerations.[5]

From some traditional conservatives, once the ends of the political order are questioned in a rational manner, the political order can be too easily delegitimized. Accepted practices of resolution and agreement, which depend upon those ends being accepted, can be undermined. Additionally, rational theories do not usually generate the type of emotional and habitual commitments needed to sustain a peaceful political order. Realists also prefer that ends never be questioned because of the urgency of their demands for accomplishment and success, especially when in conflict with enemies. Principles only muddy the waters and invite failure by either misapprehending the unwillingness of enemies to accept the same principles or by misunderstanding the power and resource limitations of a situation.

One recent case against principled claims in politics argues that principles only gain life insofar as they derive from preexisting practices. Consequently, any "abstract" or purely "rational" principles, or even demands based upon abstract "humanity," have little if any serious moral weight within a community of belief. Such moral claims can also be faulted because, as abstract and universalistic, they impose too much of an obligation; people simply cannot live up to them and so become cynical or reject them. Additionally, abstract claims alienate individuals from everyday ethical judgments. This foreignness and abstraction means that principles cannot effectively motivate people. In political life, motivation weighs in almost as much as validity, because people must be persuaded to act to avoid resort to violence or manipulation. Arid and detailed principles are not suitable for politics. If they do not motivate, they fail as effective directives, or worse, they may warrant rulers to use immense coercion to force others to do the "right thing," however implausible people find it.[6]

Another case sees the attempt to generate principles as an act of hubris made impossible by historical relativism. Beliefs discovered and bound by a community and historical age provide the only defensible reasons to act. Claims of universal rules or principles cannot be claimed and not only fail before the claims of rationality, but cannot extend beyond any one historical period that accepts their premises as valid. Additionally, these principles possess totalitarian implications. If individuals have the principles and know they are right, then they may feel warranted to act upon them using tyrannical or totalitarian coercion to implement such a world. This warrant for use unleashes nothing but harm because principled actions can ignore reality constraints and human diversity in the quest to establish hegemony.[7]

A final case emphasizes that principles dehumanize individuals and their morality. According to this critique, principles and the moral point of view reduce individuals to inhuman abstractions who possess no body or culture. The moral psychology of the moral point of view is warped since people are seen only as carriers of rights or duties with no reference to their social matrix or real world identity. All goods are held up to presumptive judgment of right when no archimedian point exists. Even theories that base themselves on "the good" must articulate such a general ensemble of capacities to define human nature that they become hopelessly abstract and need some criteria of right to define which goods are actually good. In fact, to develop a persuasive case for right, people must allude to what others already accept as good. In reality, a principled ethics violates autonomy because it presumes to dictate outcomes and denies people serious judgment since they are supposed to act upon dictated outcomes rather than actively assess the situation and consequences of an outcome. It further eliminates serious moral discourse, because it generates solipsistic rules of action without the benefit of discourse with equal beings. This world of principles devalues serious democracy and justifies a politics based upon bureaucratic specialists who administer a world devoid of communal human loyalties and deliberation.

These various critiques often converge and suggest that individuals need an ethics that is imbedded in a social context with concrete identities. Such a morality would base a plausible ethics upon "imbedded," "embodied," "encumbered," "constituted," or "historical" selves. It would not alienate people, but persuade by touching beliefs and desires. Additionally, hubris or totalitarian pretensions will be avoided because a socially grounded ethics will be bound in its aspirations to members of one political community, historically situated. Such an ethics, in politics, would decide upon its obligations after deliberation among equal citizens conjoined in mutual community.[8]

It should be clear, however, that once "political" reasons involving prudence, conflict resolution, and contextual possibilities are recognized as possessing justificatory power, the animus against moral reasons, *per se,* has little to sustain it. This essay argues that all these reasons belong in political life, perform vital functions, and none should be ruled out, nor should any one dominate political life. Consequently, admitting moral reasons into a plural world of political justification, especially one where prudence bridges principles and practice, avoids most of the realist, conservative, and communitarian plaints. Once the straw man who informs the theories is rejected, moral principles need not be banished from political life, just as prudence, context, and politics should not be banished from moral life.

Beyond these concerns, it is vital to remember, as discussed in Chapter 1, that moral principles and ideals perform critical roles in political life. These roles countermand the weaknesses of the alternative critiques. The moral point of view and principles or ideals emerge from second-order reflection. People step back and make an effort to discover points of view from which to evaluate the myriad actions, roles, and practices that make up the daily world. Second-order reflection can help individuals escape from simple acceptance of the socialized norms and identities that they have acquired from parents, culture, and interaction. As John Rawls suggests, this critical moral reflection does not take place in a vacuum, and individuals need to address their imbedded intuitions and beliefs.

The historically situated and unreflected beliefs, however, should not be romanticized in ethics. To require that all moral reflection be based only upon internalized beliefs and identity, without the discipline of second-order reflection and the demands of consistency and abstraction, limits people only to the identities and practices of a society. Some individuals who are Jewish in Aryan Germany, black in white America, or female anywhere, can look into their imbeddedness and discover a socialized sense of inferiority and a smoldering self-loathing. Conversely, people can be socialized into a casual superiority based upon nothing other than encumbered, unearned, and morally irrelevant traits like the color of skin, the ethnicity of birth, sex, or the wealth of parents. This imbedded morality leaves the background institutions, prejudices, and oppressions in place and gives the oppressed and ruling too few tools to move beyond those terms.

The abstracted political self, from which the moral point of view works, has very strong historical reasons behind it. Individuals disembody the public conception of self in order to open the public arena and rule out certain patterns of domination once justified by encumbered or embodied terms. Big people are not allowed to dominate small people; people of noble blood are not allowed to claim political power over those of plebeian blood; white people are not allowed to dominate black people; men are not allowed to dominate women; manor-born cannot dominate country-born. People born as "Smiths" or "Carpenters" are not required to be smiths and carpenters forever. Whatever terms people use to define a public persona become terms that warrant government intervention to exclude or limit others who do not possess them. They become warrants for government coercion. In the past, governments and cultures have employed encumbered or embodied concepts to justify governmental coercion to deny others their rights to self-determination or dignity within a culture. What dignity they were allowed was circumscribed and depended upon never claiming equality with the embodied elite. A person had to know and stay in his or her place. It is possible to acknowledge the importance of communal aspects of humanity for our life, while at the same time, profoundly limiting them as standards for justification in public life.

Autonomy and equal dignity as understood in the moral point of view prohibit these embodied and encumbered claims from justifying the use of government and law to exclude or benefit on these grounds. The major tool for uncovering the implications of these beliefs is recurrence to the moral point of view and its ideals and principles. The moral point of view drives individuals to impartiality and universality in assessments. All privileged claims and obligations derivative of parochial, self-serving, or morally irrelevant human characteristics are disallowed or severely questioned. It becomes especially important to discipline reflection in this way in politics because political actions and those of government affect other humans so profoundly, and political action is so central to integrity. The moral point of view or ideal notions of humanity become a forum of judgment from which people can critically reflect upon practices and institutions and accept, criticize, or reform them. Principles provide a powerful and disciplined way to stand back from the pressures of rules, orders and unexamined prejudice and preferences.

Second-order reflection from the moral point of view then opens all these institutions to scrutiny. It fortifies judgments and evaluations by providing tools to question dehumanizing, unequal, and privileged claims against other human beings. It can force others who profess to "believe" in human dignity and freedom to be exposed to the self-serving hypocrisy of their own judgments. Individuals can demand impartial and consistent reasons for these imbedded discriminations. If the culture supports such discrimination, then rationality queries the culture. If people develop principles asserting common humanity and demand that all practices be judged by them, they need to make sense of them by linking their insights to common usages. They then place communal claims in a moral tension with those of humanity. This may lead people to seek to transform cultural meanings. They may have to borrow from other cultures as Ghandi did from Christian ideals or Martin Luther King from Ghandi. But, people should not confuse the claim that moral claims must "make sense" by linking to or transforming accepted linguistic and moral practices with the fallacious claims that they must arise from and stay within existing practices.

The category of humanity and the demands for consistency and impartiality on its behalf require that all claims of difference or superiority be limited and judged by duties to humans. Difference and diversity need not be denied, but political claims of privileged power or exclusion, which can be based upon them, should always be deeply questioned. The claims of imbeddedness, encumberedness, constitutedness and their ilk carry little moral weight until people ask exactly what has been, for instance, "constituted" and by whom and to whom.

The limitations of an historical period certainly do not disqualify people from making valid claims on behalf of common humanity, nor of acting upon an increased understanding of who qualifies as human and what obligations this entails. Atemporal universality is not required to claim validity for worldwide human obligations given the knowledge and reasoned powers individuals have at one historical moment. Nor does it preclude individuals from developing purposeful and plausible implications based on reasoning of what a commitment to equal human dignity and autonomy demands. Denying the atemporal nature of obligations may limit the satisfactions to be gained from recklessly judging all past cultures by one's own standards, but certainly does not undermine obligations at present. Nor do historical limitations vitiate the demands of consistency and impartiality or the power and plausibility of universalizing claims or examining them from disinterested points of view. Such fortified reflection from the moral point of view provides a way to question the easy abuse of patriotism and exclusion and to search out obligations across the historical accidents of being born behind one set of cultural and political boundaries. As such, these principles can direct and orient in politics.

John Morley points out the power of moral questioning to challenge the tendency towards self-deception and the desire to give up conscience for tranquility (Morley 1893, 136–39). Serene self-deception or comfort in beliefs can reduce people to very sophisticated robots programmed by the expectations and internalized norms of authority and culture. If individuals only judge on these grounds, if they only reflect bound by these criteria, then they in fact surrender identity and integrity to control of others. Nothing guarantees that the norms or practices of a culture do justice to common humanity since they usually work to stabilize and legitimize an existing political order. But norms may do so by convincing people to accept internalized superiority or inferiority that simply sustain a caste, class, or feudal order.

Such moral self-reflection can make one's entire self problematic, but if, for example, individuals place themselves behind Rawls's veil of ignorance and make the thought experiment, in conjunction with others, to strip away born attributes of body and class, then they can discipline their own hypocrisy.[9] People can question their prejudices and subject themselves to an ordering forum of integrity. They can apprehend and judge and work to revise their selfhood. The moral point of view and principles suggest that people should not govern by gut intuitions, even widely shared gut intuitions. To discuss and deliberate within an unquestioned cultural matrix only guarantees that they will replicate and reinforce inarticulated prejudices and power distributions. Mere empathy within a culture is not enough, for the empathy will be defined by culturally prescribed stereotypes of whom warrants concern. Moral claims in political life can extend the range of interests and concerns to others who would normally be dismissed. One's principles should make sense of values and show why they make sense and cohere. But once persons have principles, they can dialectically assess other goods and affirm or reject them. Principles demand consistency. They challenge people when they value their goods because of their humanity and yet deny such benefits to other humans. Social lobotomy can bring selfhood of sorts, but only at the cost of giving up autonomy and truth.

Principles and the moral point of view, then, provide powerful reasons to compromise to respect the autonomy and equal dignity of fellow human beings and preserve the institutions and way of life that support human freedom and integrity. At the same time, compromise can flow from people acknowledging the moral complexity of any situation that places responsibility upon them to provide good reasons to justify actions. Individuals are judging and reflecting persons who take on the role of citizens and politicians. These are central but derivative roles since the polity can and should be judged by how it respects the basic humanity of its people.

Notes

1. This section and chapter are deeply influenced by the article "Compromise and Morality" by Arthur Kuflik (1979, esp. 41–52). Kuflik carefully analyzes how "pure compromise" as a first principle is incoherent. He then traces the relation between constitutional liberal democracy and morally valid compromise. Carens (1979) approaches the same issue from a different but insightful perspective. Both assume that people cannot be allowed to abdicate their moral autonomy in a compromise. At a minimum, people should be prohibited from compromising into complete and irrevocable enslavement and giving up protections of due process and against arbitrary interference (Kuflik 1979, 46). These set basic limits upon compromise in a world of autonomous persons.

2. The essays by Golding, Benditt and especially Kuflik in Pennock and Chapman (1979) pursue this line of reasoning. While I disagree with the full characterization of moral compromise as requiring mutual respect for autonomy and legitimate interests, I agree that these pose good, even the best, reasons to compromise. The following discussions owe a tremendous amount to these essays and to the one by Carens in the same volume. See also Warwick (1981), M. Moore (1981), and Fleishman (1981). These essays discuss the moral obligations upon public officials to seek out the interests and rights of the unorganized and inarticulate.

3. See Luker (1984) for a discussion of how an issue like abortion derives not just from the "moral" issues but how deeply these moral issues flow from the integrity and self-understandings of the participants.

4. Modern "communitarians" make these claims with monotonous regularity. For examples see Sandel (1982) and MacIntyre (1984).

5. Walzer (1983) and Williams (1985) present serious and extensive discussions of this claim. Walzer concentrates upon the political dimension while Williams focuses upon the claims for moral theory itself. Williams's attempt to deflate the pretensions of some moral theory is quite helpful. He argues correctly that the best people can expect in these enterprises is "confidence," not certainty, and that this changes the potential demands of all moral theorizing. But I believe that Williams underestimates the role the moral point of view and principles can play even in a "confident" and more pluralistic world. Without such points of reference, his own notion of "reflection" is weakened considerably in its potential to examine and direct life. Reflection then simply reflects the existing beliefs and commitments of a person or culture with very few and usually self-referential ways to critically question their humanity or injustice.

When these issues are transposed to the realm of politics, avoiding this limit of reflection becomes all the more important. Williams (1981) has used the example of special relations such as parental claims to deflate the pretensions of moral theory. The pure moralists' claims that a man would have no moral reasons for going back into a crashed plane to save his child over anyone else exemplifies his claim that moral theory violates basic intuitions. In fact, a utilitarian might argue that it is positively immoral to save a son or daughter if the man left a valuable doctor or physicist there instead.

At one level, I am not sure how much deep personal affiliations and commitments do deflate moral theory. For instance, it is not clear to me that a man committed to racial superiority, who goes back to save all the Aryans, whether he knows them or not, deflates moral duties. Rather, he instructs people to look again at the affiliations and asks which ones deserve respect rather than implying respect for commitment or affiliation *per se*. See Goodin (1985) for an attempt to make sense of range of affiliations or special commitments. More importantly, these examples do not carry nearly as much power if the issue is phrased as one of the moral requirements of political life. When people are given privileged responsibilities with coercive power, then there exists strong and plausible moral reasons to require that these special or even characterological commitments be subordinated to moral requirements. When nepotism or religious discrimination is outlawed, for instance, or when judges and officials are required to enforce laws impartially even on their families and friends, there are powerful and plausible moral, political, and prudential reasons for this approach. I would hope many of my comments in this chapter demonstrate that one can accept some of Williams's own limitations upon the pretensions of theory and still recognize how the moral point of view can augment and direct reflection on the purposes of political life.

6. Various aspects of this case are discussed by Walzer (1983), MacIntyre (1984), Oakeshott (1981), and Beiner (1983).

7. Various aspects of this case are discussed in Bickel (1975), Walzer (1983), and MacIntyre (1984).

8. This case is suggested by the work of Sandel (1982), Beiner (1983), Sullivan (1982), MacIntyre (1984), and Barber (1984). Sullivan, Beiner, and sometimes MacIntyre, all assume that people are all equal persons and this will frame any just political order. They eschew the hard work of defending this claim or pursuing the implications of it for organized political life while denigrating most liberal democratic theorists who still work assiduously upon it.

9. Rawls's veil of ignorance approach asks individuals to develop principles to govern society by placing themselves behind a veil of ignorance. Behind this veil, individuals strip themselves of knowledge about what their exact position and nature will be. Needless to say the veil can be a different levels of opacity. Once persons deny knowledge to themselves of what race, religion, sex, or even generation they will inhabit, they then seek to discover principles upon which all behind the veil would accept to order the basic class distribution of resources, goods, and rights within a society.

5

The Fundamental Political Choice

*"There is no surer way of keeping
possession than by devastation."*
—Machiavelli

"If you cannot kill your enemy, kiss him."
—Proverb

The fundamental choice of politics is whether to treat with or coerce opponents. Every individual in politics must determine how to deal with opponents. This choice, even more than a person's principles, determines the style and tone of political life and its potential for freedom, justice, and peace. Some of the rhetorically most urgent defenses of compromise in political life build upon the notion that compromise is the major alternative to a politics based upon force (Smith 1956; Biddle 1957; Crick 1972). The second great family of powerful justifications for political compromise congregate around this choice.

Bernard Crick has suggested that "political compromises are the price that has to be paid for liberty" (Crick 1972, 151). I will use Crick's term "politics" to cover these justifications, since they flow from the quality of conflict resolution within a society. Political life obviously comprises other aspects and prudential judgments encompass many other dimensions. But while humans build their communities and actualize vital aspects of autonomous life through politics, a liberal and democratic politics cannot flourish without solving the problems of security and peace.

Political justifications, as I discuss them, focus upon domesticating coercion and arriving at peaceful resolution of conflict. Coercion and force pose the most profound dangers to a free and democratic life, and many good reasons to compromise flow from justifications based upon controlling coercion and building peace. Compromises based upon avoiding violence can be more positively justified as helping to build a community of cooperation and maintain civility

These political justifications might justly be considered a subset of prudence. But coercion really does pose the fundamental choice for a political order and deserves independent consideration. A liberal and democratic political order must solve the concomitant problems of public safety and peaceful conflict resolution while avoiding tyranny or totalitarianism. Until this is accomplished, all other projects of free individuals will be jeopardized. I treat these concerns with domesticating coercion as a separate but greatly overlapping set of justifications with prudence because of the central and very dangerous role of force in public life.

People are coerced when they act predominantly from fear of painful consequences—either by infliction or deprivation—threatened against them, or from ignorance deliberately fostered. Individuals coerce when they act so as to get another to act without any regard for that person's considered judgment.[1] Coercion can involve force and violence, or manipulation and deceit; it strikes at the heart of free personality. When others deceive and manipulate people through false information, they dominate one's integrity and subvert autonomy. Coercion and manipulation are the antitheses of the activity of justification and co-promising that lies at the heart of a free politics among moral agents. When others threaten to use violence or force, they assault integrity by reducing all but the heroes and saints to bodily fear. The importance of one's desires, commitments, and reflected judgments is denied, and individuals are reduced to physical objects. Politics does not reduce to force, but until force is placated and controlled, free and democratic politics cannot flourish.

People need peace, but not the peace of slaves. Political peace promotes resolution of conflicts among citizens with minimum resort to manipulation and force. A nontyrannical political order should be able to accommodate the demands and aspirations of many groups (some of whom are suffering from oppression) and channel their grievances into nonviolent resolution. At the same time, controlled coercion can play vital roles in community and political order. Armed self-defense against enemies and constitutionally bound police coercion can create an arena within which communal ties can grow and freedom can be exercised. A fairly administered punishment for a crime after a fair trial can recognize another human being's moral responsibility for wrong far better than ignoring it or pretending the individual merely reflected congeries of social forces and needs to be "reformed."

State force stands behind legal and ritual agreements; it secures individuals in their possessions and lives. In doing so, it makes bargains and commerce possible and encourages trust to grow while discouraging habitual defection from agreements. State coercion deters free riders, arrests criminality, and protects the state and individuals from "enemies." The boundaries of this effective force define the common destiny of a community. In that community, people can create a history and practices that give them a common political identity.

The Faustian aspects of governmental force, however, always vest it with the potential to unleash tyranny or seek totalitarian control of all forms of authority. In liberal democracy, coercion is bound by the subordination of the armed services to civilian rulers. These are bound by rituals of election and accountability, due process and appeal, professional training of armed officers and open political questioning. Where possible, checks and balances can help. Ultimately, this requires the users of force to provide good justifications bound to the requirements of respecting basic values and procedures. Only when peace is secured will people actively cooperate with one another and resolve disputes with some hope of durability and fairness. Domesticating coercion remains the first responsibility of politics.

As citizens of the twentieth century, this lesson should be indelibly engraved on people's consciences. A quick perusal of the history of this century brings one face to face with the nightmares of untamed political force. The First World War, the Armenian genocide, the Stalin purges and genocide, the Holocaust, the Second World War, the Gulag Archipelago, or the Cambodian disaster of the Khmer Rouge should always sober anyone before the glittering possibilities of politics. But coercion always tempts people in politics. The obstinacy of others frustrates the drive to accomplish urgent tasks. In any disagreement with friends or foes, people can often get their way by deceit, manipulation, or force. It requires great moral discipline to give up coercion in the pursuit of great goals, and to compromise.

The world suffers no shortage of saviors who would gladly save people from the morass of politics. But the temptation to salvation through coercion endangers all of worth in liberal and democratic life.

At its core, coercion violates human integrity and the conditions under which persons affirm and develop their potential and self.[2] As Gore Vidal has Abraham Lincoln say, "We can never guarantee anyone else and, sometimes, in politics, we can't even guarantee ourselves" (Vidal 1984, 583, 584). The need for coercion can always arise despite its dangers. Enemies can resort to violence; governments can decay to tyranny; friends can betray. At times, force may be necessary for self-defense or violence may be the only way to achieve self-determination against repressive regimes.

At times an unwillingness to use coercion can cause even more coercion. In an extended self-interested negotiation, if individuals are not constrained by the possibility of retaliation if they violate agreements, they may be encouraged to continue incursions and lessen the chance of productive cooperation evolving (Axelrod 1984). An unwillingness to use legitimate force to enforce the law or stop wrongdoing may frustrate the achievement of worthy goals. The sporadic and terminated enforcement of Reconstruction in the South ended any real chance for black equality after the Civil War and encouraged southern vigilantism and refusal to come to terms with freed slaves. When federal troops pulled out, the local and state governments quickly institutionalized the social and political inferiority of blacks while tacitly permitting vigilante assaults. Dwight D. Eisenhower's later refusal to use federal power to enforce desegregation orders encouraged southern governors to defy federal power and prolong segregation (Ambrose 1984, Chap. 18).

As a counterpoint to the dangers coercion poses to liberal and democratic life, modern revolutionaries see revolutionary violence as a praxis that frees individuals from shackles of customary and political oppression. Oppressed people can band together and discover the potential to create their own destiny through violent struggle. A community can actually be forged in struggle, just as the thirteen American colonies discovered their unity in the Revolutionary War. Anarchists and existential terrorists assert their selfhood and humanity in acts of violence. These pure and compassionate murderers of innocents represent the penultimate romanticization of violence. Fascist spirituality glorifies force because human warriors transcend their degrading materiality. Warriors prove their moral superiority when the heroic spirit proves stronger than the body.[3]

But it is vital not to romanticize violence even though it may be necessary to political life. Simone Weil in her meditation *The Iliad or The Poem of Force* dispels the illusion of heroic force. She reflects that force turns a human into a thing in the most literal sense; a person becomes a corpse. "Somebody was here, and the next moment there is nobody at all." In *The Iliad,* heroes must dehumanize themselves to harden their flesh against force. The heroes are described as raging and mad animals as they tear and slash at one another. Men must descend into a killing persona and deny their most human capacities for self-awareness—thought, friendship, and sorrow. Heroism has always been touched by madness, but confronting force, madness conquers our humanity.

The Iliad always recalls that each person killed fought to live, not die. Heroes fell to their knees and begged to be spared, promising ransoms and speaking of their parents, wives, and children. Yet the heroes to whom they begged seldom stopped in their killing rage. The poem always details the smashed brains, the spilt entrails, and spurting blood, and the anguish of dying men. Every heroic death is accompanied by a recitation of those who remain behind and suffer for the death. No illusions, exaltation, or fanaticism covers the misery and finality of heroic death. Even the heroes, stripped of the "prestige of force," recognize their frailty and pathos. "The man who does not wear the armor of the lie cannot experience force without being touched by it to the very soul. Grace can prevent this touch from corrupting him, but it cannot spare him the wound" (Weil 1956, 36).

A liberal democracy should also fear violent confrontation because of the dialectic of violence. Historical experience and theories of negotiation suggest that people need to be provokable and retaliate when harmed to ensure peaceful cooperation (Axelrod 1984). But often such violence can breed violence into spiraling patterns of revenge with no way out. Hate endures longer than affections. In such a situation, the political actors become locked at the lowest level of gain and highest level of loss for both sides. As they become entrenched in the conflict, the desire to "win" can triumph over all reasonable analysis of costs, and critics will be silenced while each side continues to fight, punch drunk, almost forgetting the reasons for the fight except the dynamic of winning.[4] This is especially true when religious, ethnic, or ideological cleavages aggravate conflict. The unending civil wars and terrorism in Lebanon, Northern Ireland, or Israel cut to the heart of a civil order. These conflicts remind everyone of how vital and fragile is the creation of a secular political order that enables ethnic, religious, and racial groups to participate in a common citizenship.

In violent conflict, the law of emulation can set in and undermine the deepest strengths of liberal democracy. Governments can come to resemble what they hate most in their enemies. Whole establishments adopt special terrorist tactics, deceive their own people and elected representatives, and utilize reprisal and execution without due process or clear legal sanction. Officials grow impatient and constitutional controls give way under the duress of secret war. The violence and the fear it induces can lead people to surrender their freedom to strong leaders who can guarantee "law and order." Few people who constantly feel physically threatened have the moral strength to worry about due process. Many terrorists seek to precipitate just such authoritarianism in the West. This, in turn, would further revolutionary upheaval. Building political communities in divided societies depends upon reducing the amount of violence and defusing the effect of violence, not starting an never-ending cycle of reprisals.

Violence and coercion in politics, especially nonstate coercion, almost always plays into the hands of the authoritarians. As Lyndon Johnson saw liberals abandon him on the Vietnam war and conservatives abandon him on the Great Society, he argued against the violence, however justified, of the antiwar and civil rights groups: "Those who glorify violence as a form of political action are the best friends the status quo ever had. They provoke a powerful conservative reaction among millions of people. They inspire . . . a blind allegiance to things as they are—even when those things ought to be changed" (McPherson 1972, 447–48). Successful civil rights demonstrations provoked violence from authorities, but avoided initiating violence for fear of undermining their support (Garrow 1978). Violence puts liberal reforms on the defensive and enables sympathetic reformers to be tagged as cozeners of violence. It destroys consensus and undermines faith in the nonviolent rituals and processes of conflict resolution while polarizing political issues and making durable solutions harder. Sometimes, violence can precipitate reform, but generally, it paralyzes reformers and gives greater voice to authoritarian figures.

It is not necessary to believe humans are innately evil to recognize the human capacity to tolerate and even enjoy violence towards others. Max Weber rightly feared the "diabolic forces lurking in all violence" (Weber 1969, 126). It can bring individuals alive, establish intense camaraderie, push persons to self-sacrifice, and allow them to assert superiority. Violence can tempt and consume individuals. But at its core, it threatens the foundations of liberal and democratic life.[5]

Pure coercion objectifies people and reduces them to objects subject to control. It violates human integrity and taunts human convictions and beliefs by reducing them to nothing. It is the antithesis of liberal and democratic justification because it silences voice and warps convictions before the brute reality of superior force or manipulation. The threat of force denies virtue to all but the strongest, and forces people to retreat to isolated selves or private communities. Political violence seldom transforms individuals; when it does, it usually hardens and embitters, rather than humanizes.

Coercion also threatens community.[6] A free community thrives because its members can affirm their relations with others. They trust the respect and care of others. Their identity unites them even as they cooperate, fight, and resolve among themselves. But force poisons not only relations with oneself but with all others. A community cannot live on force alone. When people are reduced to protect themselves and maybe their own, because they can be punished for acting on their integrity, then they must lie to protect themselves and their family. Subservience becomes a habit of survival. Durable servitude then spawns universal hypocrisy. People must bribe those in power to protect what they value. Everyone must publicly adhere to the announced will and beliefs of the conquerors, and survival and accomplishment depend upon hypocrisy and deceit. No one can really be trusted, especially if the regime poisons the mind of children with its socialization. Children praised by the state for reporting their parents' revolutionary perfidy is not an Orwellian nightmare but a Stalinist and Nazi reality. Any state with religious or ideological domination breeds bribed conversion and official hypocrisy. Even those who fight the system must bend before it in their public lives. In a totalitarian order, those who do publicly denounce the system are the most likely to be informants. Tyrants always use force to isolate people from one another in fear, which prevents them from uniting to free themselves. Betrayal, hypocrisy, and corruption become functional to survival under such a regime.

Shooting people simplifies things, but politics ends with the barrel of a gun. Tyrants and totalitarians refuse to compromise with their opponents. They transcend the need to compromise: tyrannically, by breaking the body or will of their opponents; totally, by transforming the consciousness of their subjects. In either case, they deny the free actions of their opponents and reject a compromise politics, which treats with the diversity of intellect, morality, interest, or power that arises among equal and free citizens.

Since they refuse to compromise, they employ mental and physical coercion to reach their ends. Plato remarked that one of the hallmarks of a tyrant was his willingness to act out his dreams with nightmarish results (Plato 1974, IX). Whether the dark and gargantuan dreams of Hitler or the Gilbert and Sullivan absurdity of Idi Amin, the feverish fantasies of a tyrant play out as mass murder and uniquely degrading human suffering for opponents and innocent alike. Even benign tyrants have the willful possibility to unleash suffering at their whim. Over time, the exceptional discipline and commitment of "good" tyrants or liberators can be worn down by the flattery and frustration of office. In a tyrannical or totalitarian order, individuals who pursue morally independent life plans or who intellectually quest for truth or knowledge beyond sanctioned limits find themselves at constant and great risk. Personal excellence and freedom are severely limited unless one becomes a friend of the tyrant, joins the omniscient party, or holds an indispensable skill.

But tyrants have no friends and fear excessive virtues in anyone (Aquinas 1967, III, 1–18). They must atomize citizens and prevent "mutual confidence and high spirits" (Aristotle 1965, 244). The tyrant Periander illustrated this principle of rule to the messenger of his fellow tyrant Thrasybulus. Asked how to secure his reign, he walked through a field lopping off all the high stalks until the field was level (Aristotle, 1965, 135, 237–41). Tyrants often thrive best by bringing in mercenaries or raising up marginal men who owe their entire existence to the tyrant rather than to the society. In either case, the tyrant gains allies only by melding fear of himself, fear of the people, and self-interest. The logic of a tyrant endangers all who draw too close or who demonstrate too much excellence, skill, or ambition.

Totalitarian states harness excellence and ambition by yoking them to party discipline and intense indoctrination. They thus amass far greater power to exterminate bodies and destroy souls. When they succeed, they can even harness integrity by controlling the shape of convictions held by people through monopolizing information and authority. The Gulag Archipelago may regularize terror and even refine its procedural "fairness," but it still undergirds the system.

It is one of the great ironies of politics that the choice of coercion, nonetheless, hides a profound compromise. Totalitarians and tyrants must compromise with those who perform the coercion. Plato explains the profound paradox of tyrannical coercion. "The freest of men" slowly becomes beholden to the army and thugs who enforce his rule. He must pander to their whims and slowly grow in fear of them. Because the ruler has little support elsewhere, he becomes more beholden and more fearful until the one who need never compromise becomes their slave (Plato 1974, IX). Just as the Praetorian guard held a stranglehold on the Roman emperor in the second and third centuries, Hitler lost control of the SS. Stalin depended so much upon his secret police as time went on that Beria became his greatest threat and had to be killed. Every third-world dictatorship risks an endless cycle of coup and revolution in its reliance upon military coercion. Even totalitarian countries can fall prey to the paradox. In Poland, the army has displaced the communist party, creating the first communist military dictatorship.

People will compromise for good reason because they "settle for less than we want, because we also want to live without violence or perpetual fear of violence from other people who want other things" (Crick 1972, 76). Politics and compromise are "a way of ruling in divided societies without undue violence" (Crick 1972, 146), and individuals can and should compromise to keep and build peace. Unless political life is polarized by permanent class, communal or ideological cleavages, such compromises usually encourage a less vicious politics. If political actors know that they will not be destroyed or incarcerated for acting on their own convictions or interests, they will have far less incentive to coerce others when they win. If they know that by acquiring some power and voice, they have a real chance at some gain through compromise, they will have much less reason to become guerrillas or terrorists when they lose. All sides settle for less than they might get if they destroyed opponents to avoid the pendulum swing where they could be hunted. Defeats are easier to swallow when one lives to fight another day. People can always compromise to keep political possibilities and optimism open—this encourages a more peaceful and innovative political life.

In complex societies, the serendipity of politics means that persons who are enemies on one issue may be allies later. It behooves politicians to respect and compromise. Vidal's Abraham Lincoln points out to a vengeful Gideon Welles, "In politics the statute of limitations must be short" (Vidal 1984, 591). When the Catholic bishops publicly castigated President Johnson for his views on birth control, Johnson held his ire in check because "we may reach a point where the only people that will support the poverty program will be the Catholic bishops" (Califano 1975, 213). To avoid foreclosing possible alliances and future opportunities, individuals should try to respect and compromise with opponents.

Compromise can avoid terrible vendettas, which can unleash spirals of violence. If individuals enter negotiations with open offers and seek cooperation, they can sometimes neutralize patterns of mistrust and initial hostility. In game theory, by starting "nice" and not trying to stick it to the other side in the initial round of game, individuals can often initiate extremely productive rounds of self-interested coopera-tion (Axelrod 1984). By settling for less, by respecting the other side's legitimate concerns, by not humiliating or persecuting the others or by reasonably negotiating, individuals can avoid polarized and incessant conflict. Too often any bargain that begins with a stated position and says "take it or leave it" humiliates the other side and discourages interaction and the development of patterns of negotiation, recogni-tion, and trust. To offer and then seriously engage another can deflect the bitterness and seething resentment of those who feel slighted, humiliated, or ignored in the crush of political life. Machiavelli traces the exhausting and futile battles of the Guelphs and Ghibbilines in his *History of Florence*. This cycle of exile and revolution meant that no government, aristocratic or republican, could sustain itself for long, and opened the state to foreign intervention. He summarizes the logic in his reconstructed plea to the Republic, "Beware of treating Cosimo harshly for if you drive him out and he returns, he will be corrupted and more violent" (Fisher 1981; Raiffa 1982; Machiavelli 1965, IV, 27).

Compromises can allow politicians to break out of cycles of bad faith that prevent people from reaching agreements that would make everyone better off. They do this by achieving some concrete, even minor accomplishments and co-promises that hold. These can then be the basis for building more successful solutions. Compromise and trust can also occur by setting large overarching frameworks for agreement and then holding to them as they make other trade-offs internally. When the Social Security system was on the verge of collapse in 1983, the first several efforts to save the system floundered upon the inability of all sides, especially the most committed liberals and conservatives, to reach any workable agreements. The final solution emerged only after a small group of principals convened to a more private setting. Here they were not trapped by rhetorical displays or the need for public posturing. Here their overarching goal was to prevent financial collapse and bring the system into line by aiming for a package which would be financed one half by reductions in benefits and one half by increase in taxes. Within this framework, they could negotiate a number of smaller compromises and internal trade-offs, seldom men-tioning the immense moral stakes involved in the basic social contract between generations. These compromises fit under the larger rubric of getting the funds to rescue the system and were tied together in one bill. The solutions that emerged were not perfect and left some issues unresolved, but they broke a terrible impasse and salvaged the United States' basic social welfare system (Light 1985).

Players can also break out of long strings of relations where both sides lose, if they can demonstrate, even through voluntary loss or "martyr runs," that they can be trusted and wish to bargain in a positive and mutually accommodating manner. This can break a cycle where both sides are losing because of their aggressive defensiveness (Rapoport 1964, 50–52). "Nice" tactics do not win all the negotiations; they can be subverted by aggressive or vicious tactics, but over the long run in almost all types of relations, they will produce the best results. However, the initial approach and compromises must be reinforced by provocability and retaliatory willingness. A "nice" *tit for tat* strategy supports a preference for good faith compromises with a forceful response when betrayed. This in turn can lead to robust cooperation (Axelrod 1984). Eventually "conventions" and "rules" can be discovered or agreed upon, which can also break patterns of prisoner's dilemmas and vicious conflict. Sometimes they develop spontaneously and at other times they can be agreed upon in order to diffuse possible misunderstandings and violence in the future (Hardin 1982; Sobel 1972).

These patterns mean that compromise solutions can be stable and trustworthy. If neither side feels overly coerced and deeply resentful, and if some free assent is involved, then both sides are far more likely to go along with and even embrace a solution. A community where people know they will have continued interactions can give agreements even greater durability. Less enforcement will then be needed given the voluntariness. In the Social Security compromises, most participants knew they had to deal on many other issues and needed to maintain civility and build up relations of trust for other political issues (Light 1985). Of course, the more both sides accommodate each other's priority demands and approach a win/win or mutually satisfying if imperfect outcome, the more reliable and enduring will be the solution (Fisher 1981). Individuals might even compromise in order to move a solution towards more optimal gains for the other side in order to enhance the other side's commitment and trust (Raiffa 1982). Additionally, if other politicians have not been humiliated or backed into corners, they can save face and "sell" the solution to their own groups more easily. This, in turn, increases the stability and power of compromised solutions. Coerced solutions based upon fear and resentment cost more to enforce and destabilize far more easily.[7]

The alternative endings of the two World Wars point to the power of these reasons. The vengeful enforcement of the humiliating and impossible reparations against Germany embittered Germans and discredited its fledgling Weimar government. It justified a dark vendetta against France and never allowed the wounds of the war to heal. The allied treatment and reconstruction of Germany after World War II helped immensely in reintroducing a democratic and less bellicose German culture. The new German state was born and sustained with far more legitimacy. Yet during World War II, the unyielding allied demand for "unconditional surrender" needlessly prolonged the war, played into the hands of the war parties and fanatics in both Japan and Germany, and obfuscated to both allies and enemies the ultimate goals of the war.

Above all, the regular practice of compromise helps build and sustain a community of civility and institutions that all sides accept. In the heat of political battle when the stakes are high, commitments deep, and rhetoric is incendiary, politicians and citizens need deeply-held practices and commitments to moderate the temptation to coerce or vilify their opponents. Individuals might compromise at any time to maintain these traditions. David M. Potter captures this ethos in his description of the Lincoln–Douglas debates.

> In these face-to-face encounters, the rivals sometimes assailed each other with the blunt combativeness of men who believed in their cause and were not afraid to fight, but always in the American fashion of being able to shake hands after they had traded blows. This is what layman have called good sportsmanship and what scholars called consensus, and what it meant at bottom was that the values which united them as Americans were more important than those that divided them as candidates, or if not that, at least that the right to fight for one's ideas involved an obligation to fight fair and recognize a democratic bond with other fighters for other ideas (Potter 1976, 333).

Traditions and rituals of civility and conflict resolution transmogrify disagreement into communal affirmation. They reaffirm shared identity and mutual interests in living together and help moderate moral anger. Winning and losing candidates appear on the same platforms together, losers graciously concede elections and pledge loyalty, Supreme Court Justices personally greet each other each day, legislatures rule personal vituperation out of order. All these actions create emotional and psychological distance between political disagreement and personal or civic fellowship. They make possible adherence to rules of resolution and acceptance of defeat or compromise without feeling complete alienation.

Political civility increases the possibility of fruitful listening and negotiation (Fisher 1981, 17–100). If opponents possess a history of shared agreements, then they can trust promises made and can resolve differences more easily. Compromises begin and sustain these agreements. Civility then means that political battles need not poison daily social and economic lives. When the first efforts at achieving a solution to the economic perils of the Social Security system failed, two principals, Robert Ball, Former Social Security Commissioner, and Director of the Office of Management and Budget David Stockman reignited the efforts. They did so with a series of informal conversations in which they discussed "the kinds of problems we'd all face if we didn't do something about the problem. . . . They kept talking about the breakdown of government institutions, increased public cynicism, those kinds of things. It was all part of the conditioning that had to be involved in the bargaining. We all had to believe that the negotiations were important for something more than immediate political gain. We had to believe." This rebuilt a relation to begin negotiations, which were carried out in Senator Howard Baker's home and accompanied by informal activities, like watching football games together and building a sense of mutual commitment to the process and to civil agreement. They also had to make great efforts to keep Senator Armstrong, an uncompromising conservative, from disrupting the entire negotiations when he bullied his way into the process (Light 1985, Chaps. 14, 15, 16). Politicians need their opponents to listen carefully and negotiate in good faith. Although generally thick-skinned, they neither enjoy nor respond well to personal vilification by opponents. Compromises on the rules and rituals of politics serve to protect egos as well as fellowship and fruitful bargaining.[8]

Respect for civility can also breed its own standards of respect and concern, which cut across normal political boundaries. As a junior Republican Senator from New Mexico, Peter Domenici of New Mexico had worked extremely hard and fought very fair for years to push through a bill in the Senate to charge fees on barges that used the federal lock system. An ally, Senator Adlai Stevenson of Illinois, betrayed him to protect the construction of a lock in Stevenson's own state. Senator Russell Long, the powerful Democrat of Louisiana and initially a staunch opponent, rescued the bill. Long had developed considerable respect for the hard work and fair play that Domenici had demonstrated in fighting for the bill and thought he deserved the bill (Reid 1980).

A system that thrives upon mutual recognition and compromise can socialize intolerant fanatics into a loyalty to constitutional rules. John Rawls describes the logic:

> The liberties of the intolerant may persuade them to a belief in freedom. This persuasion works on the psychological principle that those whose liberties are protected by and who benefit from a just constitution will, other things being equal, acquire an allegiance to it over a period of time (Rawls 1971, 219).

Individuals might always choose to compromise to bring individuals and groups into the domain of discursive political life and accommodation and wean them away from violence. If individuals have a fair voice in politics, if they gain some of their goals, they develop a deeper commitment to the process as well as feeling they were given a "fair" chance. This solidifies their loyalty as well as softening the bitterness of their defeats. It also leads them to redouble their efforts to compete under the legitimate rules. Over time, this process can transform enemies into opponents and opponents into allies. Lenin indirectly supports this claim for the seductive powers of compromise with his bitter fear of representative government and successful trade union and labor parties. He assaults "opportunists" in Germany and Great Britain who succumb to "parliamentary cretinism" and adapt to representative democracy. In his eyes, this commitment saps the class struggle and mystifies the inexorable class war between two eternal antagonists (Lenin 1975, 546ff, 596ff).

In a world of political compromises, groups can begin on the outside and gradually acquire status and voice, but only after giving up their violence and most vicious attributes. The recent career of the Moral Majority illustrates this. It broke into American politics by mobilizing the embittered voices of seemingly disenfranchised fundamentalist and evangelical Christians. Early campaigns concentrated upon negative assaults and virulently characterized its opponents as anti-God, atheists, panderers of pornography and whatever other slanderous epithets came to mind. Initial victories spawned a counter mobilization against them and opponents characterized the group as fanatics, but the victories also gave them establishment allies. Now members had to work with its elected allies and partake in the hard work of legislative compromise. At the same time, the group has reached out to ally with

Jews over Israel and Catholics over abortion. In each case, it has had to shed its nativist hatred of Catholics and Jews. Its leader, Jerry Falwell, appeared on the same stage debating Senator Edward Kennedy, the scion of liberal Democrats. Yet the appearance on the stage before Falwell's own supporters simultaneously helped legitimize the Moral Majority but also socialized them into pluralist democracy. People cannot easily stigmatize an individual as "devil spawn" once they have seen him in the flesh, listened and applauded, and watched him exchange quips and civilized debate with their leaders. The group recently changed its name from Moral Majority, with the militant insult to the rest of the country, to the Liberty Lobby.[9]

However, these are not *a priori* advantages of compromise, and depend upon empirical claims. In modern Europe, the Euro-communists claim a commitment to liberal rights and representative democracy and have shed their commitment to overthrow the system. But Stalinists overthrew the Czechoslovakian democracy twice and still thrive in corners of France and Italy while applauding the Soviet crushing of self-determination in East Europe. The Weimar government failed to domesticate the Nazis. While the Moral Majority may slowly work its way into respectability in the U.S., the Aryan Nation, the Order and other paramilitary fascist groups harness crackpot fundamentalist theology and racism and have begun campaigns to terrorize and overthrow the government. The refusal of any group to eschew violence or build a track record of reliable peaceful accord justifies governments to use coercion in self-defense. At these limits, prudence and self-interest as well as principled defense of liberal democracy can legitimize repression against violent opponents who possess the possibility of destroying liberal democracy (Rawls 1971, 216–21).

In his provocative book, *In Defense of Politics* (1972), Bernard Crick exemplifies this approach. Crick wants to insulate compromise from ideological imperialists and protect life from excessive coercion. He seeks to do this, like some of the conservative theorists, by demoralizing politics. "Let us be brazen and simply say, 'We prefer politics;' it is better than coercion" (Crick 1972, 22–32). Specifically, he argues that there is no one common good by which to organize a state, and even if there were, individuals should not use coercion to get it, yet coercion is the only practical way to morally reform a state (Crick 1972, 26).

These reasons to compromise possess immense scope and plausibility, and they reinforce this by tracking with liberal and democratic moral concerns to respect the foundations of individuals' integrity and freedom. This match underlies liberalism's famous boast that a society of devils could organize itself under liberal and democratic principles. It leads T. V. Smith to cast his defense almost exclusively in terms of the need to maintain civility and avoid excessive violence. Smith even suggests that this is almost identical to liberal democracy (Smith 1956). But such claims, alone, do not do complete justice to liberal and democratic politics. At the core these moral principles presume that the morality of compromise is respected by not compromising some things away. The Crick approach can too often respond only to those who are organized and already powerful. It provides no independent directive to get all individuals regardless of power into the political order or to respect the relatively powerless. Nor does it have the rhetorical resources to respond to moral claims of respect and participation in the political order. Its realism is not realistic enough. But political compromises that flow from the fundamental political choice, while not sufficient, are certainly necessary to establishing and maintaining the possibility of a free and just political order.

Notes

1. See the essays by Held, Wolff, and Wertheimer in Pennock and Chapman (1972).

2. Coercion violates autonomy when it is inflicted without regard to considered judgment. However, a constrained coercion need not necessarily violate, but may acknowledge a person's autonomy and responsibility. The arrest and fair conviction of a criminal who violates a just and public law deprives the criminal of freedom but not of autonomy. Such judgment and punishment presume the criminal is responsible for actions.

3. See Sorel (1961) and Berkman (1970) for examples of the romanticization of violence and the assertion of true humanity.

4. Raiffa (1982), Chap. 6, describes the dynamics of an escalation game where the desire to "win" overrides assessments of the real costs and gains involved.

5. The following discussion draws heavily upon Shklar (1984) and Friedrich (1972).

6. For all the reasons mentioned above, coercion obviously helps to maintain community. This is especially so as it defends boundaries, deals with criminality, and can eliminate prisoner's dilemmas. For the last point, see Sobel (1972).

7. All these reasons to compromise and seek cooperation hold, but hold out no guarantees. People should not mistake the political implications of game

theory with the reality of political life. As I mentioned above, when class, ethnic, religious, or irrendentist claims overlap, the cycle of violence often seems impervious to breaking as in Northern Ireland or Lebanon. Trying to break these cycles involves far more than just building some successful compromises. Ultimately it means changing the symbolic and ritual allegiances. The famous Hatfield and McCoy vendetta for instance, ultimately ended with a marriage between the two clans.

8. See Sher (1981) for a discussion of a possible abortion compromise that draws its strength from trying to maintain civility in discussion. He proposes exchanging public complicity in abortion by ending publicly financed abortion for lowering the tone and violence of the dispute.

9. See Tesh (1984) for a sanguine view of how single-issue groups must become domesticated to succeed. See Dobel (1982) for a more deeply critical discussion. I do not address the problem leaders such as Falwell will face as distance appears between the vitriolic rhetoric he uses to true believers and the domesticated rhetoric and compromises of public life.

6
Prudence, Politics, and Compromise

*"The curse of politics is precisely that it
must translate values into the
order of facts."*
—Maurice Merleau-Ponty

People enter politics to achieve. These achievements result in consequences that entail right and wrong, good and harm in others' lives.
Individuals need to cooperate with others in a relatively unpredictable
world of unequal power, conflicting values, or differing interpretations
of the same values. In such a political world, individuals seek real
solutions in actual historical situations that will endure with a minimum
of violence. Merleau-Ponty describes this world of justification:

> A policy therefore cannot be grounded in principle, it must also compre-
> hend the facts of the situation. It was said long ago that politics is the art
> of the possible. That does not suppress our initiative: since we do not
> know the future, we have only, after carefully weighing everything, to
> push in our own direction. But that reminds us of the gravity of politics;
> it obliges us, instead of simply forcing our will, to look hard among the
> facts for the shape they should take.

A policy cannot simply be justified by its good intentions, nor is any
policy that succeeds good. But failure and incompetence are wrongs in
politics. "In order to be good a policy must succeed" (Merleau-Ponty
1969, xxxiv, xxxv).

In liberal and democratic life, success is defined and constrained by
basic commitments to human autonomy and its preconditions, equal

human dignity, social and governmental fairness, and governmental accountability undergirded by citizen participation. All actions, policies and "successes" can be challenged by invoking these considerations. These claims and purposes rein in the drive to success by any means because the means become an end. In such a world, prudent judgments give shape to values and goals and take into account the context of political life.

I aver to the traditional understanding of prudent judgment that sees prudence as more than simple cunning to achieve one goal. Rather, as a true virtue and not simply the tactically best way to achieve one's ends, prudent judgments are absolutely essential to achieving right and good in the world and possess their own moral weight and justification. As a virtue, prudence extends the penumbra of moral justification in a number of ways. First, justifications flow from the effectiveness imperative. If one has a morally defensible goals, prudent justifications flow from the attempt to create viable and do-able good, not simply to act on unrealizable intentions. Second, prudent judgments flow from facing the reality of actions; such judgments focus upon the concrete consequences for good and bad in other people's lives. Third, prudent judgments address all the dimensions of the context. This links prudent judgments inextricably with concerns of truth-seeking. Prudent judgments are built upon finding accurate and true assessments of all the consequences of actions and of learning the complexity—natural, social, economic, and moral—of a situation. Prudent judgments then address the multiple dimensions truthfully revealed in any political action. Finally, political prudence, because it is concerned with concrete political accomplishment, real and true consequences in people's lives, and do-able and viable good, covers the judgments that flow from the characteristics of political success. All these concerns give prudent judgments a powerful and persuasive weight in discussions that extend the moral penumbra to them and provide some of the best and most extensive reasons to compromise in politics.

The logic of prudence and compromise is not the logic of moral principles, ideals or rights. Nor does it provide neat rules about how to weigh and trade-off (Carens 1979, 124–26). Too often those who generate moral concerns exclusively from the moral point of view reduce prudence to a technical logic of how to derive certain conclusions from goals sought.[1] Reasons generated by reality considerations are devalued and given little justificatory power. Or, they are thrown into a grab-bag category that one ought to act, "all things considered." Although prudent reflection does not dictate outcomes, it is far more than exhortations to sympathy, detachment, and balance.[2] Beyond a point of detachment, prudence maps the agenda of concerns and reasons that a prudent politician should account for and answer to; it maps the "all things considered." Politicians can be praised for their success and condemned for their failure on the basis of prudence.

This approach to prudence understands prudent judgments as addressing the logic of moral action and implementation. It builds upon Saint Thomas Aquinas's understanding of the virtue of prudence as one of "imperative decision." Aquinas explains it as "to command the execution of what has been deliberated and decided on" (Aquinas 1974, Qu. 47, Art. 8, 9). Prudence makes possible the "doing of human acts" and the "correct marshalling of means to end" in situations where there is "no final way of reaching an agreement" (Aquinas 1974, Qu. 47, Art. 2, 5, 7).[3]

Prudence encompasses a structure of reflection, evaluation, judgment, and action whereby individuals seek to give concrete shape to their convictions. They get the best possible "fit" in the world given their principles, ideals and resources. Prudence accounts for and assesses the consequences of all dimensions. But it is far more than cunning or even Machiavelli's famed "virtù." Prudence influences the shaping of moral goals and our response to truth and moral complexity. Aquinas sees prudence as a robust virtue that impels individuals to avoid evil, but, even better, to do the "good" (Aquinas 1974, Qu. 47, Art. 8). Prudence addresses how individuals conceive the goals, the means they use to attain them, and the form of a successful political accomplishment.

Prudential justifications for compromise are rooted in the effectiveness imperative or what might be called the "duty of conscientiousness" (Benditt 1979, 26). Individuals of integrity enter politics to accomplish good. Their moral convictions and commitments define their standards of right and the nature of the good. For a conscientious person, these commitments generate imperatives to act and bring about enduring good as defined by their conceptions of right, and engage obstacles to achieving these results.

Political prudence begins when it engages reality to give shape to goals (Pieper 1966, Chap.1). Such moral action sees principles and ideals as directives to shape and motivate action in a direction despite the inherent imperfections and limits of life.[4] Political prudence, then, begins by rejecting a moral absolutism or moral narcissism about one's integrity or purity. In other words, it begins by rejecting what I called moral absolutism.

In a prudent judgment, individuals act within the tension between the possibilities of reality, and the thrust of ideals and principles. In his study of compromise, John Morley urges politicians to be "bold" in pursuing and promulgating ideas despite the need to compromise in practice with social constraints and prejudice (Morley 1893, 103–4). Prudent politicians can publicly lead, speak out, challenge, educate, and work to shift the meaning of symbols and to change opinion. Prudence does not have to be staid or conservative. For instance, if people possess little power and visibility, they might prudently challenge the status quo through imaginative tactics. Saul Alinsky recalls methods of gaining leverage when one is relatively powerless; the methods range from sit-ins and boycotts to public incidents of humor. But Alinsky rejects the moral narcissism of absolutism. His creative disruptions or Morley's boldness should be followed by a "constructive alternative" (Alinsky 1971, 130–38; Alinsky 1969).

The word "prudence" derives from the Latin "to foresee," and "foresight" is requirement of all effective action. Prudent actors should form a conception of the good or right they desire with the best attempt to foresee the consequences, including the costs. The search for consequences means people should do their best to acknowledge the historical, social and physical truth of a situation and act in accord with these facts and insights.

Prudent compromises begin when individuals seek to give concrete shape to their goals, principles, and ideals. Prudence has its preeminence as a virtue because it shapes moral claims (Pieper, 1966, Chap. 1). Almost all principles or ideals are underdetermined—they do not immediately dictate one and only one outcome in a situation. Individuals discover the act actually directed by the goal by asking imaginatively what the moral result would look like given the historical and cultural possibilities of a context, their resources, and the obstacles to realizing the goals. Deliberation, discussion with allies and even opponents will contribute to this shaping. Finally, concern with learning the truth of a situation and responding to the moral, social, and natural complexity of a situation will affect the shape of a prudent action.

If individuals are more Aristotelian and less oriented to principles, they can still carry ideals or models of action that practices sustain. People can give shape to such goals by looking to moral exemplars. Moral exemplars can be past models or living persons who embody the goals and attitudes. An individual might either follow their lead if they are living or imaginatively reconstruct what a past exemplar might have done in our situation. Stories, biographies, and the study of history can give substance to one's goals. This approach possesses real persuasive power and helps give reality to any moral view, but like all Aristotelian ethics, it remains blind to background assumptions and lacks self-reflective evaluation of the goals. For instance, a person might choose Jefferson or Lincoln as a moral exemplar, but one might also choose Hitler or Stalin. To give reality to the goals, individuals require dispositions and decision undergirded by virtue, but the goals themselves remain subject to moral question and claims.[5]

Giving shape to a goal means that politicians should work to grasp the real implications of the commitments central to their integrity. They need to get a fix on their core values and on less important values as well. For prudent and meaningful political morality, they need to know what Charles Francis Adams, a noted abolitionist and ambassador to England during the Civil War, called "the difference between surrendering unimportant points and sacrificing principles" (Potter 1976, 220).

Many goals and values will have arisen from reflection on the diverse strands within the political culture, but persons' abstract and imaginative reflection can extend or transform values within a culture. To the extent that political goals are derived from reflected or abstract ideals, they need to be grafted onto the symbolic and intuitive beliefs available within the culture to give them the greatest plausibility and motivational power. For instance, at a basic level, this knowledge of the political and historical moment affects the very act of compromising. A political actor should explore the culture's and opponents' attitudes towards promise-keeping and negotiation. The level of haggling, misrepresentation, strategic bargaining and the honor accorded those who succeed in fleecing the other side all need to be factored into any serious political endeavor to give shape to political goals (Raiffa 1982, Chap. 14).

The achievable reality of moral goals will be based on the possibilities of a political culture and the multiple means available at that moment. For example, if individuals are committed to equal human dignity and autonomy, their integrity would inspire them to seek legal, social, and political equality for women. But the political shape of this goal would differ if people lived in England or the United States. A constitutional amendment leaps to the mind as the obvious way to establish the political legitimacy of women's equality in the United States. But in a country without a written constitution and with a sovereign parliament as in England, the political resolution would look very different. Even in the United States, a conservative ally might suggest that the political guarantees could be obtained by state constitutional amendments, rather than by a national amendment. A more conservative person might also argue that the laws and codes could be changed to eliminate sexual discrimination without the risk and polarization of a national amendment.

A proponent of women's rights might even agree with a conservative after the national constitutional amendment had been defeated. Even among proponents, people might disagree about the exact shape of the amendment's wording. The obvious choice would straightforwardly prohibit discrimination against people on grounds of sex. But a moderate ally might be more interested in passage than total victory with a higher risk of defeat. He or she might ask that the amendment exempt women from combat duty and allow church-related sexual separation to continue. These two provisos could neutralize two of the most dangerous arguments against the amendment and gain a few additional votes in recalcitrant legislatures. In another country, an individual committed to women's rights and equality might fight a very different battle. In some cases, efforts to get people to take the issue seriously, akin to the plight of the suffragette movement a century ago might be in order. Issues like ending forms of slavery or improving education for women might matter far more than "equal pay for equal work" or voting rights.

The shape of achievable goals also depends upon a realistic inventory of resources and potentials for allies. The nonlinear nature of much political morality and action flows from the constant need to acquire resources and build coalitions, and many compromises flow from this need. For instance, with few official resources to seek urgent goals, leaders might prudently adopt peaceful demonstrations or devise clever schemes to call attention to their plight or cause. Individuals could prudently decide that agitation best compensated for their lack of resources or served as the best way to notify and mobilize people of a problem. As William Gladstone remarked during the English agitation against the Bulgarian atrocities, "Good ends can rarely be attained in politics without passion" (Kelley 1969, 147). With sufficient recognition and a power base, an alliance might be extended by compromise. With great institutional power and stature, individuals might resolve to keep issues in courts or counterattack with media campaigns and contributions to war chests.

So many of the justifications for action in political life hinge upon empirical claims about conditions and outcomes. Most of the seemingly side actions or indirect actions and compromises accompanying them depend upon claims that some momentum has been achieved or that some real good has been accomplished in people's lives. All this places an overwhelming priority on making accurate and truthful assessments of the reality of a situation and the range of consequences. It also makes assessing the real experiences of the people affected by the changes extremely important, for their assessments of lived good and evil should matter tremendously in judgments about whether projected good was achieved or harm avoided. Responding to the experience of people implicated in policy notifies politicians of unanticipated consequences and harms that might justify change or compromise of the initial goals.

Life may be simple, but reality is complex. Prudent reflection, then, should account for the complexity of reality and seek out the truth about an action in terms of its values, benefits, and costs. Prudent political solutions can be compromised to integrate the insights of physical and social science into its goals and use expertise to see the exact shape a goal should take in light of direct and indirect consequences. One of the more important compromises that can occur in political conflict is to agree upon methods to discover facts or agree upon one set of facts about a situation rather than throw partisan sets of factual evaluations past each other in the heat of conflict.

Environmental goals illustrate the issues very well. At one level, people often tend to discount the multiple benefits to future generations while simultaneously underplaying the nonquantifiable values like beauty, serenity or access to the untamed wilderness. Some purist environmentalists sometimes forget the sacrifices that workers might be asked to make when their economic livelihood is threatened by proposed environmental controls. At the same time, people often need studies and knowledge to determine exactly what constitutes the "safe" level of pollution. The possibilities of available and experimental technologies to solve the problem should be understood. At other times, environmental solutions may transcend normal local or state boundaries, since pollution does not respect conventional boundaries. Development-oriented leaders suggest that states might be discouraged from supporting environmental progress because pollution controls could put their indigenous manufacturers at a competitive disadvantage. Historically, state and local governments have tended to fail because excessive regulation causes industries to leave a site and invest elsewhere. Consequently, individuals should prudently seek national standards. People might prudently compromise in these areas for reasons suggested by expert knowledge and experience.

Prudence also incorporates moral complexity. As discussed in Chapter 4, most issues are impinged upon by several moral issues and principles. Generally, other moral points of view are presented by people in political life, but sometimes, prudence demands that people seek out and try to address the wrongs that a policy might inflict on others. Few people do this well, since reading another person's mind, let alone second-guessing moral commitments, borders on hubris. Far better for prudent politicians to seek to empower others to present their own points. All kinds of compromise could be defended as a prudential response to the autonomy or legitimate moral claims of others. By rejecting absolutism, prudence opens solutions to the costs and opportunities identified by moral diversity and complexity.

Prudent action acknowledges and deals with obstacles. The power and opinions of others represents the most enduring obstacles. People can discuss, debate, and cooperate, but ultimately, they may not be able to persuade other people of their point of view and still be unconvinced by their opponents. At this point, individuals might prudently choose to compromise attainable goals or outside trade-offs, even as they agree to carry on the battle by normal political means. The northern antislavery forces fought against slavery relentlessly for decades. But they ultimately had to come to terms with what Lincoln called "the necessity arising from its actual presence in the nation" (Smith 1956, 86). The southern states possessed power, legitimacy, and legal promises to protect their "peculiar institution." The South could be neither overridden nor destroyed, so efforts to end slavery short of war dragged on mercilessly. Some abolitionists call for disunion to free the North from collaboration with the slave states. Many other northern antislavery forces settled for stopping the expansion of slavery at all costs and waging a slow war of attrition to bring slavery within the South to an end after several generations. Short of that, they could wage war or let the South secede and become a permanent slave-holding country.

A hundred years later, the Southern Christian Leadership Conference challenged the legalized coercion of segregation. Their prudence led to compromises, but of a striking and original kind. They lacked sufficient power to overthrow the order and were denied political participation to challenge it. They learned in earlier demonstrations that peaceful witness would not change the minds of segregationists. But they also discovered that official violence against peaceful demonstrators would precipitate disgust and reaction in the rest of the country. Compromising their nonviolence as the only way short of despair or direct violence to gain freedom, they prudently courted official repression on the streets of Selma, Alabama. They even went so far as to target a town with a violent sheriff. Their tactics both appalled and galvanized a nation when armed southern sheriffs assaulted unarmed and peaceful demonstrators on national television (Garrow 1978). When people live in a community and seek political goals while minimizing violence, prudent judgments could lead individuals to compromise the immediate shape of goals as they compromise with the power of others and seek their own power base.

Power makes politics possible. Every citizen or politician who seeks to accomplish good in politics requires power. Any persons who seek to carve out their own destiny require power. Power gives life to dignity and freedom and makes accomplishment possible. With power, people can defend themselves and pursue their interests and aspirations when challenged. Without power, dignity and autonomy resemble eggshells ready to be crushed by the thoughtlessness or aspirations of opponents and even allies. Prudent compromises to gain and deploy power represent the most widespread forms of prudence in political life. Individuals, whether in or out of "office," always need to work to build support for their positions to attain any durable goals.[6]

Individuals begin with the need to acquire and keep a power base. Fighters for a goal have to recruit support, accommodate diverse goals and values, and neutralize opposition. In large organizations, people must fight to maintain a budget and high morale or fight for access by compromises with those above them. Elected leaders or participants in an alliance need to pay close attention to the demands of the power base. For years, Lyndon Johnson tended to the interests of the large oil and gas lobbies in Texas. This loyalty gave him the power to refuse to sign the 1956 Southern Manifesto fighting desegregation. Later he could vote for foreign aid and support the 1957 and 1960 Civil Rights Acts, because his major supporters knew he was safe on the basic economic issues. In a similar vein, the liberal George McGovern always watched over the interests and subsidies to farmers while pursuing his ambitious liberal agenda in the Senate. In workable alliances, everyone is forgiven certain votes and stands (McCarthy 1957). Independence is earned by compromises that serve the basic interests of allies and constituents (McPherson 1972, 60–68).

Many prudent compromises are made to maintain large political alliances that have cleavages of their own. Very often individuals compromise to maintain a power base intact for future gains. For instance, Abraham Lincoln, William Seward, and other antislavery

Whigs supported a slave holder, Zachary Taylor, in the 1848 election. They did so to keep the party intact while they were assiduously working to turn the party into a real antislavery party (Potter 1976, 79–96). The actual timing of goals can be compromised to ensure their feasibility.

The Whigs fell apart and most antislavery Whigs entered into the Republican party. They formed a strained alliance with the old Free Soil Party and the Know-Nothings to create a national alliance bond by antislavery. The party united both the desire of some to free slaves with others' resentment over possible competition from slaves in the newly opened states. It also allowed antislavery leaders to trade off side issues of lesser importance for their major issues. The final platform on the verge of the critical 1860 election united a commitment to a Homestead Act available to immigrants and small farmers with a promised tariff and public works for businesses. An antislavery plank held them all together by unalterably opposing the extension of slavery to the western territories. Nativists, Free Soilers, big business, and antislavery stalwarts subordinated differences and compromised to gain power without which they could accomplish nothing while others would do greater harm. The party even by-passed its most prominent spokesman, Senator William Seward of New York, because he was perceived as too radical and could not win the border states (Foner 1971, 170–84; Potter 1976, 390–2, 420–30; Jaffa 1982). They nominated a less well known and more marketable candidate named Abraham Lincoln.

On the other hand, "integrated" trade-offs can often underlie the best compromises for power. The winning coalitions in political life can be extended by moving to modify one's concrete position enough to gain sufficient allies to achieve the overall goals. People can modify positions incrementally, gaining allies each time without overtly violating basic aspirations. Sometimes individuals can logroll side issues of lesser concern to gain support for their vital issues. Compromises can always be made to extend mutual gains and broaden the base of the alliance or the commitment to the goals without diluting the original goals too severely.

Some of the most serious issues arise in compromises in coalitions when basic moral issues are on the line. In a devil's bargain, a politician supports, acquiesces in, or refrains from opposing an ally's position that he or she finds morally repugnant. Such compromises can only be justified in defense of other basic moral issues—no other justifications will support them. The alliance between Democratic liberals and

Southerners is a classic case. Northern liberals needed the southern Democrats to support basic social justice reforms. Yet even Southerners who sympathized with civil rights were paralyzed by southern voters and the willingness of opponents to seize upon racism to destroy them. Lyndon Johnson described the plight of many. "One heroic stand and I'd be back home, defeated and unable to do good for anyone, much less the blacks and underprivileged" (Johnson 1971). Without that compromise, illiberal as well as racist Southerners would have dominated the senate and no major domestic reforms could have been passed. Successful alliances grow and must constantly compromise to downplay factionalization and prevent energetic and angry factions from bolting or undermining the power base (Gamson 1975, 104–5). But devil's bargains implicate people in the substantial harms as well as in the good. They need to be justified in basic moral terms comparable to those at stake, and create a constant demand to change the terms of the bargain as soon as possible.

Keeping power might also involve another form of compromise. Mancur Olson has pointed out that most large social alliances face constant attrition from the free-rider problem (Olson 1971). Individuals who benefit from a public gain as a result of the actions of others will avoid contributing their fair share. A classic case is workers who enjoy gains won by a union but refuse to join it. Groups often need to adopt some coercive methods to gain support from nonmembers or offer them inducements to join and contribute. Time and effort and compromises in immediate gains can also be invested in garnering loyalty to an ideology that binds the groups and discourages defections. In addition, once a group gains stature and success, it usually bureaucratizes, and much effort must be diverted from the goals to keep the organizational base which stabilized past successes functioning. Individuals might compromise to maintain the efficacy of these methods or to secure the organizational base.

Prudence also extends the moral penumbra to cover the notoriously difficult concept of timing. To be effective, people must seek the "crucial moment" and rely upon what Lord Butler called "the patience of politics" (Butler 1971, 240–45). At that moment, the balance changes and resources once inadequate for achieving a purpose suddenly become adequate, risks once not worth taking suddenly become defensible. Without the change in balance, any efforts would result in squandering of resources with no significant accomplishment. This hinges upon the idea that political resources should be marshalled and not squandered. Politics does not thrive on Light Brigade charges.

Like soldiers, politicians must often wait on suffering before their eyes while they patiently build support, try to wean away opponents' allies, change public opinion, or wait for a "window of opportunity."

Skilled political actors must often devote far more time and energy to changing public opinion or symbolic meanings than forcing a solution. The oblique nature of much of political morality is evidenced most in long campaigns, which entail years of hard work and even some conscious defeats to advance positions, just as civil rights leaders carefully built up precedents leading to *Brown v. Board of Education* (Klugar 1968). Feminist efforts at consciousness-raising point to the same needs to divert efforts and energy to change the terms of justification and perceptions of individuals to promote successful action. On the other hand, groups might work to create the right time, as the civil rights demonstrators in Selma did when they risked local defeat and violence to galvanize national support for voting rights (Garrow 1978). To sustain action, individuals need to link their goals and ideals with the passions and commitments of ordinary citizens. Prudence makes this connection.

Often, individuals may have to wait for a propitious, even grisly, event to catalyze action. Lyndon Johnson used the assassination of John Kennedy to mobilize support for moribund social and civil rights reform bills. Televised racial assaults in Selma, Alabama became a springboard for Johnson to attack segregation. By refusing to use violence or manipulation, individuals in a liberal and democratic world must use the imperfect devices of politics; this means building power bases, watching the strength of opponents, and knowing when to strike (McPherson 1972, Chaps. 5,9,10; Evans and Novak 1966, Chaps. 7, 16, 17, 19; Johnson 1971, Chap. 7). As William Seward said of his antislavery commitment, "my life is chiefly dedicated to the advancement of a reform that I think cannot be hastily or convulsively made" (Potter 1942, 26). Timing justifies compromise, but only as a supplement to action and foresight imperatives.

Finally, time sometimes forces a choice upon individuals. At that moment, they have no more time to build a power base or change public opinion. As Machiavelli might have said, *fortuna* has swung and individuals must rely upon their past prudent foresight and efforts. People may try to stall but be denied this by opponents or demands of the moment, and action may follow without sufficient preparation, resources, or knowledge. At the beginning of the Civil War, Lincoln acted with "masterful inactivity" as he desperately tried to keep Virginia and the border states in the Union. He was willing to surrender all federal presence in the South, and guarantee slavery in place to enable a peaceful reconciliation. When hostilities were finally forced, this position strengthened his hand with doubters and gained him strategic advantages in the border states. But ultimately he had to act and respond to the secession (Potter 1976, 320ff; 1942, 159ff, 319–24). In similar circumstances, despite one's best efforts, individuals may have to compromise because the timing and situation were forced upon them.

Prudence defines the logic of moral action, which shapes successful solutions in political life. This means many justifications flow from the realities of imbedding solutions in the peculiarities of political life as opposed to other realms of actions. As discussed in Chapter 1, political success means that the behavior and often the beliefs of people have been changed, and this is measured in terms of durability, minimal necessity for coercion or manipulation to attain it, and its actual effect on the way people live. In a liberal democracy, these outcomes can also be challenged pragmatically on terms of whether they comport with or enhance basic constitutional processes and values, and the freedom and dignity of citizens, while remaining true to the rule of law in society. These concerns frame another set of prudential justifications for compromise.

A durable political success must be supported by symbolic justifications accepted by most citizens. Only this will link one's aspirations to the commitments and loyalties of people. The link between symbols and goals will help the changes become internalized social practices, and enable the change to occur without massive coercion. Success is not measured in revolution but in the changed behavior and perceptions that constitute the unreflective daily practices of people and institutions. Successful compromise gains the promise of citizens to live with a solution.

To gain durability, politicians need to pay attention to the accepted rituals of public legitimation and either play by the rules or change the rules. Programs need to be justified by practices and language that people understand and accept in their daily lives. This sometimes requires immense effort just to change accepted modes of justification. Both the civil rights and women's movements, along with public leaders, have devoted immense time and energy just to change the public terms of identification and judgment. Today even opponents of civil rights for minorities and women have to pay public lip service to the ideals. At any stage, individuals might compromise in the public presentation of their goals to adapt to the language and rituals of compromise in the speed of direct attainment to change the rules or terms of justification.

Once a political outcome has passed through and been legitimized by the accepted rituals of conflict resolution and governance, it still needs to be adequately funded and must endure successive political and institutional challenges. This means it must ultimately adjust to the self-interest, especially the economic self-interest, of the people. Any loyal citizenry will sacrifice their interests to a common good, especially in time of trials. But no nation consists of saints capable of indefinite self-sacrifice. Short of whipping people up into perpetual hysteria or permanent revolution, political solutions must conform to the needs and aspirations of the self-interest of citizens over the long run. For instance, the thin but widespread commitment to protect the environment for future generations must coexist with intense resentment by people who fear that environmentalism means a no-growth economy and shrinking economic opportunities. Welfare programs should not only respect the dignity of the poor but need to quell the resentment of individuals who do not want to see their "hard-earned money" supporting wastrels. Compromises can always be made to knit interests into the fabric of political solutions to give them strength.

For example, most policies touch people's lives hardest in their pocketbooks. In modern states, to commit is to finance, and durable policies need stable financing. Given the moral problems with taxation, the costs to those who are taxed, the political volatility of taxes, and their capacity to hurt economic growth, a whole set of special moral obligations and prudential concerns should surround every form of taxation and public expenditure. Compromises might be made to address limited resources, the dangers of a backlash from raised taxes, degradation of compliance with the tax code or methods to guarantee efficiency of expenditures.

In a classic political ploy, one could prudently compromise in the articulation of goals by working to transform the language of discussion from one based on moral and principled claims into one based on interests. While this risks hiding some of the moral issues, it can diffuse the rhetorical polarization and incivility of discussion. While daunting principles seem uncompromisable, when several principles are at stake, it becomes more acceptable. When the underdetermined principles take on concrete and fungible shapes, negotiation and discussion can occur with less acrimony and with less confusion of commitments of integrity to principles with the commitments to liberal and democratic procedures and concrete and politically viable out-comes. Focus on interests, even morally supported interests, also gives a greater degree of precision to articulation and makes trade-offs more feasible. The negotiations to save the Social Security System in 1983 took place in a morally charged atmosphere, but one where the actual trades were discussed in specific terms of interests, money, and concrete and divisible issues. This enabled a workable solution to be compromised even as everyone knew the profound moral stakes (Light 1985).

As discussed at length in Chapter 5, prudent judgments always should account for problems of enforcement and coercion. Govern-ment always manifests a Faustian aspect when institutions are granted special permissions to use coercion with legal immunity and moral exoneration of officials. Those who possess power to enforce can also turn on the population they protect and oppress them. All military dictatorships—communist, capitalist, and third world—soberly remind us of this pervasive danger. Politics transforms conflict and coopera-tion from coercion to peaceful encounter undergirded by coercion. That coercion can always be used to destroy the political process.

Such justifications for compromise might be summed up by the minimum abuse imperative. People should design laws and institutions with an eye towards their minimum possible abuse. The more knowl-edge required to solve a problem and the more moral perfection required of the enforcers, the more people should be willing to compro-mise in the enforcement. Additionally, institutions should be designed with an awareness of the capacity of leaders and officials, even of their integrity and great commitment, to subvert or abuse the authority they have been given. In a similar sense, prudent judgments often rein in the regulatory conscience of society because the more personal and pervasive control becomes, the more likely it is that abuse of power and corruption of institutions will occur. The corrosive effects on police of enforcing prohibition or many vice laws exemplifies these types of issues over which individuals might compromise in their goals and methods. A good thought experiment would be to ask what would happen to an institution set up to implement a policy if people diamet-rically opposed to the law gained control.

This minimum abuse imperative should also be taken seriously by theorists and intellectuals who promulgate justifications for actions. They should ask what happens in reality when government officials, harried bureaucrats and put-upon leaders grab hold of a theory to justify an action. For instance, one might construe an interesting and finely qualified justification for torturing human beings—a potential nuclear terrorist presents a nice example (Levin 1982). Given that bureaucracies regularize action, and leaders tend to use the weapons in their arsenal, and given that participants in an action become hardened, the finely honed qualifications that the theorist defined to limit proscribed action wither in practice. Limitations that in theory make sense and justify the practice fall away, and the practice extends naturally as the professionals become hardened and "perfect" their technique, and government officials find torture morally easy to use. The history of the Inquisition and its evolution into a governmentally controlled form of church terror illuminates how nicely qualified exceptions can become brutal norms. The growth of mass bombing of cities during World War II exemplifies the same process. Torture, censorship, and most finely qualified forms of repression are institutionally addictive. To ignore this when people justify actions and recommendations is morally and prudentially irresponsible.

History gives little comfort about high morale, talent, and commitment to public servants over time. Nor should anyone ever assume that they and their allies will always control the reins of government. Additionally, the tendency of bureaucracies to aggrandize power and expand their agenda should be anticipated in all solutions. Bureaucrats burn out, new leaders take over, even the most well-intentioned officials can succumb to the pathologies of political life (Friedrich 1972). Compromises can flow naturally from the minimum possible abuse imperative because good solutions should always account for the pathological possibilities.

In a similar vein, prudent judgments always seek to respect the need for openness in political life. Saint Thomas Aquinas argued that prudence meant that a person must be "teachable." Most politicians normally seek to keep their options open because decision closes them in and makes enemies. They must be sensitive to the possibilities around them given the restless change within society and live their lives in what Bernard Crick calls the subjunctive mode—what might be or might occur (Crick 1972, 151). In this mode, politicians should be open to the unanticipated consequences of their actions and capable of revising policies if they fail or generate great harm.

Openness aligns with and reinforces the central role of truthseeking in prudence. Individuals should always be open to the reality of situation, the claims of others, especially their experience and assessments of the rights and wrongs of an action. This openness supports truth because prudent individuals should be open to persuasion by the ideas and claims of others.

A politician might struggle mightily and compromise prudentially to gain a small but vital precedent rather than accept a clear loss on much greater immediate claims. Theodore Roosevelt often pursued this strategy and settled for a precedent that opened the political system up for larger gains later. The Meat Packing Act of 1906 entailed a series of compromises and was fraught with what Roosevelt called "purposeful ambiguity." But Roosevelt compromised on the number of inspectors and in other areas to gain the principle of federal control, that could later be extended (Bailyn 1981, 66–68). Civil rights leaders always sought voting rights protection as the most important in their compromises. The vote opened the system and enabled blacks to create their own political base and pursue their own goals (Johnson 1971, Chap. 7).

In a different vein, people might leave the actual public justifications of a policy or law rhetorically vague or general. To the extent that public explanation of actions remains general and at the highest level of rhetoric, it can pull in the maximum number of assenting individuals, and makes it possible for each side to defend the compromise to its own allies in its own terms. This maximizes the possibilities for widespread consent, enabling broader coalitions to be built since each side can enter for concrete action but need not agree on the actual justifications or interpretations for the actions. Any number of compromises can be made on avoiding closure for these reasons. Such rhetorical compromises help stabilize solutions, make agreement easier by not demanding complete agreements that affect integrity too deeply, and engage and exploit the moral and intellectual diversity of political actors. It turns the diversity into a strength rather than an obstacle.

The last form of prudential openness defends frameworks that are preconditions for later success. Most antislavery leaders firmly believed that slavery could become "ultimately extinct," as Lincoln put it, within the Union. Consequently, antislavery politicians agreed to complicated moral compromises in 1850, for instance, enforcing the hated Fugitive Slave Act to return runaway slaves to their masters. Lincoln and most Republicans believed that slavery would wither away if only it could be kept from expanding. Republicans would tolerate it in place and use federal power and patronage to pressure for its demise while according it due constitutional protections. But the Republicans adamantly refused to allow the extension of slavery to the territories (Foner 1971, 215–25; Potter 1976, 45ff.). On this point, Lincoln and his allies were unshakable, even to the point of precipitating the Civil War. These Republicans would fight to guarantee "ultimate extinction" within the Union rather than permit an independent, permanent, and expanding slave empire to the south (Potter 1976, Chaps. 8, 13, 19). To compromise for less and acquiesce in continued evil involves great dangers and depends upon clear analysis of possibilities and the accuracy of empirical claims. It also depends, like timing, upon a continued thrust for change. Openness without action guarantees the status quo.

Prudence, then, defines the pervasive logic of moral implementation that shapes imperative morality. Prudential justifications flow from how people conceive a goal, how they seek to gain it, and from the peculiar aspects of political success. In this prudence completes the triumvirate of families of justification that dominate political justifications. To the extent these families converge on each other, they provide the strongest and most pervasive justifications for compromise and action.

Notes

1. See Bricker (1980) for a technical example of this approach to prudence. Bricker adds an interesting twist to Aquinas's concern with foresight. He suggests that prudence can best be understood by seeing it as a technical strategy to determine what kind of future self we wish to be in making present decisions. The discussion suggests an important dimension often ignored in politics, that political actions can, in fact, change the type of persons living in a community. But narrowness of analysis shows the unhelpfulness of such analytic approaches for comprehending political prudence.

2. Beiner (1983) suggests political judgment and prudence inhere by definition in situations where principles and moral differences do not apply. Instead, political judgment requires that people disinterestedly seek through sympathy to understand other members of the community.

3. Aquinas provides and discusses his own list of attributes. This list both differs from and considerably influences mine. In Question 49 of the *Summa Theologiciae,* he enumerates the following components: memory, insight or intelligence, teachableness, acumen, reasoned judgment, foresight, circumspection, and caution.

4. See Galston (1980) for a more benign and plausible account of the role of ideal or "utopian" theory. This defense complements many of my comments upon the role of moral claims in politics in Chapters 1 and 4. In both accounts,

principles do not reduce to determining imperatives that overrule all other political and moral considerations.

5. See MacIntyre (1984) and Beiner (1983) for studies of how moral exemplars can humanize and guide our aspirations. Such stories can certainly help educate and clarify goals, but they also respond to and carry the prejudices and limits of a political culture. MacIntyre and Beiner both seem to assume we will only tell "stories" that support freedom and human dignity.

6. Neustadt (1964), Seidman (1980), and Mintzbeg (1983) examine the role of persuasion and compromise even when we hold "official" power.

7. Enelow (1984) provides a technical discussion of this mode of compromise in legislatures.

7

The Trouble with Compromise

"The most dangerous is that temptation
that doth goad us on to sin in loving
virtue."—Measure for Measure

Life offers no panaceas, and politics and compromise are certainly part of life. Accordingly, no one advocates compromise for its own sake. Even its most ardent proponent, T. V. Smith, acknowledged that it is "superior as a means, inferior as an end" (Smith 1956, 44). Like all activities, it can be perverted and abused, especially so since it often possesses an inherent moral ambiguity and tension. This essay explicates the nature and role of compromise in politics and defends it as a cornerstone practice of liberal and democratic political life. But any explications or defense must come to a proper appreciation of the dangers and limits of an activity. Born in imperfection and complexity, compromise possesses its fair share of both.

Controversy is built into compromise, and there are no guarantees that people will compromise well or that all compromises will be good. Compromises are quintessentially human actions fraught with imperfection and limits. They require evaluation and judgment on a wide range of prudential, political, and moral concerns. The troubles with compromise begin because the very activity of compromising can undermine the assumptions necessary to its prudential, political, and principled justifications.

In this essay three dimensions have been used to assess the good or right of a compromise. First, it can be evaluated according to the goals of the those entering into the compromise. Second, it can be evaluated

139

by whether it comports with the basic values of liberal and democratic life and supports or strengthens the institutions vital to that life. Third, a compromise can be evaluated by examining its execution and results in light of the standards of a successful political endeavor including whether it holds, is perceived as legitimate, or can be accomplished with a minimum of coercion or manipulation.

The major problems in light of these standards develop internally. Paradoxically, the activity of compromising tends to undercut the reality conditions that ensure a good compromise. Successful compromise depends, above all, on the commitment, skill, and integrity of the politicians exercising power and pursuing goals. The act of compromising tends to corrode every aspect of these assumptions. First, compromise can sap moral integrity and commitment. Second, compromise can lead to an attrition of the power base. Third, compromise can blur and subvert the goals. In a different vein, compromise as the political norm can reinforce the status quo and entrench already existing inequalities and moral stagnation.

The integrity of individuals lays the baseline from which compromises proceed. Political actors need to be clear-eyed judges of concrete outcomes and be capable of honestly evaluating actions according to their values and goals. Individual integrity grounds effective judgments and depends upon persons' capacity to resort to internalized forums of judgment and to honestly assess oneself and actions by these criteria. Compromising often entails helpful ambiguity and individuals need moral benchmarks to which they can refer, or people need groups who embody these benchmarks and to whom they are accountable.

Persons committed to goals should not only remain answerable to them but also energetically and tenaciously strive for the goals. Given the inevitability of frustrations and failures, this moral tenacity, even optimism, is an oft underestimated virtue in political life. To gain the political goals, people need to ally commitment and tenacity with the skillful acquisition and deployment of power. This reaches its fruition in liberal and democratic life when individuals can demonstrate in a publicly confirmable manner that they have achieved concrete and durable good and right. Given the ambiguity and stresses of compromise, this public dimension of justification is absolutely essential, for people can delude themselves or a small cadre that they have accomplished a goal when they have only served themselves.

Individuals stretch convictions and virtues when they compromise and can lose touch with their moral benchmarks while falling into self-deception. They can overvalue their own power and status, and compromise their effectiveness in the process. Their drive and direction can dissipate in the exercise or enjoyment of power and compromise. In all these cases, the basic assumptions of viable and energetic integrity can be undermined by compromise. Even Edmund Burke's apologiae for compromise warn that no one should "barter away the immediate jewel of his soul" (Burke 1970, 37).

Thomas More appraises the problem with dark irony in the first book of Utopia. His discussion takes on even greater poignancy when one realizes realize that More himself was struggling at the time with offers to enter public service and leave the life of a scholar and humanist. In the first book, More has just tried to persuade his remarkable friend, Raphael Hythloday, to enter government since Hythloday's wisdom and energy could help the commonwealth to flourish. When Hythloday expresses exasperation and even contempt over the obstinacy of reality and futility of politics, More replies: "You must not abandon the ship in the storm because you cannot control the winds." Politicians should use the "indirect approach" and must "seek and strive to the best of your power to handle matters tactfully. What you cannot turn to good you must make as little bad as you can." More chides Hythloday for demanding to speak out as a moral prophet and recommending impossible policies, rather than enter the hard work of political persuasion and compromise. Raphael responds with a stinging indictment of the moral attrition of political life:

> By this approach I should accomplish nothing else than to share the madness of others as I tried to cure their lunacy. . . .
>
> As to that indirect approach of yours, I cannot see its relevancy. . . .At court there is little room for dissembling, nor may one shut one's eyes to things. One must openly approve the worst counsels and subscribe to the most ruinous decrees. He would be counted a spy and almost a traitor, who gives only faint praise to evil counsels.
>
> Moreover, there is no chance for you to do any real good because you are brought among colleagues who would easily corrupt even the best of men before being reformed themselves. By their evil companionship, either you will be seduced yourself or, keeping your own integrity and innocence, you will be made a screen for the wickedness and folly of others (More 1964, 51–2).

The power of Hythloday's indictment still rings true. Secret intentions to do good do not vitiate the harm collaborated in. But Hythloday makes an icon of his integrity and worships his own purity. What appears to be a moral stance is nothing more than a form of selfishness, even immaturity. Hythloday vacillates between seeing morality as absolute rules that cannot be violated except at the cost of one's integrity, and anger over his inability to effectuate utopia immediately upon a rhetorical appeal to the council and king. More's position on the effectiveness imperative and imperfection of reality corresponds far more closely with the theory of morality and responsibility that informs this essay. Hythloday linked integrity and purity, but such purity too often breeds either impotence or tyranny. The force of integrity ultimately requires that right be done, not that evil be tolerated from fear of contamination. More's position and decision to enter politics, however, do not nullify the force of Hythloday's criticism. Entering politics entails moral risk and More's later martyrdom for taking a stand on principle haunts the entire discussion.

Compromising politicians can come to value their own power more than the goals they once pursued. Power is enjoyable. It brings the satisfaction of accomplishment, but it also brings recognition, deference, high status, and sometimes fame. At a darker level, power enables individuals to crush their opponents, reward their allies, and gain ends with less concern for other's positions. Power and success can inflate self-worth and addict people to the joy of dominating and succeeding.[1] Few citizens gladly give up power once they possess it. Every politician is tempted to compromise simply to keep power and position, regardless of initial priorities. As Burke remarked, "power rarely reforms itself" (Burke 1970, 166).

Robert Caro portrays this archetypical interaction of power and personality in *The Powerbroker,* his classic biography of Robert Moses. As a young and idealistic reformer, Moses had been constantly frustrated in his efforts to reform New York City public planning. After his early failures, he resolved to gain enough power to achieve his goals. He compromised with the city political machines and elites and curried alliances with contractors, unions and powerful politicians. Eventually he succeeded in gaining independent power and transformed New York City with a profusion of parks, beaches, schools, and parkways. The politicians learned to depend upon him, because he could deliver vital contracts to their allies and produce visible signs of success in his placement of new construction. Initially Moses curbed many abuses and did much to make New York a more beautiful and humane city.

But Moses became inured of the corrupt practices and increasingly built his power upon an interlocking network of favors among unions, contractors, banks, and public officials. He came to terms with corrupt bidding practices and privileged contractors and lax inspections to fulfill his dream of rebuilding New York's public infrastructure. To ensure his independence, he created networks with public works officials in the state capital and later in Washington, D.C. He used innovative attempts to free public officials from corrupt electoral pressures to create fee and tax authorities with no accountability to the public. By the zenith of his career, he had insulated himself from all effective electoral accountability and ruled his own empire. Immune from normal political pressures, he could even intimidate reform mayors and governors like Fiorello La Guardia and Herbert Lehman. Moses simply ignored local or neighborhood associations. After defying Presidents and deeply influencing federal legislation, he embarked upon an unrivalled spree of building public housing and highways. In the process, he wrecked neighborhoods, abetted urban sprawl and formalized the ghettos of the city. When his first generation of dynamic and independent subordinates departed, he increasingly treated his subordinates and enemies with disdain, even cruelty and revenge. Surrounded by "yes" men, he dismissed any information that demonstrated his own achievements' contribution to New York's urban sprawl and ghettos. In the end, the reformer became the "boss" who both mastered and succumbed to the methods of those he fought to displace. His experience exemplifies the dangers of compromising oneself for power and then confusing one's own power with the goals (Caro 1974).

Compromises and incremental changes can insidiously sap energy and commitment and can lead individuals to overvalue their power for its own sake, even when they are no longer accomplishing their committed goals. During the Tory ministries of Disraeli, many Tories bitterly complained that to keep power, they had to vote "black as white." On great commitments like disestablishing the Church of England or extending the franchise, the Tories voted against their consciences and traditions to keep the ministry in power (Marsh 1979, 215–42). In the end, Disraeli's last ministry drifted along with no major goals except to keep the liberals out and enjoy the rewards of office (Blake 1967, Chap. 30, 24). Disraeli summed up his own problem well when he referred to a Gladstone ministry as a "range of exhausted volcanoes."

Perhaps no American event exemplifies the capacity of power and compromise to corrupt as the disputed election of 1876 (Woodward 1951). Democrat Samuel J. Tildon won the popular vote. In a remarkably corrupt electoral count, the election was thrown into the House of Representatives when Tildon failed to garner enough votes in the Electoral College. Tildon had run on a militant reform record, and the Republicans were desperate to keep control of the power and governmental largess they had ruthlessly exploited over the previous eleven years.

After arduous negotiations, the Republican leadership managed to detach a number of southern Democrats away from their party affiliation with promises of increasing federal subsidies to the impoverished south. In particular, they agreed to underwrite the building of the Texas and Pacific Railroad which was ardently desired throughout much of the South. In addition, the Republicans agreed to remove the remaining federal troops from the south and accept the "Redemption" of states by the very conservative and racist regimes that had replaced the Carpetbaggers. At the same time they agreed to paper guarantees that the Negroes' rights would be respected. Underneath the negotiations, some Republicans hoped that they could create a new alliance with older southern Whigs who would be economically conservative but build on the Negro vote.

In the House, the Republican candidate Rutherford B. Hayes was awarded the election when the southern Democrats opted for a Republican candidate. The Republican leaders of the party of Lincoln and abolitionism had grown tired of its commitment to Negro equality. Keeping control of patronage and furthering subsidies for big business mattered far more to them, and they played on the southerners who feared Tildon's reformist record and opposition to public works and corruption. Even while publicly acknowledging their duty to protect the Negro in the South, the Republicans compromised what few commitments they still retained to regain the White House. They consoled themselves that the southern Whigs would work to keep the votes of Negroes and thus guarantee their rights. The withdrawal of troops and the official end of national control in the South guaranteed the final "Redemption" of the south and the end of Negro freedoms for seventy-five years.

Compromise and power can insidiously mute the rage or optimism that kindles a reformer or dampens the intensity of belief that energizes a politician. Politicians can become Morley's despised "man of the world" who can no longer take aspirations to reform seriously because he has lost his commitments. Compromise becomes too easy, an unreflected norm, rather than a problem. For Morley, Lord Halifax, "the trimmer," exemplified the problem. Halifax remained a staunch republican in his convictions, but never made serious efforts to let them influence his actions, as he refined "trimming" to a way of life. By such constant trimming, ideals and convictions lose any operative force or content. Yet "what purpose is served by an ideal, if it is not to make a guide for practice and a landmark in dealing with the real?" Morley suggests, "If an ideal has no point of contact with what exists," it has become "not much more than the vapid outcome of intellectual or spiritual self-indulgence" (Morley 1893, 226–28). He might have added self-deception.

Once politicians feel no qualms about compromise, they often have lost part of their moral compass. At this point allies become extremely important because they remind politicians of the goals to which the leaders are ostensibly committed, but the political actors may no longer push as hard or negotiate as sharply. Since they know their opponents personally, they cannot pretend that all opponents are enemies or Satans. Over time, they might even come to sympathize with the views of the other side or at least understand them. Too often, this understanding, cut off from moral impetus, can enfeeble, just as judgment without understanding can destroy.

As leaders spend time negotiating and working with the elite or the opposition, they can lose touch with their own allies and aspirations. Recognition by the elite and co-option are two of the most highly valued and common methods of dealing with political dissent (Gamson 1975). Union leaders are often cut off from the floor after their elections as they spend most of their time in public life, managing large bureaucracies, and meeting face to face with their counterparts in management. Even workers who must sit in on labor-management councils and help run factories often end up accepting much of management's point of view (Piven and Cloward 1977, Chap. 3).

Compromise comes even easier when a person not only thrives under the rules of the game, but assimilates them and values them as highly as his or her own political goals. In the English parliament, the moderates of both parties value the parliamentary procedures and civility far more highly than the radicals, and are willing to give the other side their due in major controversies. The radical wings, however, value parliamentary procedure less than the attainment of their goals (Searing 1982, 244–55). In most representative bodies, the moderates are as committed to arriving at consensus and making the rules work as they are to any substantive goals.

Most successful and durable groups centralize and bureaucratize. In both cases, institutional and careerist stakes go up. Individuals can easily value office and institutional preservation more highly than the purposes for which they were instituted. Second- and third-generation leaders of a group may be far from the original impetus and struggle that gave moral coherence and drive to its founders. Their own concerns may focus more heavily on keeping the institutional and monetary apparatus in shape. Too many Roman Catholic and Christian churches remained quiescent, trying to protect their institutional basis, when confronted with the terrible rise of Nazi power. They sacrificed their convictions to institutional preservation. In the end, they lost both.

Ultimately integrity remains an internal personal phenomenon. Persons internally reflect upon goals and convictions, then they make the best effort to judge before their consciences how their actions and accomplishments comport with their goals. Persons of integrity seek some coherence, alignment, or unity both at the level of conscience and selfhood and between conscience and actions. Integrity presumes honesty in this process of self-evaluation. But the political world offers constant frustration as well as the temptations of power, assimilation and institutional identification. Failures or changing commitments can assault self-esteem and introduce the moral pain of guilt or shame as well as cognitive dissonance. The cognitive dissonance occurs because the gap between real accomplishments, goals and commitments and ideal self-images, convictions and ideals, widens, almost to the breaking point. People often respond to this pain, not by working to lessen the gap, but by changing their goals or modifying their standards or evaluations of the successes and commitments (Buchanan 1978, Chaps. 4–6).

Under the tensions of moral ambiguity or failure, individuals can deceive themselves. They can hide the implications of acts from themselves, or simply refuse to examine them. More actively, they can convince themselves that actions that violate convictions or stem from base motives actually conform to convictions (Fingarette 1969; Hauerwas 1977). Very often, when people make a commitment, even after considerable personal turmoil, they will reconstruct their decision and beliefs to eliminate moral ambiguity once the decision has been made. Each serious compromise splits people, since they know both good and wrong. No one likes to live with constant moral ambiguity, especially when promises must be fulfilled to remain an effective politician. People will often then rationalize their commitments and decisions, and hide from the complexity or incongruity that they may have seen before the decision (Janis and Mann 1977). This rationalization actually helps political compromise work, but it can induce self-deception, which destroys or cloaks the moral benchmarks that made it possible for a person to compromise well.

Individuals also can come to identify themselves with their offices and goals, as Robert Moses did, and identify themselves as "indispensable persons" for gaining vital moral goals. When this situation exists, all opposition to the incumbents and their compromises to keep power becomes opposition to the moral goals themselves. Honorable leaders untouched by venal purposes can simply lose perspective under the crush of events and cling to power because they believe in their own indispensability. After the start of World War II and after the demonstrated failure of his policies, Neville Chamberlain still believed that he alone could end the crisis. He stumbled through a demoralizing prosecution of the first months of the war and only resigned after much of his party deserted him (Cooper 1953, Chaps. 15, 16). Ironically, Churchill, who replaced Chamberlain, clung to power too long at the end of his career for similar beliefs about himself.

Because of the internal nature of integrity and the problems of temptation and self-deception, political morality possesses an inescapably social dimension. People need to check with others to confirm if their own evaluations of moral principles and ideals, even their own meanings for moral terms, comport with what other people believe. Individuals who profess to share values and who become allies in political battles become especially important. Even as consciences can be distorted in solipsistic reflections, social and political discussion and accountability can force individuals to check their judgments against reality with some serious questioning. But many leaders will go out of their way to subvert serious moral and political accountability or debate. To quiet their consciences, such leaders need to corrupt or silence friends, allies, and opponents. Power-holders notoriously resent moral rebukes and honest reporting of bad news. Like the Persian tyrant, they will cut off the head of the bringer of bad news and often ostracize dissenters. The limitless capacity for self-deception is magnified by the "group think" of coteries. Politicians will surround themselves with sycophantic advisors, who reinforce the illusions and blindness of the leader with reassurances of integrity and success. These advisors will censor moral dissent and disruptive information (Janis 1982; Dobel 1980).

Compromises can undercut the power base of a political group and cripple its ability to do good. This nullifies the second major assumption of successful compromising. Compromises can alienate leaders from the power base, rendering both ineffectual. The base coalition can disintegrate under the centrifugal pull of a compromise. The coherence and drive of a group can be wounded when compromises domesticate a group or lead them to accept symbolic justifications, which subvert the real goals.

A successful coalition requires skilled leadership accountable to the alliance members. The ethical legitimacy and almost certainly, integrity of the politicians depends upon their accountability to the group. Leaders should answer to and explain their positions in light of the actual goals that the members seek. These dialogues and challenges clarify and test the efficacy of the politician's positions, and give leaders an opportunity to change the ideals and images of their allies. As discussed above, compromises that involve powerholding and contagion by opponents can undermine both commitment and accountability while separating leaders and followers.

Initially, many leaders emerge in the turmoil of protest. When leaders gain power, they often try for good reasons to rationalize their legitimacy and emphasize elections and procedures over the rough and tumble methods that first gained them clout. This emphasis grows greater in successor generations. Once secure, they often become preoccupied with the "responsibilities and satisfactions of that office" (Piven and Cloward 1977, p. 300).[2] Leaders must administer and maintain their organizations as well as deal with the elite and other power wielders. Individuals begin to believe that they possess access because they are perceived to be "strong" and "reasonable." Wedded to behind-the-scenes negotiation and organizational legitimacy, they actively discourage their most feared tactics—disruption and protest. This fear of open confrontation gradually wears away the leaders' credibility within their group, alienates grass roots activists and slowly causes them to lose leverage with the elite. Some leaders will go so far as to purge their "extremist" elements to maintain their position and ability to "deliver" a now docile organization. This undercuts the group's ability to mobilize its membership and dissipates energy on internal battles to consolidate control. Bureaucratization demands more money and specialists, and this makes groups more dependent upon dues and internal coercion or upon outside largesse rather than on the power of motivated members. As the group is tamed, leaders can slowly be weaned from its original goals. They learn to speak a different language, to dress differently, and so enter public life and office. The "shoulder rubbing" effect subtly separates legitimized leaders from the moral urgency of their followers' plight (Piven and Cloward 1977, Chap.5).[3]

Even if leaders remain accountable and committed, compromise can often dissipate a power base. Most political coalitions are constituted by members with differing intensity of commitment and often with different, but yoked together, goals. A compromise will sometimes break up the unified power of the coalition because it will satisfy some more than others, and further dull the commitment to fight. Robert La Follette, the great progressive leader, repudiates compromise for this reason: "Half a loaf as a rule dulls the appetite, and destroys the keenness of interest in attaining the full loaf. A half-way measure . . . is certain to weaken, disappoint, and dissipate public interest" (La-Follette 1960, vii).

Immediate and marginal gains will often lead some members of the coalition to drop out and paralyze future efforts. After the redistribution of land during the early part of the French Revolution, the peasants opted out of the revolutionary mainstream. They tenaciously fought to protect their gains and later became the backbone of Bonapartism and monarchical restoration. In the welfare rights movement in New York City, after certain grievances had been placated, many of the most vocal supporters dropped out and stymied efforts to gain further concessions (Piven and Cloward 1977, Chap. 5). Sometimes a compromise, which satisfies one group, will infuriate other allies and lead them to defect. The old Whig party was torn asunder in the 1850s by its compromise with slavery and the Know-Nothing(s). It lost northern antislavery Whigs to the Republicans and immigrants to the Democrats (Potter 1976, 239–56).

Too often, small reforms can be the enemy of big reforms. They dampen the fervor of the group. A proabortion activist described the dynamic, "Well, there's nothing to set back a good cause like a little tiny reform. You know, they reform a little bit and then they sit on their duffs for ten years" (Luker 1984, 96). Lenin indicted successful labor unions for the same set of reasons. In his eyes someone like Samuel Gompers bought breathing space for the American craft unions by trading off wage gains for quiescence on social and political issues. But as the English saying goes, "Give an Irishman a horse and he'll vote Tory." When workers gain a decent standard of living, they will seldom push for major social change unless jolted by a depression. Often, comfortable workers will lose their own desire to proselytize and close off their unions to others to protect higher wages. American craft unions became "labor aristocrats" and collaborated against the emergence of industrial unions and fought against the extension of labor's political agenda. "Craft selfishness" and economic compromises can turn organized workers against unorganized laborers (Lenin 1975, 566, 575, 588; Lindblom 1977, Chap. 1).

Every compromise involves a battle to attain "moral ascendancy" in public discourse. The stakes are high. The authority of a group or law presupposes a community of meaning that validates authority. These symbolic justifications set the limits of what is perceived as "just repression" (Gamson 1975, 140–42). The shape of a debate and justification deeply affects the self-image of a group and community and the possibility of persuading people to change in the future. In a compromise on abortion, for instance, the future possibilities are profoundly affected by whether a policy is justified primarily in terms of the autonomy of the mother and the mother's safety or in terms of granting moral and legal status to the fetus. The Republican Party was founded on a mix of public rhetorics—antislavery could be justified on moral, constitutional, political, or economic grounds. The economic and constitutional arguments extended the foundations of support but watered down the fervor of moral stalwarts (Foner 1971, 59–64, 78–86). These differences revealed profound fissures in the party when it battled over the extent of Republican Reconstruction. Constitutional and economically inspired Republicans moved much more slowly and carefully in seeking political and social equality for blacks. The more far-ranging radical Republican proposals to create an independent and educated black yeomanry after the Civil War were often defeated by defections of those who adhered to the political or economic antislavery positions (Les Benedict 1974).

Any laws or compromised political outcomes will be justified in ways that lead to acquiescence and reassurance. One of the major functions of law and decision is to reassure citizens that a problem has been addressed. Rituals and symbols can sometimes hide real outcomes from people. At the same time, they can lead people to accept as solutions formal laws with no substance (Edelman 1964; Morley 1893, 132). But laws and court decisions often represent only a symbolic statement of intent; the real work of changing behavior and gaining compliance is yet to be done. If people do not realize this, a compromise can paralyze efforts to change the system when many individuals demobilize after a bill has been passed or a court decision handed down. But, the day-to-day reality of politics depends upon constant effort in courts, administrative agencies, and at grassroots levels to maintain pressure in areas as diverse as civil rights or environmental protection. The compromise for the 1957 Civil Rights Act set a vital precedent and reassured most Americans that some substantive progress was being made in civil rights. It had almost no significant impact on the lives of people and policy, except to crystallize consensus. Similarly, *Brown v. Board of Education* ordered an end to segregation in schools and mandated the order to be carried out with "all deliberate speed." In fact, it took years of compromised compliance to begin serious enforcement of the Court's mandate, while many citizens thought segregation in schools had ended.

Finally, if individuals compromise and accept the broad terms of policy with which they disagree, they are reduced to speaking only in instrumental terms to try and change policy. Many individuals who held a more pluralistic and complex view of third world politics found themselves unable to influence discussions of the Vietnam War. Instead, they had to adopt the terms of an institutional anticommunism and dogmatic domino theory, which precluded them from being able to seriously question the goals of the policy. In addition, they had to discuss the instrumental success of bombing or land reform, rather than take on the pathological anticommunism that ritually justified the Vietnam quagmire. Almost every major dissenter on the policy found that efforts to affect the policy were constantly frustrated by the adoption of this world view (Halberstam 1969; Dobel 1982; Gelb and Betts 1979; Berman 1982).

Compromises can ultimately subvert an individual's goals by opening traps that undermine the ability to define and reach the goals. Compromised integrity and power fall into the "effectiveness trap" (Thomson 1968, 1973). Here, a person seeks access to policy makers. Policy is usually determined by small groups with their own informal consensus. To earn access, a person must adapt to the mores and assumptions of the group, much as Thomas More suggested to Hythloday. If a person opposes and wants to change a policy, he or she must mute the criticisms and tailor recommendations to the group's perceptions. The leader's needs and blindnesses must be accommodated to maintain credibility. Only credibility in the group gains effectiveness and influence. Yet the very process of getting power and earning trust usually implicates people in policies they may despise. Further, when dissent becomes known, dissenters may be asked to perform even more collaborative actions to prove their loyalty and earn the right to dissent. But the dissent erodes credibility anyway, and people gradually participate more in the policy they oppose, even as they lose their influence. To gain power, they risk integrity; to keep integrity, they risk power. Compromise can often destroy effectiveness either way (Dobel 1982).

In the leverage trap, individuals compromise goals to gain an ally and become subverted by the ally's agenda. Once people publicly commit their position, their own credibility is on the line and the ally then possesses an extreme amount of flexibility. The allies can use the commitment to ratchet up costs, because they are now needed while balking at fulfilling their part of the bargain. If individuals break their promises to such allies, the validity of one's promises and political morality will be cast into doubt. The ally uses this to extract more aid, while giving less than promised. The weak can, in fact, tyrannize the strong.

The leverage trap can be generalized into a sort of sunken investment or tar-baby trap. Compromises often involve partial or incomplete commitments. But once people have invested money, personnel, resources, or prestige into a policy or organization, it becomes very difficult to pull back for reasons of public credibility. So, compromises, which might seem at the time to be only initial testings or limited partnerships, can quickly grow into full-scale moral and resource commitments that were totally underestimated at the time of the compromise.

A willingness to compromise fits nicely with a strategy of incremental change. But this approach can possess several problems. First, people can become too enamored of compromise and success. Even to his admirers, Lyndon Johnson sometimes seemed willing to accept crumbs when a half-loaf was not available. At those moments, it often made more sense to continue agitation and education, of which a public defeat would be one aspect, rather than divert energies and risk losing support with false victories (McPherson 1972; Evans and Novak 1966). Second, an open and incremental politics invites massive side compromises with special interest groups. Major policy initiatives can be amended to death, plugged full of loopholes, and yet passed as one whole piece of legislation. Too often, the end result falls disastrously short of any serious aspirations. Opponents rely upon the fact that proponents want the bill passed and will tolerate a considerable number of side issues or amendments as long as the bill itself remains intact. At some point, the substance of the bill may be compromised, but sponsors focus upon maintaining a winning coalition. This gives reluctant allies and opponents a chance to nickel and dime the bill to death in exchange for support in the final passage. The process by which President Reagan's 1981 tax cut proposal ended up generating massive federal deficits parallels the ability of lobbyists and marginally important members of congress to fill the bill with revenue holes because the White House desperately desired to pass the bill regardless of the compromises of revenue (Greider 1982).

The nature of compromise in bureaucratic life magnifies the danger that compromise will defeat the purposes of the goals. Bureaucracies must give reality to the symbolic aspirations of law and policy and fit limited resources and expertise with very large jurisdictions. For ease and efficiency, they routinize actions to offset understaffing compared to their missions. Most bureaucracies for good reason prefer parsimony in coercion. Consequently, they seek to gain maximum amounts of "voluntary" compliance, usually by lowering expectations to levels acceptable to the recalcitrant. By asking less, they avoid massive resistance. Very often, in the United States, regulators try to respect the initiative and power of federalism. They do not want to treat states and localities like "conquered provinces." Over time, they try to regularize federal relations and maintain "professional," even cordial contacts with local administrators whose behavior they must change. At the same time, they must work in a world where the resisters learn the regulators' methods and can constantly initiate new ways of avoiding the law. All this leads officials to dilute their enforcement methods and seek lowest-common-denominator solutions, which get the largest compliance.

The implementation of the 1965 Voting Rights Act represents just such a case. A small staff of lawyers and paralegals, around thirty-five officials, were responsible for monitoring over a thousand local and county jurisdictions to foster improved black participation and prevent any local changes from diluting black political strength. Understaffed, they faced a high level of local hostility as well as opposition from the Republican administrations under which they served. Additionally, the local officials pursued a wide range of tactics such as gerrymandering, changing the location of voting machines, eliminating elected offices, and annexations to dilute or frustrate black voting strength. The federal officials also had few overt enforcement penalties or incentives available to them and were extremely sensitive to the imperatives of federalism. So all the good reasons to compromise—fitting resources with the job, minimizing coercion, avoiding abuses, and respecting local democracy, fostering openness to learning—led them to compromise many serious efforts to foster increased black opportunities for political power. Instead, they focused on demanding "preclearance" from local officials before new changes were implemented. This led to some incremental changes, predominantly by preventing abuses, but resulted in far less good than could have been done (Ball et al. 1982).

When Lyndon Johnson began his campaign to pass the 1965 Voting Rights Act, he refused to compromise or even consider compromise. Johnson's reasons bear recollection, "I knew the slightest wavering on my part would give hope to the opposition's strategy of amending a bill to death" (Johnson 1971, 157). Very often, the willingness to compromise encourages the opposition. It gives them an incentive to continue to oppose, because they are being rewarded with substantive change for their opposition. If individuals compromise all the time on anything, it can even encourage opponents to nullify actions with violence or become enemies. Reasonableness or internal differences might be regarded as a sign of weakness. This in turn encourages harsh and extreme posturing by the other side to move people closer to their position since they know their opponents to be accommodating (Raiffa 1982, Chap. 8). Compromising with true enemies can make a situation even worse. Allies will view compromises as a "sell out" of their interests, while enemies will be encouraged to be obdurate. John McNaughton, Assistant Secretary of Defense in the mid-sixties and a thoughtful architect of Vietnam policy, summarized the dilemma as American policy-makers perceived it:

> We are in a dilemma. . . .it may be that while going for victory we have strength for compromise, but if we go for compromise we have the strength only for defeat—this because a revealed lowering of sights from victory to compromise (a) will unhinge the GVN (Government of Vietnam) and (b) will give the DRV (Democratic Republic of Vietnam) the "smell of blood" (Gelb and Betts 1979, 128).

Dwight Eisenhower's response to Senator Joseph R. McCarthy illuminates the problems. Eisenhower had achieved many of his greatest successes as a conciliator and compromiser. He had held the grand alliance together with just such skills and also helped rebuild the Atlantic community. During the major crises of his administration, he seldom took the advice of his hawkish advisors to commit his resources or military might. His techniques included waiting on controversies, letting others play their hand and trying to defuse conflict while avoiding getting involved militarily if at all possible. This style paid handsome dividends in his crisis management, but debilitated his civil rights efforts and made a mockery of his efforts on McCarthy.

Eisenhower had become an anticommunist as an aftermath of the

Cold War. Like many Republicans, he worried over security and the liberalism of many Roosevelt administration holdovers. Additionally, he needed the support, or at least acquiescence, of the old guard Republicans for his own initiatives in Congress. Yet he despised McCarthy and his demogogic assaults upon individuals and the government. Eisenhower hated censorship and blanched when McCarthy began his campaign against the United States Information Agency to purge books from library shelves, a campaign that whipped up nationwide book burnings. McCarthy even attacked Eisenhower's old mentor and friend George Marshall in his everwidening and irresponsible net of innuendo and assault. Finally, McCarthy formed his own "pro-American network" to become a sort of second government in the American government and inform to McCarthy on any suspected anti-Americanism. This affronted Eisenhower just as McCarthy's campaign against the army angered him.

But throughout his campaign and administration Eisenhower refused to attack McCarthy by name and even refrained from a public defense of George Marshall. On one hand, Eisenhower did not want to alienate the old guard; on the other, he sympathized with McCarthy's goals, if not his methods. But above all, he felt that he would only give McCarthy greater credibility by "getting into the gutter" with him. Eisenhower was convinced that McCarthy would hang himself, if given enough opportunity. So Eisenhower compromised on his policy, lived in silence with a demagogue he hated and periodically would privately help a friend. He even gave a speech against book burning, which he refused to follow up with support for his beleaguered USIA. But in fact, Eisenhower did almost nothing to stop McCarthy, and McCarthy's supporters took the silence as tacit support. Additionally, Eisenhower set up his own internal security system that purged over two thousand bureaucrats in order to do McCarthy's dirty work for him. Instead of mollifying McCarthy, this simply encouraged him to take on more targets. The Robert Oppenheimer security hearings, where the head of the laboratory that developed the atomic bomb was denied his security clearance in a kangaroo court, was initiated by the administration, in part, to ward off McCarthy.

Meanwhile, several of Eisenhower's own appointees, especially at USIA, languished without public support. The State Department was similarly crippled by McCarthy's attacks. The resulting purges and demoralization of many bureaucracies not only hurt American policy-making, but helped cement the pathological anticommunism that blinded so much of the decision-making on Vietnam.[4] Eisenhower's

compromised silence abetted McCarthy at almost all turns and prolonged McCarthy's power by giving the diffuse and scared opposition
no point of reference or protection. His compromise involved him in
collaborating in actions he distrusted, and encouraged and empowered
the opponent he despised while undermining his own government.

Compromises depend upon promises to live by a solution and play
by the rules of the game. Compromises over time generally reinforce
the status quo. Process and vested property are generally more highly
valued in compromises than provision of equity or substance for the
underclass. Moderates, Whigs, and Conservatives lend credence to
this truth by their preference for compromise. Usually, liberals and
radicals of both the left and right distrust it most deeply. The moral
urgency of the reform imperative moves them more deeply, while they
value the institutional means of conflict resolution less or indict the
entire structure of society as hopelessly corrupt or unjust.[5]
In a political compromise, politicians meld ideals and power into
workable policy. As politicians, they seek out or confront expressions
of concern and realities of power and opposition. These arise from
organized groups in the population. Any successful compromise must
accommodate the groups who hold great power and stature. At the
very least, success must be crafted so as not to alienate them permanently or evoke active subversion. In this politics, organized groups
can express their will and exercise power. Unless all groups are
organized and possess adequate voice, then compromises benefit the
organized over the unorganized. Even in a totally organized society,
no one has an incentive to seek out what may be the common good or
public interest on issues. Minorities, even majorities, who are either
unorganized or lack the prerequisites of power will regularly lose out
in the political system of generalized compromise.[6]
The history of President Reagan's 1981 Tax Bill and budget cuts
illuminates the problem. David Stockman, President Reagan's Budget
Director, announced that the new Conservatism sought to reduce taxes
and the budget, but in an equitable manner. "We are interested in
curtailing weak claims rather than weak clients. . . . We are willing to
attack powerful clients with weak claims" (Greider 1981, 13). The new
administration would pursue efficiency with equity and Stockman
worked tirelessly to cut domestic policies helping the poor, confident
that the powerful would sacrifice equally.
Once the bargaining began to cut the budget and reform taxes, his
principled equity collapsed. Strong lobbyists protected their subsidies
and pet projects. Vitally needed members of congress parlayed their

votes on the margin into promises to protect or help their own constit-uencies. Placed in competition with the Democrats to design an ap-pealing tax bill, the White House caved in on special preferences like keeping sugar subsidies worth 2 to 5 billion dollars while ruthlessly cutting welfare programs. Stockman ruefully commented on "certain wages" that had to be paid as the revenue side of the bill collapsed and special interests were placated or protected. Any notion of equity was sacrificed in the need to win with organized groups holding the power. Stockman sums up the limits of compromise in unequal but organized systems where "weak clients" suffered for their weakness: "Power is contingent. . . .The client groups know how to make themselves heard. The problem is, unorganized groups can't play this game" (Greider 1981, 60).

This poses one of the most profound problems of pluralistic democ-racy. Formal constitutional protections of autonomy and dignity too often undervalue the importance of having the requisite resources to take advantage of the formal guarantees. Without relatively equal political resources and a solid baseline for all citizens, the formal politics ends up consistently benefiting those with wealth and power. The formal justifications provide vital symbolic justifications to chal-lenge the system to acknowledge new groups and to help actively in the empowerment of all citizens. But even such principled criticisms and justifications might overvalue process and existing property rights at the expense of the basic necessities of life and dignity for all citizens. Equal respect for freedom values moral integrity and expression of life plans very highly. Rather naturally, it encourages individuals to delib-erate on and respect articulated and vested interests, especially if the interests had been garnered under legitimate rules. This sensitivity means that those who possess great amounts of property and articu-lately defend them will be respected and accommodated. Those with-out property or the skills to defend their interests will also be accom-modated, but very slowly and with great weight given to due process and others' legitimate claims. Equal respect and autonomy emphasize slow accommodation and sensitivity to claims and procedural rights; they do not necessarily value basic needs highly, unless society adds what John Rawls would call a "baseline" of primary goods for each citizen. This baseline would ensure the basic goods needed to begin autonomous reflection and action upon our own life plans. Without such a baseline, substantive equality and real political power will be regularly undervalued in the name of formal liberty for all citizens (Rawls 1971, Chap. 2).

If compromise is raised to a cultural norm, it can easily lead to social stagnation. If individuals presume to compromise before they battle to fulfill moral values, they blunt their own moral energy and critical eye towards society. Premature and universal compromise can only engender cynicism in both leaders and the young. Toleration and respect become confused with moral indifference. Moral reform and questioning is undervalued and not rewarded while individuals are encouraged to make their mark and fortune by conforming to economic and social norms. No driving moral energy or vision challenges people to reform the deficiencies and injustice of the political order. It becomes a time in which John Morley gloomily pronounced that "the souls of men have become void." Morley excoriated the dangers of a "shrinking deference to the status quo" and a too easy "accommodation with error," which an ethos of compromise can breed (Morley 1893, 32–35, 19–21, 45–48, 75, 213–215). Compromise as a way of life, can kill intellectual and moral integrity. Everything becomes a game with payoffs and it spawns a cynical society of "gamesmen" committed only to their own advancement and satisfaction. Without loyalty or integrity, they accept the game on its own terms and succeed. They win but never challenge or change the order that rewards them (Maccoby 1976).

On the other hand, the limits to compromise can induce some individuals to use refusal to compromise as a tactic in politics. A Washington staffer described how President Reagan used this tactic, "He'll stonewall until he's sure he's got a good compromise. It'll look like he's set in concrete, but he knows when it's time to move" (Light 1985, 180). Southern "Fireaters" stonewalled throughout the 1840s and 1850s, and were able to swing solutions in their direction because Democrats needed them and all sides feared their threat to secede (Potter 1976, Chaps. 2, 4, 10, 15, 17). Southern Democrats used similar strategies to stymie civil rights reforms while radical Republicans tried the same strategy to hold the Republican party to a progressive reconstruction (Foner 1971, 110–11; Les Benedict 1974).

Extreme positions can also enable a cause to recruit moral activists and get money from radical backers. Moral appeals galvanize members, and absolute claims about single issues simplify the moral universe. If a group can organize money, votes, and shock tactics around a single issue such as abortion or gun control, they can magnify their power in a fragmented electorate or representative body (Dobel 1982a). By refusing to compromise, groups can grab headlines with outrageous rhetoric and symbolic acts. If skillful and aggressive, extremists can shape the tone of the debate and agenda while putting opponents on the defensive with virulent and *ad hominem* attacks.

These are not moral absolutist claims per se. Rather, they hinge upon the "prudential" claim that more good can be accomplished by refusing to compromise in political life. The argument possesses significant weaknesses. First, these individuals exploit the civility and willingness of others to compromise. Both these are significant historical accomplishments worth defending. As in an iterative bargaining game, the militants win big only as long as the others play by the rules and in good faith. After a period of time where they lose to the militant tactics, other groups will adopt a similar position and the political coin will be debased. Single issue groups spawn clones on the other side. Pro and anti groups arise around each issue and polarize the terms of discussion and election. They encourage politicians to posture on symbolic votes and avoid serious negotiation about problems. Moral complexity is masked behind one issue, and one position illegitimately overvalues all other issues. Voters literally lose control by focusing upon these issues to the exclusion of others. Many moderates either leave political life or are forced out by the stridency of demands and the need to assemble gerry-rigged coalitions of money and single-issue groups rather than rely upon broad-based parties (Dobel 1982a).

Constant militancy can also backfire. First, "purity can mean impotence" if a group cannot change or accommodate the rhetorical discourse of a society. Second, groups can become a liability if their stand has spawned militant opposition groups who carry as much weight. Most politicians distrust militant allies and when militants lose strength, the politicians will often distance themselves from them. If this happens, they will suffer attrition and can end as pariahs or in political backwaters. Third, militants can unite reluctant allies and solidify moderates with the other side of the issue. Not only can "no compromise" unite opposition despite differences, but it can stiffen their will and intensify conflict. No one should forget the real costs and moral liabilities of intransigent politics.

The last trouble with compromise is that sometimes, people simply should not compromise. If opponents are using coercion or intransigence to deny the basic autonomy and dignity of fellow citizens, individuals should be uncompromising in their opposition to both means and end. Even if individuals must move carefully, they can resolutely press to end the oppression. If the stakes are extremely high, if people gain sufficient noncoercive power, and if opponents' past intransigence has foiled serious efforts at the goal, one's own intransigence may be the prudentially, politically, and principled correct strategy. Compromise cannot solve all the problems of political life and carries its own problems. Lyndon Johnson campaigned for the 1964 Civil Rights Act by announcing in advance that he would not compromise. He had seen too many civil rights initiatives broken by compromises with intransigent opponents. He had done so himself in 1957. This time, he placed all his supporters on the spot and alerted his opponents that their past tactics would not work. The bill passed intact.

Political compromise is a practice grounded in prudential, political, and principled reasons invoked by politicians seeking to accomplish good in a complex and obstinate world. As defensible practice, compromise depends upon the power of its reasons. These reasons depend upon a series of reality assumptions for their validity: politicians must possess integrity and accountability as they pursue goals; individuals need to muster and deploy power successfully to achieve the goals; the goals must have a verifiable reality. But the very process of compromise possesses a countervailing dynamic that can subvert each of these assumptions. While compromise should be the central practice of a prudential and liberal-democratic politics, any justifications for a good compromise must account for these limits.

Notes

1. *The Powerholder* (Kipnis 1976) traces some of the most obvious changes or what he calls the "metamorphic effects of power" in individuals. Buchanan (1978) examines other changes in personality brought on by the combination of power and stress when individuals confront frustration and deference. Janis and Mann (1977) examine how the psychology of decision and commitment involves one's self-esteem and tends to harden a person's commitment as well as narrow the perceptions of alternatives. Haroutunian (1949) provides a provocative and wide-ranging testimony to the dangers of untrammelled seeking and possession of power. In an unpublished essay "Temptations of Power," I analyze ethical rationalizations used to justify keeping power for its own sake.

2. Only charismatic leaders escape this tactical preoccupation, but their successors must confront it. Any charismatic figure who bargains for concrete gains faces similar problems.

3. Piven and Cloward (1977) discuss these problems in telling detail for the union, civil rights, and welfare rights movements. No one who advocates effective and moral compromise can afford to ignore their sobering lessons.

Gamson (1975) discusses a wider historical variety of groups without nearly as much detail. He charts the consequences of recognition, centralization, and bureaucratization in protest movements.

4. This summary is drawn from Ambrose (1984). See Merson (1955) for a searing indictment of the consequences of Eisenhower's compromising on his own appointees to the USIA.

5. Reactionaries might feel the same way, but invert the argument. They might believe that any changes, like small tilts on a sensitive gyroscope, will destabilize the political order and lead to wild and erratic swings or changes. They will adamantly oppose compromise on most issues. In this case, they and the radical uncompromising left lock in polarized conflict. They differ from genuinely moderate conservatives who entertain a multiplicity of values and try to do justice to them, or from realistic conservatives who compromise, because they know it strengthens the political order in the long run.

6. See Carens (1979, 133–37) for a more technical and aggressive discussion of these problems. But compromise can also enable new groups to enter more easily and enable small but organized minorities to leverage their position into some power in coalitions that need them. As conflict is socialized and politics is opened up, it becomes more possible for minority groups to gain power for themselves in larger coalitions (Schattschneider 1960).

8

A Good Compromise Is Hard to Find

*"Integrity without knowledge is useless and
knowledge without integrity is dangerous
and dreadful."—Samuel Johnson*

Compromise lies at the center of the web of the moral and political relations of liberal and democratic life. The practice of meeting others, taking their concerns seriously, asking them to take one's own concerns seriously, and making binding agreements and compromises rightly represents the pervasive medium of engagement and accomplishment in such a politics. The practice gives reality to the moral claims that individuals possess a dignity and freedom that warrants their pursuit of their own destinies. Compromising with other persons acknowledges their status as legitimate participants in the political order and their integrity, which presumes their capacity to assess, promise, and abide by agreements. In many compromises, the interests of others are recognized as worthy of concern, even respect. To the extent that compromises involve mutual gains, they acknowledge all participants as "victors" or gainers in the exercise of politics with a right to those gains. This conclusion will pull together the case made in previous chapters. It will summarize the defense of political compromise and unite the justifications with the problems of compromising to present a series of maxims about compromising well.

The beauty of compromise as a moral-political practice is that it amalgamates so many diverse motives into these acts of mutual recognition and respect. In reality, many people might compromise grudg-

163

ingly and not even intend to show mutual respect for the other side, which they may dislike intensely. The participants may enter a compromise for many diverse motives and still profoundly disagree over many things. They might compromise more out of recognition of the other side's power and the need to accommodate, more than any other reason. But the public actions of politics, such as negotiation, voting, legislating, or making public agreements, transform diverse motives into public rituals of respect and acknowledgment. The public reality and precedents as well as the experience of meeting and compromising turn compromises into such recognitions, sometimes despite the wishes of the participants.

This symbolic dimension to political compromise underlines how the moral consequences of the rituals and practices reinforce its political importance. The possibility of compromise encourages individuals and groups to enter the political order. It extends the range of active politics and makes any group that can organize even a minimal amount of power a serious potential participant. Groups denied dignity, if they can gain some power, can gain recognition of that power, and apprehension of their dignity will often follow. It allows room for the prophetic and agitational dimensions of moral life to flourish in politics and yet still be tempered in the forge of compromise solutions. Within this loud and rambunctious world, compromising among individuals and groups over time creates the possibility that bonds of communal commitment and recognition will grow and that diverse and pluralistic societies will do more than coexist in simmering incomprehension.

The political realities and moral thrust work together to build a political culture where individuals expect to be acknowledged and to work with others in attaining their goals. The internalized sense that politics involves "fair give and take" breeds a pervasive expectation on the part of political actors to acknowledge and take individuals and groups seriously. People presume that good political solutions will involve listening to and negotiating with others and seeking solutions that do justice to the widest possible range of interests and points of view. Such a political culture encourages public civility and a sense that norms of accommodation are important to the long-term well-being of everyone's goals. The openness to compromise coupled with the serendipity of politics means that all political actors are potential allies in attaining goals; it encourages a public citizenship that cuts across the polarizing tendencies of so many dimensions of economic and social life. All these work to support the baseline contribution of the political order—to create and sustain a community where individuals can seek their goals and cooperate and compete with others without resort to tyrannical coercion or totalitarian manipulation. Compromises maximize the potential for widespread assent by pulling many groups and individuals into the process and outcome as well as making future revision of problems a viable alternative to revolt.

Compromise as I have used it in this work, arises as a serious and difficult practice because of its morally problematic nature. Persons of integrity motivated to seek goals inspired by their ethical ideals and principles experience the moral tensions of compromise in several dimensions. First, they may accept less than the outcome demanded by their commitment to a moral goal, less than would be morally acceptable under ideal conditions. Second, they may have to work much more slowly and sometimes obliquely to arrive at the goal, and even then they may achieve much less than they sought. In both settling for less and accommodating the slowness and obliqueness of political life, individuals know the tension that the imperative nature of their moral commitments still carries, even as they work through the fabled, "all things considered" world of moral theory. Third, individuals might have to cooperate in ways they find morally problematic to achieve a given goal; or engage in side-trades; or acquiesce to others' morally questionable goals to ensure support for their own goals. Lastly, they might have to collaborate in implementing flawed programs in order to attain other vital, moral aims.

This entire account of compromise has presumed a sense of moral pluralism whereby individuals of integrity can possess a number of incommensurable moral commitments. While these commitments might have rankings, this account further assumes that these commitments, while generally underdetermined, cannot necessarily be unified along one dimension of assessment as an absolutist or utilitarian might. It also assumes that even though acting upon one imperative may, in fact, be the right and good thing to do, this does not nullify the force of the other moral issues involved. Thus, compromise can be both justified and problematic at the same time, unlike the accounts of an absolutist or utilitarian.[1]

A whole range of moral, political and prudential justifications warrant compromise as the central practice of democratic and liberal political life. But its tensions and ambiguities mean that compromising *per se* cannot be relied upon to produce a just, humane, and viable order. It can go a long way in this direction, but ultimately compromise as a norm can be too accommodating of power and existing inequalities of power and wealth. Compromises then become a means to reinforce patterns of domination and oppression rather than instruments for a more just political and social life for all citizens (Hallowell 1944). Asymmetries of power, skill, or information can lead individuals to compromise away basic rights and subvert their dignity. Stable coalitions can compromise among themselves and dominate other groups and minorities without reference to people's freedom or dignity. Additionally, as I emphasized in Chapter 7, the very tensions of compromise, combined with the reality of power, can lead individuals and groups to deceive themselves about the actual intent and consequences of compromise.

Any claims that compromise should be the preferred moral-political practice of a liberal and democratic society then depends upon the limits of compromise being addressed. Good compromises can flourish, and compromise as a practice can be recommended and relied upon best in a political order that has several characteristics. First, potential compromises should be bounded by values and institutions that protect values that individuals are not allowed to compromise away. These constitutional boundaries are crucial to the protection of the basic preconditions for dignity and free decision-making among citizens. Second, the political order should make every effort to empower the largest number of citizens. Only then will people have any reliance that compromises reflect diverse interests and that compromisers have at least tried to respect diverse viewpoints. Third, the more equally basic political resources are distributed, the more seriously compromise can be relied upon. At the very least, the threshold of effective power and entrance into the political arena should be very low. Good compromises should extend or strengthen any aspect of these basic systematic requirements needed to legitimize compromise as a norm.

Finally, compromise can be relied upon as the preferred option of political morality only if political actors are required to give public justifications for their compromises and be held accountable for them. Giving reasons for actions is an act of primal political respect. Without being bound by that respect, individuals can feel free to coerce or manipulate to get their way. As the Greeks first recognized, justifying actions is central to the political life of free citizens. But even more so, the demand for public justification offsets the dangers of compromise going awry due to self-deception.

Compromises are enmeshed in complex judgments not just of moral valuations and weightings but of empirical claims about resource limits and historical possibilities, the need to gain power and to deploy it, the nature of momentum and movement, or the fit between accomplishment and moral aspiration. This requires the giving of reasons and constant checking. For instance, a political actor compromises to gain power that will make further action possible rather than risk defeat and lose the opportunity to make a significant difference in people's lives as well as to establish the group's credibility. Such claims depend completely upon public exposure to determine their genuineness. The compromise might make a significant difference or it might not, but the public needs to hear the justification, experience the consequences, and judge for themselves. Similarly, any claims to gain power must be publicly tested by continuous questioning from supporters about whether or not the power is being used for its intended purposes, is being monopolized by the possessors, or is being put to other uses. The consequential nature of political morality absolutely requires public justification and accountability to the people who entrust their support or power to political actors and who experience the consequences of those actions. Good compromises should be defensible against the challenges raised against it from any of the three families of justification. They prove themselves good to the extent that individuals can justify them in an open and accountable manner without resorting to great coercion or manipulation.

What constitutes compromising well? The question always possesses at least two dimensions. From the agents' point of view, people accomplish enduring gains. Individuals gain as much in concrete terms as they could reasonably expect, given their resources, opponents, and historical possibilities. They do this without subverting their commitment or accountability and without undermining their power base. The compromise leaves open the possibility both of refining or increasing gains, and dealing with problems that arise. These gains require reasonable, not excessive, amounts of coercion to gain widespread support or compliance.

Externally, a compromise can be judged by its responsiveness to moral issues beyond those that justify initial goals. In a liberal democracy good compromises respect or enhance the personal autonomy and dignity of citizens and strengthen liberal and democratic institutions by satisfying legitimate aspirations, by empowering disenfranchised citizens, or by opening a closed system to greater public participation. To the extent that a compromise addresses the moral, natural, and social complexity of an issue and minimizes adverse side consequences, it can be evaluated to be "good." When the compromise meets expectations and satisfies grievances, it strengthens a viable and flexible order and legitimizes a liberal and democratic world. The stability and viability, as well as justice, of the political order provide other external vantage points. Good compromises also make civility possible, sometimes by uncivilly opening the door to groups previously denied access, and all good compromises respond to the need to limit coercion and minimize their abuse.

These frames of reference define initial starting points from which to judge compromises. These standards, like any evaluations in political life, should build on moral, political, and prudential reasons discounted by their dangers and pitfalls. Good justifications reflect the context of accomplishment and should remain essentially rebuttable. Tensions exist among the various families; people should expect innovation and extension in political justifications and life. It is hard to imagine a good compromise where politicians deliberately gain less than they could, change their allegiances and beliefs, and silence and disarm their allies while seeking to close the issue to all future discussion. Nonetheless, exceptions could surely arise for any criteria. The Bill of Rights or the Thirteenth, Fourteenth, and Fifteenth Amendments deliberately set out to prohibit violations of freedom of speech and religion, and to outlaw slavery. Interpretation of complex questions leaves open certain aspects of these issues, but the political order, rightly, sought to ensure these freedoms as completely as possible.

Good maxims unite empirical considerations with morality as any consequentialist ethics must. The actual justifications of a good compromise gain power and plausibility when the families of justification reinforce one another, as happens in the best maxims. This convergence provides the strongest and best justifications for action. For instance, the arguments for compromise to preserve liberal democracy already discussed demonstrate the power of this convergence.

Good political-moral claims should be designed to help real individuals do the right thing. Long and obtuse derivations as well as overly refined and qualified principles written in obscure languages are of little help to real persons of integrity, struggling to do the right thing in a very complicated world. Committed politicians confront a world of self-interest, ambition, opposition, conflict, scarcity, cooption, zealotry, resource and time constraints as well as moral, social, and physical complexity. Political actors, whether as citizens or officeholders, are embarked on a moral enterprise justified by trust and delegation as well as coresponsibility for the lived welfare of individuals in the community. They must shape goals, judge, improvise, and act; they must compromise. Moral-political maxims unite moral and empirical considerations and provide a midlevel of standards of judgment for political actors.

Political maxims advise and direct but can be refuted with other good reasons. They do not obligate, like strong moral principles, but oblige conscientious individuals to take account of them. They provide ground for good and legitimate judgments about compromises. The claims made throughout the essay and in this chapter do not end criticism and evaluation. They present the initial framework for judgement and challenge that reflective citizens and politicians should consider when they compromise.

Good compromising like good ethics begins with knowledge about one's commitments. The success and goodness of compromises depend upon the integrity and skill of individuals as they exercise discretion in making the compromises. But no clear rules exist to define integrity while compromising. At best, individuals can recur to an examination of conscience that covers the vital dimensions of the action and question themselves or be questioned when they compromise. It is vital that individuals possess maps of their own commitments, especially of their core commitments and the actions required of those core values. They need to know the uncertainties about outcomes and where the commitments underdetermine required actions. This gives them the benchmarks of what should not be compromised and what should shape and direct their actions. To the extent that core values are less clearly determined, more room for compromising exists. To the extent that core values compete, some room for compromise among the commitments exists. Similarly, the less vital values and even indifferent areas need to be charted. Good compromises often sacrifice values, and the better compromises lose less in important areas. As Representative Daniel Rostenkowski, Chair of the House Ways and Means Committee told his fellow House conferees upon entering into negotiations on the final shape of the bill to rescue Social Security, "We want to lose whenever we can, because we're going to beat the hell out of them on the big ones" (Light 1985, 218–19).

Individuals who act as citizens and officials in a liberal democracy need to remember that public life entails a special set of core commitments that build upon and co-exist with personal core commitments. Concerns to protect the institutions and processes that give life to liberal and democratic values should nest at the core of these commitments. These commitments are ultimately justifiable in terms of basic personal moral concerns, but they possess their own weight and should always temper any commitments and actions derived from personal moral commitments and integrity. In a sense, this makes all ethics of citizenship a continuous compromising and calibrating among personal and public commitments. In this work I have argued that these commitments do not exist as two separate or independent realms, but as interdependent sets of obligations and warrants that should coexist as productive tensions. Compromise in liberal democracy with its built-in capacity not just for gain but for a continuing fight makes the tension a bearable and productive one.

The temptations of power and the tendencies towards self-deception and cooption run like an undertow in political life. A good compromiser avoids being swamped by these problems. In a good compromise, individuals keep their moral benchmarks intact amid the confusions, frustrations, and satisfactions of politics. While little may be accomplished without the intense involvement of individuals of great ego and ambition, political actors should beware of personally staking too much of their personal self-esteem. Their self-interests can always distort their evaluation of outcomes, and people should question what outcomes they would accept if their own self-interests were not involved. A good compromise does not overvalue one's own gain or indispensabilty as opposed to the concrete worth of the compromise. A good compromise calibrates self-interested gains versus the real goals sought. In a good test, individuals might ask whether or not they would pursue the same compromise if another person held the power and gained the credit. In good compromises, politicians should not accept mere acquisition of sterile power as sufficient to justify a compromise, for there is no simple identification of one's own advancement with advancement of goals.

Political integrity is intimately associated with others who question and push political actors. Followers, allies and friends anchor that integrity and commitment as individuals sail the dangerous currents of exercising power. In a good compromise, people keep their accountability to allies. Holding a commitment to democratic and peaceful procedures should weigh equally, even more so, than commitment to common and ideal goals. At the core, good compromisers struggle to keep their empathy and contact with the moral urgency and roots of their goals. The psychological and moral tendencies of successful democratic politics and compromises often undermine moral independence. Accountability reminds individuals that compromises have concrete effects upon people who rely upon them. Whenever people find themselves purging dissenting allies to defend a compromise, the compromise has problems. In a good compromise, individuals should give up only what is necessary to meet the power and legitimate moral positions of the other side.

The honesty of politicians is maintained by accountability. A good compromise should always be defensible to allies in public terms; the politician should be able to demonstrate a connection between the compromise and the goals sought. Good compromises minimize the need to be enforced against allies and friends. Every politician should seek to avoid having to unleash troops upon his own allies and friends. The moral and psychological costs will devastate the politician's conscience and power. In the course of politics and especially given the dynamics of committing to and defending ambiguous compromises, people can legitimately change their minds. If politicians lose their bearings or change their minds—the two are not synonymous—they should try to change their followers' point of view or change sides. Compromises can sometimes force either course of action for followers or for leaders who take issue with their constituents.[2]

Devotion and single-mindedness are often needed to pursue causes in political orders. These mindsets are seldom attuned to complexity, yet good compromises accommodate complexity and uncertainty. Few concrete solutions embody the exact delineants of what is required by interests or principles. Unanticipated effects always follow from every human endeavor in complex natural and social systems. Most issues cluster around a nexus of several moral principles or interests. A good compromise accommodates reasonable uncertainty about outcomes as well as complexity.

Given the uncongeniality of many single-minded partisans to such concerns, good compromisers need to be attuned to keeping the system open and empowered so that all the relevant issues are brought to the fore. Most interests and moral complexity stems from the freedom and dignity of persons. To the extent that people possess power and knowledge to defend their own freedom, the obligation of individuals to internalize these concerns lessens considerably. But compromises, except in limited cases of self-defense or the enforcement of basic rights, should not assault the foundations of autonomy.[3] Extraordinary moments do arise when compromisers should consciously restrain themselves in order to respect the principled rights of others who are not and cannot be represented. Good compromises should recognize future generations, children, or the disenfranchised.[4]

Compromising well requires not only knowing oneself but knowing one's opponents. Compromising presumes that all sides agree to abide by the solution and play by the rules. In politics, promises remain inherently conditional upon the others' promises. Compromise becomes more viable and defensible the more people can rely upon opponents' good faith and trust their adherence. In a working liberal democracy, mutuality of trust and respect, coupled with an historical record of accommodation, helps make it the preferred way of doing things. In such a system, compromise avoids many of the more dangerous attributes of missignalling weakness or encouraging intransigence. A good compromise builds upon or helps create mutuality and historical records of accommodation.

Opponents stagger neat equations and unquestioned maxims. Humans act in politics with ingenuity, innovation, and tenacity. Self-interest, ambition, weakness, and temptations to power afflict everyone and influence political actions. The deeper the commitments, the higher the stakes, the more likely opponents will view each other as enemies and the more obstinate they will be. The five-decade battle to bring political and social rights to blacks in the southern United States demonstrates the problem. White segregationists incessantly ignored court orders throughout the forties, fifties, and early sixties. The preferred strategy of litigation pursued by Presidents Eisenhower and Kennedy inspired them to prolong litigation, resist enforcement, and invent new obstacles. As black voters increased during the fifties, states initiated literacy and other tests. Local registrars selectively and viciously enforced these tests to keep black citizens from voting. Southern federal judges threw out cases that challenged those tests and slowed the progress of black participation. When white primaries were outlawed, segregationists changed registration procedures and locations, and redistricted to frustrate would-be voters. In the end, local law enforcement authorities unleashed violence upon demonstrators and blacks seeking to register. Even today, many southern localities ignore or sidestep the provisions of the 1965 Voting Rights Act (Ball 1982; Garrow 1978). In the end, only consistent federal actions and enforcement could begin to solve the problem. No good will, trust, or willingness to abide by solutions existed on the segregationist side. They would accept no compromises that did not amount to capitulation by the blacks. In such a world, only coercion, the least effective and desired alternative, makes solutions possible. Only after coercion had made it clear that basic rights would not be abridged could the possibility of a democratic community arise among whites and blacks. A good compromise should not reward or encourage intransigence and militancy. Rather, it should domesticate dissent and open the political order to nonviolent and nonoppressive resolutions. At the same time, a good compromise can always try to pull others into a circle of community and mutual obligation.

If the good faith of opponents cannot be trusted and if the "others" view people as enemies, then the possibilities of compromise are extremely limited. Individuals must fall back upon guaranteed enforcement or mutual deterrence to back any promises. These political solutions might evolve by creating some beginnings of mutual trust and accommodation. Some community might form as individuals grudgingly come to terms with coercively backed realities. But all compromises at this level remain tenuous. Resistance and subversion of compromises haunt all attempts to build a record of trust and reliable foundations for compromise. There may still be good reasons to compromise with professed enemies or adamant opponents in order to avoid cycles of vendettas and lose/lose dilemmas. Individuals may want to create networks of contact to avoid being trapped into dehumanizing and tactically blind images, as the fifties' anticommunism did. This kind of contact can also help avoid vicious escalation games where the dynamic of winning and the fervor of competition overrides any reasonable assessments of loss and gain for either side (Raiffa 1982, Chap. 6). Nonetheless, when coercion and bad faith are brandished against people, they nullify the best moral and prudential arguments to compromise. Good compromises with enemies and untrustworthy opponents are narrowly justified, must be monitored carefully and built upon limited possibilities and expectations of success. Such compromises should be built upon sturdy enforcement and provocability.

Knowing opponents requires careful judgments about their willingness to abide by or be domesticated by compromises. Politicians posture and preen in the heat of battle. Few politicians can resist invoking enemy imagery during debates; others may promise unbending resistance or unyielding commitment to principles and positions (Cook 1980). Beyond the posturing, the taking of stands, and the rhetoric indigenous to political life, a compromiser needs to judge whether or not politicians can and will compromise. Most understand the difference between dramatic posturing and concrete accomplishment. Citizens in liberal democracies, who have not concluded that politics necessarily defrauds, also understand this vital distinction. Most negotiating practices involve some posturing despite the fact that such posturing can trap leaders into untenable positions, which they must later recant or bury.

Politicians build records of reliability and accomplishment within the drama of political life and conflict. This is why knowledge of history is so central to effective prudential and moral compromise. People can know and recognize whom to trust. In a similar vein, it is vital to distinguish violence that compensates for lack of alternative instruments of power, violence that grows from pent-up frustration and powerlessness, and violence designed to incite terrorism or civil war. Good compromises can transcend the rhetoric of unyielding conflict and domesticate nonrevolutionary violence. In these cases, a good compromise addresses the first form of violence because it solves a legitimate moral, political, and social problem within a working political order. Good compromises have the potential to wean individuals from violence into fair and democratic politics.

People need power to accomplish good in politics. Power gives life to autonomy and dignity; it also solidifies oppression. The Faustian dynamics of gaining and exercising power threaten to subvert the direction of compromise. Additionally, compromising is fraught with dangers to a power base. A good compromise should be sensitive to the role and needs of keeping power as a means to an end. In a good compromise, power is deployed to accomplish goals, not just to sustain itself.

The test of any good compromise is whether or not people actually have to compromise. If they compromise when it is not required either by the obstinacy of reality or the moral legitimacy of opponents, then individuals are justly open to charges of incompetence, opportunism, or complicity with opponents. Often, a compromise may amalgamate power for later goals. In this case, people are not required to act, but they judge that an unforced compromise gains later opportunities. Many are tempted to collect power for power's sake, but at the same time power seldom survives if unexercised. Its successful use gains more power. In these cases, good compromises depend upon historical and empirical claims about themselves and actions, but the farther away from identifiable goals compromises for power occur, the more questionable they become. On the other hand, a good compromise should always account for keeping sufficient power to pursue good in the future and maintain a capacity to monitor and implement the accomplishment.

No good compromise should surrender a group's legitimate ability to exist or defend itself, and no good politician compromises the basis of a group to accomplish goals. Often, goals encompass symbolic or ritual victories. The substance of accomplishment requires perduring effort after the public consolidation of support. Additionally, political outcomes can always be assailed and undone in the future. Even closed outcomes like the Thirteenth through Fifteenth amendments were crippled by initiative from segregationists and federal indifference. Jim Crow laws recreated the economic and political aspects of slavery in the south without its more heinous social dimensions, even after the enactment of these amendments. Consequently, no compromise should emasculate power to monitor, defend, or re-agitate for a solution. Only when politicians believe that strong official enforcement will continue or that sufficient trust exists to gain voluntary compliance should they risk large losses of political power for official gains. Good compromises do not leave people powerless.

Amalgamations or coalitions might be used to magnify power or, more to the point, extend goals. Alliances or amalgamations can also be opportunities to move allies closer to a point of view. Any good compromise with other groups should work to extend the power base on the range of vital issues. At the same time, marginal or purely symbolic gains should not unduly decimate ranks of an alliance or discredit leaders. Nonetheless, most politicians must expect some defensible slippage in support when concrete accomplishments unequally satisfy members of the coalition. In time, future pushes for change and proven results should allow good leaders to rebuild their base. A good compromise should allow for extension of the power base, not its contraction. At worst, it should accept an attentuation of power for gains that outweigh the loss and allow for replenishment

Because of their ambiguity, compromises always invite backlash. Opponents will still remain opposed and use the "defeat" enshrined in the compromise to mobilize supporters. Some of the indifferent may be affected by the compromise and suddenly become active opponents. Even allies alienated by its incompleteness or "sell-out" aspects could lash out against it. Backlash poses peculiarly virulent problems for success because they are uniquely centered on the compromise. Backlash can be used, especially with the indifferent or ex-allies, to realign support around a host of other issues. A good compromise always seeks to abridge any backlash effect or provide tools to address the concerns it represents.

Good compromise leaves open opportunities for future change. Keeping an organized power base or resources of power is obviously one precondition for future movement. This future is protected by rejecting excessive coercion and repression within the political order. The long-term role of coercion should always be lessened by good compromises. The actual shape of future changes often depends as much on the symbols and rituals of legitimacy as on lowering the level of repression and keeping power. Each different group will have to convince its constituents to abide by a compromise. But the public record and rhetoric will justify a compromise and give it a legislative, judicial, or political history. These records and rhetorical resources will explain and justify the compromise for future generations. The language of public justification of a good compromise should be compatible with the long-term aims and existence of a group.

A politician should account for all these concerns in seeking to implement goals. Problems which must be acknowledged and weighed arise in traditional trade-offs. One recurring problem concerns the dilemma of keeping access in institutions of power versus maintaining the political base or autonomous power. Every group or person confronts this. To gain access and defend compromise, leaders should maintain allies outside and should avoid devastating morale. Compromises should not be sold as panaceas or revolution. To oversell can undermine internal morale if expectations are not met, while the gap between real accomplishment and expectations can destroy citizens' confidence in their leaders or in the political order. Massive differential gains can also undermine morale by fostering internal disruption. Devil's bargains can also sap élan, for no members of a group like to see themselves or their leaders consistently supporting leaders of groups whom they normally oppose on major issues. They fear their leader's contagion and can lose confidence in their own sense of commitment. Good devil's bargains need time limits and durations to avoid the long-term costs to the alliance, unless long-term communities of mutual commitment can be built.

Finally, a good compromise endures because both sides live up to their promises. More importantly, it means that a compromise can contribute to a history of trust, civility, and cooperation, even if grudging cooperation, which makes a life of minimal coercion possible. To encourage a good compromise, it should be subject to minimum abuse. Constructing institutions or laws that are subject to minimal abuse makes sense for all political actions, given the concentrations of authority, power, and resources involved in legitimate governance. Lessening possibilities for abuse is necessary because compromise possesses morally problematic aspects to the parties and needs to be kept open for re-examination. A good politician will take account of the quality of people available to administer and enforce solutions, the level of knowledge, moral virtue, and commitment required, and the future interpretations and changes in government, all of which might lead to abuses of the authority constituted for the purposes of the compromise.

In the assessments of citizens, the internal dimensions of compromise coexist with the more external systemic and moral assessments that make the practice one that has a sound moral and political priority. In these aspects, a good compromise should preserve the openness of the political order. Given the moral attrition of power, the vagaries of power bases, the tendency to ossify the status quo, and the imperfection of all outcomes, openness serves as an antidote to the troubles with compromise. Openness in politics helps keep politicians accountable to fellow citizens as well as to their consciences. Open futures enable power bases to be reassembled as well as to disintegrate and force politicians to attend to the aspirations of their allies. But openness also presents the risk that great political accomplishments will later be undone.

While everyone would like some total victories or final solutions in politics, they can never achieve final closure short of a cross between *Brave New World* and *1984*. But this openness of any compromise or solution makes change and further questioning of the status quo possible. It enables unanticipated wrongs or harms to be rectified, and solutions can be refined to gain more good. A counterdynamic is built into compromise to move towards revision and challenge as opposed to the tendency of compromise to stabilize the status quo. Openness means that authority must be relegitimated in the eyes of participants. This makes acquiescence easier when losers know they can continue the struggle. This further enhances the role of persuasion and politics rather than coercion in the political order. The less open a compromise makes the political order, the greater the questions that should be posed of it.

Compromises should strengthen liberal democracy, just as they increase openness. The moral principles that underlie liberal democracy are substantially embodied in the act of compromising, but one major dilemma haunts compromise, just as it does "liberal" "democracy." Liberal values suggest the need to close certain avenues of discussion and prohibit certain oppressive practices in order to give liberal life meaning. These areas are defined as noncompromisable for moral, prudential, and political reasons so that human individuality, autonomy, and dignity can flourish. Slavery, oppression, and discrimination on the grounds of religion, political belief, birth, race, sex or ethnicity—all the aspects of encumbered or embodied selfhood—are forbidden. A constitutional order can seek to proscribe the infringement of certain rights and shape future rhetoric around certain rituals and claims of justification. It seeks to close the vaunted openness. Yet, no constitutional order subject to revision can permanently close an issue. Only a strong political culture and committed activism on behalf of the protected freedoms will give them life. Humans can pervert and subvert any text, as the post-Reconstruction South shows on the issue of racial equality. Nonetheless, good compromises should be framed to respect and strengthen the limits necessary to give the practice moral reliability.

Compromises, like liberal and democratic institutions, should justify themselves by producing experienced results congruent with the values that legitimize them. For like compromise, with which I have yoked them, these institutions must earn the free support and active participation of citizens. Good compromises in democratic and liberal orders should not generate outcomes that create permanent political minorities. If these minorities suffer depredation of their basic liberal and democratic rights, such as equal participation, mutual and self-respect, freedom of religion or conscience, equal provision of basic needs or fairness in conflict resolution, then adherence to liberal democracy cannot justify a compromise. These violations of the principled foundations of compromise severely question any political and prudential compromises.

Prudential and political reasons will not persuade politicians or citizens who always lose in compromises. This is especially true when people seek their basic liberal and democratic due. Tradition or symbolic loyalties might lead citizens to seek cooperative rectification of their grievances. But if the political order does not respond to denials of their autonomy and dignity, they can justly resort to militancy or violence to fight for basic rights. Any group of people who are formally equal but possess none of the basic tools of political power confront awful odds in the political arena. They are doubly confounded by the symbols and rituals that justify their demands but support inequality and institutions that stultify their actions. Too many liberal democracies comfortably give these disenfranchised citizens the right to air grievances and then ignore them because they possess none of the tools of power. Compromises in such a world can only guarantee dissatisfaction and injustice. Citizens might literally resort to violence or militancy to gain some bargaining chips in the power equation of an unequal political world. These tactics might also reflect a group's coming of age and its need to show power and gain the official recognition that has been previously denied (Gamson 1975, Chap. 6).

The democratic process and logic of compromise can be respected as long as political militancy and violence are used to restore fairness to a power distribution or call attention to problems systematically ignored by citizens. Such strictures are hard to delineate and suffer from a Sorcerer's Apprentice effect—they can easily get out of control or spawn mirror-image militancy or backlash—that undercuts the whole process of domesticating dissenters or getting even minimally coercive solutions. But as long as militancy does not rage out of control or spill over into terrorism or violent revolution, they reflect no fundamental break in the political order, but supplement the limits of political compromise. Politicians normally committed to compromise might even applaud militancy from their supporters, because the demonstrated militancy outside the institutions of power gives them leverage in office and gains visibility for the cause. Civil disobedience, not usually associated with compromise, represents the most remarkable compromise of all. It allows passions and demands to flourish in liberal democratic political life, while stopping short of violence. Good compromises respond to justified and structurally generated militancy and violence. But in the long run, these compromises should promote adherence to liberal and democratic norms and empower citizens, rather than encouraging violence and militancy.

Beyond openness and liberal democratic concerns, a good compromise answers to natural, social and moral complexity. All the concerns addressed in the sections on prudence and politics can be brought up to question a compromise. At its core, a good compromise results in the best fit between expressed goals and achievement, "all things considered," and people should be acutely aware of the "all things considered" aspects central to political life. Each of them provides grounds for justification in politics.

Most compromises hold. They hold because "all things considered," individuals have sufficiently good reasons to live up to their compromises. This acceptance is enhanced if both sides believe they received a "fair shake," either as an opportunity to fight for their goals or as the recipients of some commensurable rewards or protections. This willingness is increased further if both sides feel the other side is also sacrificing something or did not gain all they sought. Both sides believe that no one dominated the outcome. This clearly does not define the "integrated solutions" discussed in Chapter 3, but it does emphasize that workable compromises are almost never capitulations. Nonetheless, within each compromise lies the possibility not only of good or right accomplished, but of harm or wrong done. These possibilities should not drop completely from sight in a good compromise.

Once a compromise has taken hold, the moral ambiguity and tension that made it an ethical conundrum often drop out. Once individuals have committed themselves to a particular plan, they redefine the advantages and disadvantages and rationalize the acceptance. The more actively people commit, the longer they live with the compromise, the more unwilling they become to reopen discussion of its moral ambiguities (Janis and Mann 1977, 279–308). Sunken costs, desires to go on to other causes, institutional and political inertia all help stabilize compromises (Downs 1967). These psychological and institutional tendencies strengthen compromise, but mean that the harms or wrong of a compromise often fall out of the political and symbolic equations. To take root, any policy needs a strong sense of its rightness, and no one interested in successfully enshrining a compromise is anxious to see its dark side aired.

This tendency towards silence is aggravated by the nature of skilled politicians. Many politicians, especially electorally successful ones, possess attributes such as a sense of humor, affability, a desire to be liked, and a corresponding willingness to adapt and see all sides of an issue. They learn to acknowledge the power of others and seek workable consensus. Many are happier building consensus and accomplishment than tearing them apart. Skilled politicians will be justly proud of their capacity to unite diverse interests into winning coalitions and deliver results. This skill sometimes leads them to underestimate or underplay the harm or wrong left by a compromise. If compromises confirm people in power or gains, they will be even less likely to dredge up its moral limitations.

A good compromise should achieve more good than harm, do more right than wrong. Correlatively, a good compromise should not end all consideration of the wrong or harm wrought. Consequentialist ethics does not need to reduce to forms of utilitarianism, which sum out the harms or wrong done. In these forms, maximizing the overall utility of a situation remains an unqualified good, and moral terms as wrong or evil do not apply to the direct or indirect consequences because the overall result is good. As in subtraction, they simply drop out.[5] In a consequentialist ethic, such as the one supposed by this essay, people can assess harm and wrong done from a variety of moral ideals and principles that do not collapse into one unidimensional assessment.

This keeps awareness and knowledge of harm and wrong alive, even as individuals compromise. People then remain responsible for all aspects of the action. A good compromise allows all moral dimensions to be kept alive and motivates individuals to maintain some momentum beyond the compromise to rectify or compensate for the wrong. Acknowledging harm or wrong done stretches the moral imagination, shapes better and less harmful solutions, and lays the foundations to justify future remedial action.

This means, again, that the political system must be open to unanticipated harms or wrong caused by the compromise. Good compromises should also embody compensation, not for good not yet accomplished, but for wrongs actually inflicted. People should, however, bear in mind the difference between wrong and harms done. Slave owners may be "harmed" by taking away their slaves. People might harm the profitability of firms and increase prices by outlawing child labor practices. But no one wrongs another when taking away benefits gained by exploitation or wrong to others. Any action, not just compromise, should seek to avoid wrong. In many cases, harm visited upon innocent or new individuals by a compromise constitutes wrong, but other harms, especially those done to illicit beneficiaries, should weigh far less in continuing agendas. At the same time, good prudential or political reasons might exist to compensate for harms in order to implement a reform or defuse opposition. Many antislavery advocates, in fact, advocated compensating slave-owners just to minimize the backlash.

To the extent that a system is open and democratically empowered, these demands are lessened upon any one politician. Groups and individuals will let leaders know about harms visited upon them. To the extent that leaders remain accountable to fellow citizens, they will answer publicly for harms or wrongs visited upon groups or good left undone. But, in fact, in no liberal democracies are all groups mobilized and represented. Even if they were, a permanent minority might not be able to defend itself against a stable dominating coalition. At best, pluralistic societies mobilize only some citizens. Even so, many articulate groups are not democratically responsible to the groups they purport to represent. Consequently, it should not be simply assumed that existing pluralism within liberal democracies guarantees good compromises. The self-limiting moral imperatives of compromise are needed to both extend the practice and overcome its practical limits.

The dynamic of politics and compromise points to a disconcerting break between the nature of political morality inside and outside institutions of government. Office holders command the symbolic, financial, and coercive resources of the state. They are delegated power for vital legal and common purposes and possess far more responsibility to respect the autonomy and dignity of others than do ordinary people. The possibility of abusing power should weigh far more heavily upon public servants because they are delegated power on the conditions that they respect and extend the autonomy of all citizens, including opponents, and the exercise of their power is bounded by law and procedure. For them, the common good and a disinterested viewpoint become serious obligations implicit in the roles they assume. These obligations impel them to transcend partisan interpretations and create policy that will be compatible with democratic and liberal civility while moderating the need for direct government coercion. As public servants and trustees of power, they may have active obligations to seek out unrepresented groups when decisions are made and take into account these unarticulated interests.[6] None of these obligations fall so forcibly upon citizen politicians outside the institutions of governance.

Officials "play by the rules" to gain and consolidate their success. Their loyalty and adherence to the rules is partially mandated by law, but also inspired by the need to secure allies and acquiescence from the other participants. Public office pushes them to decisions with tangible consequences and coercive backing in a way no citizen-politician confronts. Public officials are charged with achieving and enforcing concrete actions backed by state power. This constrains them to ensure adequate financing, to worry about the level of coercion needed, and to guarantee legitimacy and widespread compliance. Within any bureaucracy, these concerns are magnified by the pressures of bureaucratic life to compromise with the career and institutional demands of people around them. To implement policies, officials need to compromise with the constraints of official life and legitimacy.

Because they are both obligated to and need to compromise, officials sometimes compromise too easily. As power holders, they are more vulnerable to the corruption of their commitment, especially as they experience the daily frustrations of trying to make policy work. All the temptations of power plague them, as well as the corrosive effects of day-to-day negotiations with opponents and the need to satisfy some opposed demands to ensure concurrence. The ethos of negotiation, central to reducing reliance upon coercion, can lead them to value civility and even cordiality and devalue stridency within the institutions. Comfortable with success, constrained by their reality, officials may combine passionate commitment with moderate means at a time when moderate means simply do not suffice.

Citizen politicians outside government are not so bounded. In fact, they often must create the pressure needed to galvanize officials. Burly politics outside gives officials leverage and direction. Prophets, agitators, witness bearers, and all citizen "activists" give the system its moral energy. They seldom need to value compromise as highly as those who bear the responsibility of office, but this breach should not be exaggerated. Citizen-politicians must hold together coalitions over time, the larger the coalitions, the more compromises are involved in keeping them functioning. Leaders should not delude themselves. They compromise internally both to shape solutions and keep movements alive. If a group becomes established, politicians will negotiate face to face with rivals and reach out to new allies. Ultimately, they may have to join with the allies in government to plan and negotiate concrete plans. At some point, they may even be asked to "put up or shut up" and join the institutions of power to work for their goals. Success will force them to engage the severe limitations imposed by reality when evaluating, supporting, and lobbying with their legislative, bureaucratic, and other allies. When groups and citizen politicians possess enough power and recognitions, they might prudentially decide to use militant methods, but these become exceptions rather than the rule. Militancy, unless used in self-defense, in fighting for recognition, or regalvanizing a musty alliance, can too often become self-defeating. In politics, citizen-politicians should not hide from the reality of their actions while devaluing the liberal and democratic ethos within which they function.

The role and actions of Lyndon B. Johnson in the history of the great twentieth-century civil rights laws illuminates the richness and difficulty of good compromising. No major national civil rights laws had been passed in the United States since the 1870s. Legal segregation pervaded the south, de facto segregation the north. Black voting, power, and politics had been blunted across the land. A coalition of conservative Republicans and southern Democrats hamstrung the United States Senate each time civil rights legislation was proposed. Southern filibusters guaranteed the failure of any attempt to make serious change.

By the late fifties, black political agitation and liberal aggressiveness had injected civil rights into every major controversy. The *Brown v. Board of Education* decision had assaulted the concept of "separate but equal" as a code to justify oppressive segregation and exclusion in the south. Enforcement was slow and halting because black political power remained ineffectual. In the late fifties, Eisenhower and moderate Republicans proposed a civil rights voting act. They acted from a commitment to political equality and a desire to regain the black political vote for the party of Lincoln. Moderate Republicans and liberal Democrats coalesced in the Senate to push for President Eisenhower's legislation after it had passed the House. The vital provision of the law gave the United States Attorney General the power to issue injunctions against a wide variety of civil rights abuses.

Lyndon Johnson, an ambitious and extremely astute legislator from Texas, was the Senate Majority Leader and would become central to all the compromises of the next eight years. Johnson had voted against every civil rights law in his twenty years of service, but he refused to sign the desegregation manifesto that vowed opposition to the *Brown* decision. Desperately desiring to break beyond his position as a "southern" senator and become a national figure and Presidential aspirant, he saw a civil rights victory as means to accomplish his goal. As his career advanced, he became increasingly committed to civil rights and became its major supporter in the sixties.[7]

Johnson believed in victories, not in noble defeats, and excelled at creating viable coalitions by using trade-offs on issues and personal favors as well as forceful persuasion. He strongly believed that no civil rights bill with a federal injunctive power could be passed by the Senate. A southern filibuster would kill the bill and irreparably split his Democratic party. Johnson sought to avoid the defeat and internecine war. First, he threatened the southerners with the possible end to a filibuster. Then he cajoled southern leaders, especially his friend and mentor Richard Russell of Georgia, not to filibuster a bill that was eviscerated of federal injunctive power and that required jury trials for contempt citations. The loss of federal injunctive power would all but doom most major federal initiatives and spread litigation out for years; the jury trial requirement would make it very difficult to get convictions against local officials who defied the laws. No southern senator could hope for reelection unless he either filibustered or allowed a bill that had been properly emasculated to pass. Most feel, correctly, that Johnson firmly believed that he faced a choice between no bill and a diluted bill. Meanwhile, Eisenhower, never a reliable supporter of civil rights, vacillated on the injunction and gave the southerners renewed hope they could get a window-dressing bill.

Johnson's prudence and astute actions produced a compromise that was a symbolic victory and set a significant precedent, but one that actually required little serious change. During the debates, he kept his counsel and took no public position on the bill. Using every IOU and trade-off at his disposal, he quietly persuaded moderates and a few liberals (who owed him favors) to ally with conservatives to pull the injunction power as well as mandate trials for criminal contempt citations.[8] The bill passed but had little serious enforcement power. Johnson explained it this way:

> We obtained only half a loaf in that fight, but it was an essential half-loaf, the first civil rights legislation in eighty-two years . . . There was no way we could have persuaded a majority of the southerners to agree to that provision. To have pressed for the impossible would have been to destroy all hope of the possible, a legislative guarantee to protect voting rights. Once this first guarantee was on the books, the path was open for later legislation extending federal protection into every area of civil rights (Johnson 1971, 156).

It represented far less than half a loaf, but all his justifications remained solid prudential justifications to change the symbolic terms, open the system, and set a vital precedent. The principle became enshrined in public law and rhetoric, even if still ineffectively implemented.

As president, Lyndon Johnson possessed far more power and independence than he had as a legislator. Civil rights agitation pressured for an end to southern atrocities and the unjust distribution of power in the south, and aroused the nation's anger. At the same time, grief over the assassination of President Kennedy made the civil rights bill a memorial to the slain president, giving the principle greater clarity and urgency. The balance of power had changed, and President Johnson prudently refused to compromise; he had seen the "moderating" process destroy too many bills: "I made my position unmistakably clear: We are not prepared to compromise in any way . . . I knew the slightest wavering on my part would give hope to the opposition's strategy of amending the bill to death" (Johnson 1971, 157).

Johnson strove mightily to avoid complete polarization and avoided incendiary rhetoric because he wanted to maintain his ties to both sides. Nonetheless, the battle in the Senate was fierce. Everett Dirksen, the conservative Republican minority leader from Illinois, was given the spotlight by Johnson to encourage Dirksen's support against the filibuster. This time the power equation, and the rhetorical and political climate had evolved—Johnson's tactics worked and the bill passed.

The civil rights agenda needed the capstone of a powerful piece of legislation to guarantee voting rights protection. Johnson's administration had begun work upon such a bill, but was worried over pushing it too fast. But even as the administration worked and hesitated, Martin Luther King and the southern civil rights coalitions initiated a series of marches in Selma, Alabama. The marches themselves emerged from compromises between the more aggressive and the nonviolent members of the civil rights movement. They were designed to precipitate violence against demonstrators and pressure the President to initiate the legislation. Johnson privately resented the pressure of the protests and felt he was being forced to move too soon, but he reacted strongly when the demonstrators were humiliated and beaten, as they hoped, by Alabama police. On national television and before a joint session of Congress, he proclaimed "We shall overcome," and masterminded the 1965 Voting Rights Act.

During this eight year period, Lyndon Johnson, the master politician, rightly deployed most of the best justifications to forge good compromises. Driven by principle and ambition, pushed by liberals and civil rights protesters, he constantly strove to match the possibilities of a moment with concrete accomplishment consistent with a principled commitment to equal rights. Above all he knew the power and limits of his opponents. For years he had worked with them as a southerner and made every effort to not just respect their dignity and position, but to give them every chance to exhaust their own ploys and tactics. In the end, no southerner could complain that he had been humiliated or had not had a fair chance to influence governmental policy. In the process, President Johnson kept the Democratic alliance intact but frayed after both 1957 and 1964–65.

At the same time, he built his own power base carefully. He used power as well as self-interested and principled side trade-offs with blistering effect. He constantly sought to expand his base and persuade moderate Republicans to support his bills. He even swayed liberals to vote for pragmatic changes in the 1957 bill. At the core, he aimed for concrete accomplishments, but settled, during the 1957 campaign, for opening the political possibilities with a largely symbolic victory. The victory set an important precedent and changed the standards of rhetoric and commitment. All the changes Johnson proposed aimed predominantly at opening and empowering the system. In the end, he was willing to risk the need for coercion against the southern segregationists, largely because he had historically seen their lack of good faith and their success in using coercion to blunt black aspirations. At the same time, he managed to keep the Democratic alliance intact for future gains in other areas.

Later, when the timing and opportunity presented itself, even in 1965 when he resented being forced to act, he seized the initiative and used the possibilities of the moment to gain public support. He subordinated his own ego and turned the civil rights bill into a memorial to Kennedy while giving Everett Dirksen great credit, all to gain the victory. At the same time, when the power constellation shifted and he recognized that stakes were sufficiently high, political, prudential, and principled reasons led him not to compromise. The successful forging of these bills, which helped transform the American legal, rhetorical, and political landscape, illustrates how the maxims, especially as they reinforce one another, lead to good compromises.

A good compromise achieves the most good attainable given the goals people seek and the power and resources they possess when they confront the possibilities of the historical moment, and their opponents. The achievements endure by gaining widespread legitimacy with least amount of coercion necessary. These successful outcomes adapt to social, natural, and moral complexity. Their legitimacy is earned in open questioning by proving that they comport with people's basic values and interests and achieve right and good beyond the harm and wrong they encompass. Ultimately, good compromises open to the possibility of refinement in light of ongoing politics and knowledge. Good compromisers seldom have time to touch on each of the major concerns, but in an open and empowered society, almost all the challenges will be raised. The responsibility to raise them lies with active and responsible citizens.

Burke once remarked, "There is however a limit at which forbearance ceases to be a virtue." A strong and principled preference for compromise suggests that the achievement of a goal through democratic persuasion is always preferable to achievement through coercive enforcement of settlements. This preference, however, does not rule out resorts to violence or militancy as methods to assert heretofore denied claims, nor does it rule out resort to just revolution in extreme circumstances. If a political order makes all compromises capitulation; if compromises consistently sacrifice future hope and never change a public discourse that delegitimizes people's aspirations; if every effort to compromise exposes lives and the power base to threats; and if a compromise does not ensure that the other side will "live with" the settlement or "fight fair" by public rules, then compromise gives way to justified militancy and coercion and politics to revolution or tyranny.

The fight for reform and advantage never ceases. Too often, tragedy and tyranny harrow this political world. Individuals and groups sincere in their righteousness wrestle on darkling plains to dominate or destroy. Often, the best of each side is destroyed or corrupted. Sometimes, the victors, gnarled by bitterness or exalting in righteousness, claim cruel victory only to betray their ideals in their anger and pride. Sometimes, exhausted enemies bitterly settle and wait restlessly for renewed conflict, at other times, exhausted and irreconcilable, they welcome a tyrant to save them from their enmity. Good politicians can grope towards accommodation only to lose their moral compass, giving too much, receiving too little. In this world, political compromise guards the borderlands between tyranny and tragedy.

Notes

1. See Nussbaum (1986) for a compelling and insightful account of the implications of such a moral position.

2. These maxims build upon the analysis in previous chapters. They distill the experience of many politicians' memoirs, my own interviews with public servants, and the analysis of moral attrition discussed earlier. They draw extensively upon McCarthy (1957), Fleishman (1981), Warwick (1981), Dobel (1978 and 1982) and Lenin's masterpiece *Left-Wing Communism—An Infantile Disorder,* especially Section VIII, "No Compromises."

3. No plausible autonomy or dignity-based claims warrant political oppression of others. Little moral weight need be given to claims of segregationists who want to protect "their way of life," or to slaveholders who wanted respect for their property rights. Prudence and politics might lead to compromise, but not to morality.

4. Arthur Kuflik (1979, 51–53) summarizes the active link between integrity, action, and compromise. He argues that "integrity is compromised, not when one acts, but when one elects *not* to act, on what one ought to be done, 'all things considered.' " Kuflik argues that individuals can compromise without sacrificing integrity if they compromise: nonmoral interests; mistaken or doubtfully held moral demands; on claims of the other side that are legitimate; because of doubts about concretely correct solutions, or because one values peaceful settlement which fosters mutual understanding and respect.

5. A rule utilitarian might suggest that utility can be maximized by creating habits of remorse or dispositions to guilt for "harm" they bring about in maximizing the good. These theories, however, possess a remarkable degree of disingenuousness. They ask individuals to feel guilt, regret or shame for actions, which are really good by the terms of the theory. Such theories require great amounts of self-deception on politicians' parts, and they tend to

fall apart under the press of reality. The theory asks individuals not to spell out to themselves the full consequences of utilitarianism, which depend upon strong moral duty to maximize the good outcome. Level-headed utilitarians in hard situations will simply see that guilt or regret are inappropriate responses to achieving good.

6. See the essays in Fleishman (1981) that discuss the positive obligations of government officials.

7. This account is drawn from Johnson (1971), McPherson (1972), Garrow (1978), Kearns (1972), and Evans and Novak (1966, Chaps. 7, 16, 17, 22).

8. The bill's provision could be enforced by civil contempt that did not require jury trial, a fact that Johnson knew and used to sell this provision to waverers (Evans and Novak 1966, 134–35).

Epilogue

When the Athenian law-giver Solon had finished his discussions with King Croesus, he set out upon a journey to see the world. From his experiences, he would distill practical and workable guides and laws for his own land. He began a *theoria*. This aspect of the root of theory should remind people that every responsible individual in a free political order becomes a law-giver in his or her actions as a citizen. For individuals not only journey in their life, but are enmeshed in the open, wild, and unexpected travels of politics. Moral reflection and principles as well as prudent and political reflection are absolutely necessary to find direction and meaning on the political journey.

In political life, ethics and justification differ from principled or ideal morality in the same way actual travel in a countryside differs from reading a map. A map presents a two-dimensional drawing of the countryside, which orients individuals to basic directions and locations. People can easily lay down straight line journeys across a map without knowing climate, passable ground, or clear trails. Simple directions about which way to go or a detailed description of the destination are not much help; even memorizing the map and directions does not always help. The map orients and, allied with a personal moral compass, the map can keep persons pointed in the proper direction. But individuals must ford streams, climb steep hills, backtrack, ration food and energy, maintain their party's cooperation, avoid and defend against ambush or wildlife, conquer terrain changes, bad weather, and sudden catastrophes. Usually, people cannot reach a goal by following clean, straight lines on a map. A map or compass that points people through an impassable trail or a pass dominated by bandits only starts one's problems. If several strong ethical forces tug at a person, even the compass might spin crazily and give confused or inconstant readings.

Today, of course, many sophisticated maps chart highways and mark hostels or gas stations. Signs identify stops and locations while police patrol the roads. Most ethics, political and otherwise, occurs unreflectively and follows previously charted practices and procedures. Posted directions, paved ways, and institutionalized coercion channel many decisions. Conflict resolution procedures resolve many quandaries and disputes. Politics focuses considerable energy on fine-tuning these pathways and practices. But political agents also chart and build new thoroughfares, repair old ones, set new destinations, blaze new or uncharted areas, and enter borderlands inhabited by enemies. Accidents, crime, and failure afflict almost all areas of the system and introduce active and complicated dimensions.

A serious political ethic tries to draw richer and more detailed typographies, tracing more dimensions to the world. These maps should be usable by real people. They should not just provide typography; they should warn people where monsters and hardship dwell and identify proven trails. Based on older maps, exploration, and experience, such a political ethics will sketch out the equipment and training needed to handle problems and more predictable crises. The normal problems and emergencies will be enumerated and discussed as accompaniments to the maps. A compass without a map, a map without a compass, and either without knowledge and equipment spell failure or irresponsibility. Ultimately, individuals in the field of politics must survey the land and conditions and decide the proper direction in a particular situation. Its maxims, which should unite prudence, politics, and principle with assessments of dangers and limits, should exist as tools of judgment, not determinants.

To see political life as a journey also focuses on the openness, diversity, and unpredictability of the real world in which people must travel and judge. Friends, allies, and opponents act and introduce both unpredictability and innovation into any travel towards a goal. In such a world there are no havens, only temporary respites. Very little remains stable or solved for very long, and individuals must always struggle to make sense of things or to make things right.

The best individuals should ask for is a justified politics. It may not seem like much, but it has profound implications for persons, for it shifts the burden of responsibility squarely to individuals making up a political community. The giving and receiving of reasons presumes each person is a free and reflective individual capable of meaningfully examining the justifications. People offer, judge, and accept or reject the reasons in political life and also decide which reasons will move them to action. This entails each individual in responsibility for the quality of governance and politics in their society. Justified politics makes each person a citizen.

To believe in the activity of justification and a justified politics entails individuals in the defense of a free and open politics. True reasoning only exists in open discussion where charges and challenges can be offered to reasons, and individuals can answer with reasons that persuade. Whenever coercion or manipulation unduly limits the challenges or outlaws reasons and questioning, politics and authority is not justified, and tyranny or totalitarianism has replaced it. The activity of justification, then, does not presume neutrality or relativism, but builds upon the autonomy of equal and reflective individuals capable of dignified and free action. This, in turn, should lead people to seek to empower all the citizens and keep politics open.

To make sense of things and accept reasons as right or good presumes the existence of a web of meanings, a community in which the reasons are offered, discussed, and judged. People need communities to accomplish right and good and make sense of their lives. But a tragic tension exists at the core of every community of belief. Just as individuals are responsible for the quality of the reasons offered and accepted, communities tend to close and privilege their own terms of justification. They will exclude not just reasons but people who do not accept the reasons or fit their definition of privileged status or knowledge. Any community tends to intensify inculcation of values and practices to make terms more concrete and persuasion more efficacious. Communities always tend to close their circles of meanings and membership.

An individual committed to individual autonomy or equal dignity for humans should profoundly distrust the tendency to close terms and membership and to privilege knowledge. Any individual or community that stops discussion and justification on privileged grounds that "you would not understand," or sets standards of admission that require people to abandon their ability to reflect with imagination and discipline, should be resisted. All groups that claim privileged knowledge for themselves and their kind use the warrants to stop the process of justification and dominate or exclude all who do not share their privileged immunity to reason and question. Anyone committed to a justified politics should always oppose those who would create Gulags of the spirit and call it community.

Individuals in liberal and democratic life determine the limits and strengths of the quality of reasons by their own willingness to raise issues of principle, politics, and prudence. Above all, as citizens they are responsible to raise moral demands for dignity and autonomy and challenge the closure and covert oppression towards which all political communities are tempted. Within a justified political order, individuals determine the possibility for justice by their willingness to offer and respond to claims of humanity and right. Only an open-ended discussion inhabited by citizens capable of judging and acting well can wring humanity, justice, and viability from political life.

Bibliography

Adkins, Arthur W. H. 1975. *Merit and Responsibility: A Study in Greek Values*. Chicago: University of Chicago Press, A Midway Reprint.

Alinsky, Saul D., Rep. 1969. *Reveille for Radicals*. New York: Random House, Vintage Books.

———. 1971. *Rules for Radicals: A Practical Primer for Realistic Radicals*. New York: Random House.

Ambrose, Stephen E. 1984. *Volume II, Eisenhower—The President*. New York: Simon and Schuster.

Aquinas, Saint Thomas. 1967. *On Kingship to the King of Cyprus*. Trans. by Gerald Phelan, rev. and ed. by I. Eshmann, O.P. Toronto: The Pontifical Institute of Medieval Studies.

———. 1974. *Summa Theologiciae,* Vol. 36, *Prudence*. Part 2 of second part (2a 2ae), questions 47–56. Ed. and trans. by Thomas Gilby, O.P. London: Blackfriars.

Arendt, Hannah. 1965. *Eichmann in Jerusalem: A Report on the Banality of Evil*. New York: Penguin Books.

Aristotle. 1965. *The Nicomachean Ethics*. Trans. by Sir David Ross. London: Oxford University Press, The World's Classics.

———. 1965. *The Politics*. Ed. and trans. by Ernest Barker. London: Oxford University Press, Galaxy Books.

Axelrod, Robert. 1984. *The Evolution of Cooperation*. New York: Basic Books.

Bailyn, Bernard, et al. 1981. *The Great Republic: A History of the American People,* 2nd Ed. Lexington, Mass.: D.C.Heath.

Ball, George. 1984. "White House Roulette." *New York Review of Books*. November 8, 1984, pp. 5–11.

Ball, Howard, David Krane, and Thomas P. Lauth. 1982. *Compromised Compliance: Implemention of the 1965 Voting Rights Act*. Westport, Conn.: Greenwood Press.

Barber, Benjamin R. 1984. *Strong Democracy: Participatory Politics for a New Age*. Berkeley: University of California Press.

Beiner, Ronald. 1983. *Political Judgment*. Chicago: University of Chicago Press.

Benditt, Theodore M. 1979. "Compromising Interests and Principles." In J. Roland Pennock and John W. Chapman, eds., *Compromise in Ethics, Law, and Politics*. New York: New York University Press, Nomos XXI, pp. 26–37.

Berkman, Alexander. 1970. *Prison Memoirs of an Anarchist*. New York: Schocken Books.

Berman, Larry. 1982. *Planning a Tragedy: The Americanization of the War in Vietnam*. New York: W. W. Norton Company.

Bickel, Alexander M. 1962. *The Least Dangerous Branch—The Supreme Court at the Bar of Politics*. Indianapolis, Ind.: Bobbs-Merrill Company.

———. 1975. *The Morality of Consent*. New Haven: Yale University Press.

Biddle, Francis. 1957. "The Necessity for Compromise." In R. M. MacIver, ed., *Integrity and Compromise: Problems of Public and Private Conscience*. New York: Harper and Row, The Institute for Religious and Social Studies, pp. 1–9.

Blake, Robert. 1967. *Disraeli*. New York: St.Martin's Press.

Bok, Sissela. 1978. *Lying: Moral Choice in Public and Private Life*. New York: Pantheon Books

Bolt, Robert. 1960. *A Man for All Seasons*. New York: Vintage Books.

Bricker, Phillip. 1980. "Prudence." *Journal of Philosophy* 77, pp. 381–401.

Buchanan, Bruce. 1978. *The Presidential Experience: What the Office Does to the Man*. Englewood Cliffs, N.J.: Prentice Hall, Spectrum Books.

Burke, Edmund. 1900. "On the Beautiful and Sublime." *Orations and Essays*. Ed. Aldine. New York: D. Appleton and Co.

———. 1970. *The Philosophy of Edmund Burke*. Ed. by Louis I. Bredvold and Ralph G. Ross. Ann Arbor: University of Michigan Press, Ann Arbor Paperbacks.

Butler, Lord. 1971. *The Art of the Possible: The Memoirs of Lord Butler*. London: Hamish Hamilton.

Califano, Joseph A., Jr. 1975. *A Presidential Nation*. New York: W. W. Norton.

Carens, Joseph. 1979. "Compromise in Politics." In Pennock and Chapman, eds., *Compromise in Ethics, Law, and Politics*, Nomos XXI, pp. 123–41.

Caro, Robert A. 1974. *The Power Broker: Robert Moses and the Fall of New York*. New York: Alfred A. Knopf.

Connolly, William E. 1974, 1983. *The Terms of Political Discourse*. Princeton, N.J.: Princeton University Press.

Cook, Terence. "Political Justifications: The Use of Standards in Political Appeals." *Journal of Politics* (May 1980), pp. 511–33.

Cooper, David Duff (Viscount Norwich). 1953. *Old Men Forget: The Autobiography of Duff Cooper*. London: Rupert Hart-Davis, Soho Square.

Crick, Bernard. 1972. *In Defense of Politics,* 2nd Ed. Chicago: University of Chicago Press.

Dobel, J. Patrick. 1977. "Bearing Witness and Human Rights." *Christian Century,* September 7, 1977, pp. 751–53.

———. 1978. "The Corruption of a State." *The American Political Science Review* (September), pp. 958–73.

———. 1980. "Coterie Politics." *Dissent* (Fall), pp. 385–88.

———. 1982. "Doing Good by Staying In?" *Public Personnel Management* (Summer), pp. 36–47.

———. 1982a. "Mail Order Ethics: The Nature of Irresponsible Campaign Contributions and the Politics They Finance." *South Atlantic Quarterly* (Autumn 1982), pp. 376–86.

———. 1985. "The Primacy of the National Community." *South Atlantic Quarterly* (Spring 1985), pp. 161–74.

Donagan, Alan. 1977. *The Theory of Morality*. Chicago: University of Chicago Press.

Downs, Anthony. 1967. *Inside Bureaucracy*. Boston: Little, Brown and Company.

Dworkin, Ronald. 1977, 1978. *Taking Rights Seriously*. Cambridge, Mass.: Harvard University Press, A Harvard Paperback.

Edelman, Murray. 1964. *The Symbolic Uses of Politics*. Urbana, Ill.: University of Illinois Press.

Enelow, James M. 1984. "A New Theory of Congressional Compromise." *American Political Science Review* (September 1984), pp. 708–18.

Evans, Rowland, and Robert Novak. 1966. *Lyndon B. Johnson: The Exercise of Power*. New York: New American Library.

Feinberg, Joel. 1970. *Doing and Deserving*. Princeton, N.J.: Princeton University Press.

Fingarette, Herbert. 1969. *Self-Deception*. New York: Humanities Press.

Fisher, Roger, and William Ury. 1981. *Getting to Yes: Negotiating Agreement Without Giving In*. Boston: Houghton Mifflin.

Fleishman, Joel L., Lance Liebman, and Mark H. Moore, eds. 1981. *Public Duties: The Moral Obligations of Government Officials*. Cambridge, Mass.: Harvard University Press.

———. 1981. "Self-interest and Political Integrity." In Fleishman, Liebman, and Moore, eds., *Public Duties: The Moral Obligations of Government Officials*, pp. 52–92.

Follett, Mary Parker. 1949. *Freedom and Coordination*. London: Management Publications Trust.

Foner, Eric. 1971. *Free Soil, Free Labor, Free Men: The Ideology of the Republican Party before the Civil War*. London: Oxford University Press, Galaxy Books.

French, Peter A. 1983. *Ethics in Government*. Englewood Cliffs, N.J.: Prentice Hall.

Friedrich, Carl. J. 1972. *The Pathology of Politics: Violence, Betrayal, Corruption, Secrecy, and Propaganda*. New York: Harper and Row, Publishers.

Galston, William A. 1980. *Justice and the Human Good*. Chicago: University of Chicago Press.

Gamson, William A. 1975. *The Strategy of Social Protest*. Homewood, Ill.: The Dorsey Press.

Garrow, David J. 1978. *Protest at Selma: Martin Luther King, Jr. and the Voting Rights Act of 1965*. New Haven: Yale University Press.

Geertz, Clifford. 1973. *The Interpretation of Cultures*. New York: Basic Books.

Gelb, Leslie H., and Richard K. Betts. 1979. *The Irony of Vietnam: The System Worked*. Washington, D.C.: The Brookings Institution.

Gewirth, Alan. 1978. *Reason and Morality*. Chicago: University of Chicago Press.

Golding, Martin P. 1979. "The Nature of Compromise: A Preliminary Inquiry." In Pennock and Chapman, eds., *Compromise in Ethics, Law, and Politics*, Nomos XXI, pp. 3–25.

Goodin, Robert E. 1982. *Political Theory and Public Policy*. Chicago: University of Chicago Press.

———. 1985. "Vulnerabilities and Responsibilities: An Ethical Defense of the Welfare State." *American Political Science Review* (September), pp. 775–87.

Greenwalt, Kent. 1984. "The Perplexing Borders of Justification and Excuse." *Columbia Law Review* (December 1984) pp. 1897–1927.

Greider, William. 1981. *The Education of David Stockman and Other Americans*. New York: E. P. Dutton.

Griffiths, A. Phillips. 1972. "Ultimate Moral Principles: Their Justification." In *The Encyclopedia of Philosophy*. New York: Macmillan Publishing Co., reprint edition, vol. 8, pp. 177–82.

Halberstam, David. 1969. *The Best and the Brightest*. New York: Random House.

Hallowell, John H. 1944. "Compromise as a Political Ideal." *Ethics* (April), pp. 157–73.

Hampshire, Stuart, et al. ed. 1978. *Public and Private Morality*. Cambridge: Cambridge University Press.

Hardin, Russell. 1982. *Collective Action*. Baltimore: John Hopkins University Press, A Resources for the Future Book.

Harmon, Michael M. 1981. *Action Theory for Public Administration*. New York: Longman.

Haroutunian, J. 1949. *The Lust for Power*. New York: Scribner's.

Hauerwas, Stanley. 1977. "Self-Deception and Autobiography: Reflections on Speer's *Inside the Third Reich*." In Hauerwas, ed., *Truthfulness and Tragedy: Further Investigations into Christian Ethics*. Notre Dame, Ind.: University of Notre Dame Press

Held, Virginia. 1972. "Coercion and Coercive Offers." In Pennock and Chapman, *Coercion*, Nomos XIV, pp. 49–62.

Homer. 1975. *The Iliad*. Translated by Robert Fitzgerald. Garden City, N.J.: Doubleday, Anchor Books.

Jaffa, Henry V. 1982. *Crisis of the House Divided: An Interpretation of the Issues of the Lincoln–Douglas Debate*. Chicago: University of Chicago Press.

Janis, Irving L., and Leon Mann. 1977. *Decision Making: A Psychological Analysis of Conflict, Choice, and Commitment*. New York: The Free Press.

————. 1982. *Groupthink: A Psychological Study of Policy Decisions and Fiascoes*, 2nd Ed. Boston: Houghton Mifflin Company.

Johnson, Lyndon Baines. 1971. *The Vantage Point: Perspectives of the Presidency 1963–1969*. New York: Holt, Rhinehart and Winston.

Kearns, Doris. 1976. *Lyndon Johnson and the American Dream*. New York: Harper and Row.

Kelley, Robert. 1969. *The Transatlantic Persuasion: The Liberal-Democratic Mind in the Age of Gladstone*. New York: Alfred A. Knopf.

Kipnis, David. 1976. *The Power Holders*. Chicago: Chicago University Press.

Kluger, Richard. 1968. *Simple Justice*. New York: Random House, Vintage Books.

Kraditor, Aileen S. 1967. *Means and Ends in American Abolitionism: Garrison and His Critics on Strategy and Tactics, 1834–1850*. New York: Pantheon Books.

Kuflik, Arthur. 1979. "Morality and Compromise." In Pennock and Chapman, eds., *Compromise in Ethics, Law, and Politics*, Nomos XXI, pp. 38–65.

Kuhn, Thomas. 1970. *The Structure of Scientific Revolutions*. Chicago: University of Chicago Press.

La Follete, Robert. 1960. *La Follete's Autobiography: A Personal Narrative of Political Experiences*. Madison, Wis.: University of Wisconsin Press.

Lenin, V. I. 1975. *The Lenin Anthology*, Robert C. Tucker, ed. New York: W. W. Norton.

Les Benedict, Michael. 1974. *A Compromise of Principle: Congressional Republicans and Reconstruction 1863–1869*. New York: W. W. Norton.

Levin, Michael. 1982. "The Case for Torture." *Newsweek*, June 7, 1982.

Light, Paul. 1985. *Artful Work — The Politics of Social Security Reform*. New York: Random House.

Lindblom, Charles E. 1977. *Politics and Markets: The World's Political-Economic Systems*. New York: Basic Books.

Luce, R. Duncan, and Howard Raiffa. 1957. *Games and Decisions: Introduction and Critical Survey*. New York: John Wiley and Sons.

Luker, Kristin. 1984. *Abortion and the Politics of Motherhood*. Berkeley: University of California Press.

Maccoby, Michael 1978. *The Gamesman*. New York: Bantam Books.

Machiavelli, Niccolo. 1965. *The History of Florence*. In Allan Gilbert, ed. and trans., *The Chief Works and Others*, Vol. III. Durham, N. C.: Duke University Press.

———. 1961. *The Prince*. George Bull, trans. Harmondsworth: Penguin Books.

MacIntyre, Alasdair C. 1984. *After Virtue: A Study in Moral Theory*, 2nd ed. Notre Dame, Ind.: University of Notre Dame Press.

MacIver, R. M., ed. 1957. *Integrity and Compromise: Problems of Public and Private Conscience*. New York: Harper & Row, The Institute for Religious and Social Studies.

MacPherson, C. B. 1968. *The Real World of Democracy*. London: Oxford University Press, A Galaxy Book.

Marsh, Peter. 1979. "The Conservative Conscience." In Peter Marsh, ed., *The Conscience of the Victorian State*. Syracuse: Syracuse University Press, pp. 215–42.

McCarthy, Eugene P. 1957. "Compromise and Politics." In MacIver, ed., *Integrity and Compromise*, pp. 19–28.

McCormick, Richard A., and Paul Ramsey, eds. 1978. *Doing Evil to Achieve Good: Moral Choice in Conflict Situations*. Chicago: Loyola University Press.

McPherson, Harry. 1972. *A Political Education*. Boston: Little, Brown and Company, An Atlantic Monthly Book.

Merleau-Ponty, Maurice. 1969. *Humanism and Terror: An Essay on the Communist Problem*, trans. by John O'Neill. Boston: Beacon Press.

Merson, Martin. 1955. *The Private Diary of a Public Servant*. New York: The Macmillan Company.

Miller, Nicholas. 1983. "Pluralism and Social Choice." *American Political Science Review* (September), pp. 734–47.

Mintzberg, Henry. 1983. *Power In and Around Organizations*. Englewood Cliffs, N.J.: Prentice Hall.

Moore, Glover. 1953. *The Missouri Controversy 1819–1921*. Lexington: University of Kentucky Press.

Moore, Mark H. 1981. "Realms of Obligation and Virtue." In Fleishman et al. eds., *Public Duties*, pp. 3–31.

More, Saint Thomas. 1972. *Utopia*. Ed. by Edward Surtz, S.J. New Haven: Yale University Press.

Morley, John. 1893. *On Compromise*. London: Macmillan and Company.

Nagel, Thomas. 1978. "Ruthlessness in Public Life." In Hampshire, ed., *Public and Private Morality*, pp. 75–92.

Neustadt, Richard E. 1964. *Presidential Power: The Politics of Leadership*. New York: A Mentor Book.

Nussbaum, Martha C. 1986. *The Fragility of Goodness: Luck and Ethics in Greek Tragedy and Philosophy*. Cambridge: Cambridge University Press.

Oakeshott, Michael. 1981. *Rationalism in Politics and Other Essays*. London: Methuen.

Olson, Mancur. 1971. *The Logic of Collective Action: Public Goods and the Theory of Groups*. Cambridge, Mass.: Harvard University Press.

Pennock, J. Roland, and John Chapman, eds. 1972. *Coercion*, Nomos XIV. Chicago: Aldine-Atherton, Inc.

———. 1979. *Compromise in Ethics, Law, and Politics*, Nomos XXI. New York: New York University Press.

Phillips, D. Z., and H. O. Mounce. 1970. *Moral Practices*. London: Routledge & Kegan Paul.

Pieper, Josef. 1966. *The Four Cardinal Virtues*. Notre Dame, Ind.: University of Notre Dame Press.

Pitkin, Hanna Fenichel. 1972. *Wittgenstein and Justice*. Berkeley: University of California Press.

Piven, Frances Fox, and Howard A. Cloward. 1977. *Poor People's Movements: Why They Succeed and How They Fail*. New York: Pantheon Books.

Plato. 1974. *The Republic*. Trans. by G. M. A. Grube. Indianapolis: Hackett Publishing Company.

Potter, David M. 1942. *Lincoln and His Party in the Secession Crisis*. New Haven: Yale University Press.

———. 1976. *The Impending Crisis: 1848–1861*. Completed and ed. by Don E. Fehrenbacher. New York: Harper Torchbooks, The New American Nation Series.

Raiffa, Howard. 1982. *The Art and Science of Negotiation*. Cambridge, Mass.: The Belknap Press of Harvard University Press.

Randall, James G. 1945. *Lincoln the President, Volume I*. New York: Dodd, Mead and Co.

Rapoport, Anatol. 1964. *Strategy and Conscience*. New York: Harper & Row.

Rapoport, David C. 1984. "Fear and Trembling: Terrorism in Three Religious Traditions." *American Political Science Review* (September), pp. 658–77.

Rawls, John. 1971. *A Theory of Justice*. Cambridge, Mass.: Harvard University Press.

———. 1985. "Justice as Fairness: Political not Metaphysical." *Philosophy and Public Affairs* (Summer), pp. 223–51.

Reid, T. R. 1980. *Congressional Odyssey: The Saga of a Senate Bill*. New York: W. H. Freeman.

Riker, William H. 1982. *Liberalism Against Populism: A Confrontation Between Democracy and the Theory of Social Choice*. San Francisco: W. H. Freeman.

Rohr, John. 1978. *Ethics for Bureaucrats*. New York: Marcel Dekker.

Rorty, Richard. 1979. *Philosophy and the Mirror of Nature*. Princeton, N. J.: Princeton University Press.

Sabini, John, and Maury Silver. 1982. *The Moralities of Everyday Life*. Oxford: Oxford University Press.

Sandel, Michael J. 1982. *Liberalism and the Limits of Justice*. Cambridge: Cambridge University Press.

Schattschneider, E. E. 1960. *The Semisovereign People*. New York: Holt, Rhinehart and Winston.

Schick, Frederic. 1984. *Having Reasons: An Essay on Rationality and Sociality*. Princeton, N. J.: Princeton University Press.

Searing, Donald D. 1982. "Rules of the Game in Britain: Can the Politicians be Trusted?" *American Political Science Review* (June), pp. 239–58.

Seidman, Harold. 1980. *Politics, Position, and Power: The Dynamics of Federal Organization*, 3rd ed. New York: Oxford University Press.

Sen, Amartya K. 1977. "Rational Fools: A Critique of the Behavioral Foundations of Economic Theory." *Philosophy and Public Affairs* (Summer), pp. 317–44.

Sher, George. 1981. "Subsidized Abortions: Moral Rights and Moral Compromise." *Philosophy and Public Affairs* (Fall), pp. 361–72.

Shklar, Judith N. 1984. *Ordinary Vices*. Cambridge, Mass.: The Belknap Press of Harvard University Press.

Smith, T. V. 1956. *The Ethics of Compromise and the Art of Containment*. Boston: Starr King Press.

Sobel, Howard. 1972. "The Need for Coercion." In Pennock and Chapman, eds., *Coercion*, Nomos XIV.

Sorel, Georges. 1961. *Reflections on Violence*. Trans. by T. E. Hulme and J. Roth. New York: Collier Books.

Sullivan, William M. 1982. *Reconstructing Public Philosophy*. Berkeley: University of California Press.

Tesh, Sylvia. 1984. "In Support of 'Single-Issue' Politics." *Political Science Quarterly* (Spring), pp. 27–44.

Thompson, Dennis F. 1980. "Moral Responsibility of Public Officials: The Problem of Many Hands." *American Political Science Review* (December), pp. 905–16.

———. 1981. "Moral Responsibility and the New York City Fiscal Crisis." In Fleishman et al., *Public Duties*, pp. 266–85.

———. 1983. "Ascribing Responsibility to Advisers in Government." *Ethics* (April), pp. 546–60.

Thomson, Jr., James C. 1968. "How Vietnam Could Happen? An Autopsy." *The Atlantic* (April).

———. 1973. "Getting Out and Speaking Out." *Foreign Policy* (November), pp. 49–69.

Vidal, Gore. 1984. *Lincoln: A Novel*. New York: Random House.

Walzer, Michael. 1973. "Political Action: The Problem of Dirty Hands." *Philosophy and Public Affairs* (Winter), pp. 160–80.

———. 1983. *Spheres of Justice: A Defense of Pluralism and Equality*. New York: Basic Books.

Warwick, Donald P. 1981. "The Ethics of Administrative Discretion." In Fleishman et al., *Public Duties*, pp. 93–130.

Weber, Max. 1969. "Politics as a Vocation." In H. H. Gerth and C. Wright Mills, eds., *From Max Weber: Essays in Sociology*. London: Oxford University Press.

Weil, Simone. 1956. *The Iliad or the Poem of Force*. Wallingford, Pa.: A Pendle Hill Pamphlet, Number 91.

Weinstein, Donald. 1970. *Savonarola and Florence: Prophecy and Patriotism in the Renaissance*. Princeton, N. J.: Princeton University Press.

Weldon, T. D. 1970. "Political Principles." In Peter Laslett, ed., *Philosophy, Politics and Society*. Oxford: Basil Blackwell.

Wertheimer, Alan P. 1972. "Political Coercion and Political Obligation." In Pennock and Chapman, eds., *Coercion,* Nomos XIV, pp. 213–42.

Williams, Bernard. 1978. "Politics and Moral Character." In Hampshire, ed., *Public and Private Morality,* pp. 55–74.

————. 1981. "Persons, Character and Morality." In *Moral Luck: Philosophical Papers 1973–1980.* Cambridge: Cambridge University Press, pp. 1–19.

————. 1985. *Ethics and the Limits of Philosophy.* Cambridge, Mass.: Harvard University Press.

Wills, Garry. 1980. *Confessions of a Conservative.* New York: Penguin Books.

Wolff, Robert Paul. 1972. "Is Coercion 'Ethically Neutral'?" In Pennock and Chapman, eds., *Coercion,* Nomos XIV, pp. 144–47.

Woodward, C. Vann. 1951. *Reunion and Reaction: The Compromise of 1877 and the End of Reconstruction,* 2nd rev. ed. Garden City, N. Y.: Doubleday Anchor Books.

Index

Abolitionists, 10, 13, 19
  role in Missouri Compromise, 65–
  66
  tactics 20–21. *See also* Garrison,
  William Loyd
Abortion, 117 n. 8, 150
  moral complexity of, 87–88
Absolutism (moral), 3, 23–24, 27, 80,
  165
  compared to prudence, 126, 159
  structure of justification, 22–24
  techniques to undermine compromise, 24
  utilitarianism, and, 63
Abstract principles, critique of, 92–
  93
Acceptance, and justification, 54–55
Access, 151
Accountability, 103–104, 143, 170–
  173
  entails citizen responsibility, 51–52
  maintains honesty, 171
  offsets self-deception, 147, 167
  supports integrity in politics, 147–
  148, 170
Accuracy, and prudent judgment,
  125–126
Activists, and moral reform, 183
Acquiescence, to law, 150–151
Adams, Charles Francis, 123
Advise, status of maxims, 169–170
Agents, political, 38–39. *See also* po-
  litical actors

Agitators, 124, 126–127
  compared to public officials, 183
  compromise integrates in politics,
  164
  role in changing political agenda,
  18–21
Alinsky, Saul, 31, n. 7, 122
  on agitation and compromise, 21
"All things considered", 165, 179
  condition of moral principles, 120–
  122
Allies, 20–21, 36, 82, 127, 142–143,
  152
  compromises with, 124–128
  effect on shaping goals, 45–46,
  124–125
  importance to integrity, 145–146,
  170
  justifications to, 36, 45–46
Ambiguity, relation to compromise,
  140, 146–147, 180
Antiabortion, 45–46
Anticommunism, as a justification,
  151, 154–156
Antislavery movement, 65–66, 71,
  126, 181
  as complex coalition, 10–14, 150
  compromise for power base, 127–
  128
  compromise with Union, 135–136
  relation to Republican party, 10–14
Aquinas, Saint Thomas, on prudence, 121, 134, 136, n. 3

Aryan Nation, 85, 115
Arendt, Hannah, 38
Aristotle, 6, 24
Armstrong, William, Senator, 22, 113
Assent, compromise builds, 165
Antiwar movement, 106
Associational autonomy, 85–86
Authenticity, 26–27
Autonomy, 36, 85–86, 127, 157
    justification for compromise, 9, 59,
        70–72, 81–83
    limits of, 55, n. 2, 85–86
    places limits on compromise, 81–
        82
    requires process, 76–77, n. 10
    tension with absolutism, 22–23
    threatened by coercion, 102–103
asymmetry, moral, 88

Background institutions, 94–96
Backlash, and justifying compro-
    mise, 52, 132, 175
Baker, Howard, Senator, 113
Ball, Robert, 113
Baseline, resources in politics, 157,
    164
Bargain, compared to compromise,
    59–63
Basic rights, 171–172
Benchmarks (moral),
    allies help provide, 147–148, 169–
        170
    importance to good compromises,
        140, 169
Benton, Thomas Hart, 24
Berkman, Alexander, 23, 39
Bickel, Alexander, 30, nn. 4, 5
    case for compromise versus moral-
        ism, 15–17
Black yeomanry, 11–13, 150
Boundaries, 103
Bribery, 29, 107
Brown v. Board of Education, 16,
    130, 151, 183–184

Budgets, 127
    hide moral complexity of deci-
        sions, 61–62
Bureaucracy, 153–154
    tendency to compromise, 145–146
Bureaucratization, motive to com-
    promise, 148–149
Burke, Edmund, 14–16, 187
Butler, Lord, 129

Calhoun, John, 29
Capitulation, continuum with com-
    promise, 59, 68–69
Carens, Joseph, 76, n. 9, 98, n. 1,
    161, n. 6
Caro, Robert, *The Powerbroker,* 141–
    143
Catholic Church, 146
"cause", as justification for action,
    39–40
Chamberlain, Neville, 147
Characterization,
    giving moral significance to experi-
        ence, 47–50
    role of justification in, 49
Charismatic leaders, 31, n. 9, 160,
    n. 2
Citizens, 52–53, 169
    focus of responsibility, 54–55,
        102–103
    determine nature of good justifica-
        tions, 166–167, 192–194
Civil disobedience, as a compromise,
    48, 179
Civil rights groups, 106, 135
Civil rights legislation, 127, 151, 160
Civil War (American), 10, 15, 104
Civil war, 50, 105–107
Civility, 17–18
    compromise helps build, 164, 168
    moralism undermines, 15, 159
    as justification for compromise, 53
    role in politics, 102, 112–115
Clay, Henry, 65–66

Cognitive dissonance, 146
Coalitions,
  dominating coalition, 181
  require compromise, 148–149, 175, 183
Coercion, 14–16, 44, 104–105, 129, 133–134, 153
  definition, 36, 102–105
  basic problem in politics, 102–104, 116, n. 6, 172–173
  to limit as a justification to compromise, 52–53, 63–64, 109–111, 176
  relation to promising, 41, 67–68
  moral status of, 106–107, 116, n. 2. *See also* violence
Commensurability, 62
Commitment (moral), 9–10, 31, n. 8, 56, n. 2, 130
  evaluation builds upon, 61–63, 169
  and integrity, 36, 169
  source of obligation, 42, 121–123, 172
  undermined by compromise, 140–145. *See also* integrity
Communitarians, 91–94, 98, n. 4
Community, 66–67, 92–94, 168–169
  coercion helps and threatens, 103, 107–108
  compromise helps build, 68, 83–84, 173
  limits of, 26, 93–98
  of meaning, 41, 45, 150–151
  moral tension within, 27–28, 192–194
  role in politics, 51–52, 106, 111–112
Compensation, 87, 180–181
Complexity (moral), 125–128
  as justification for compromise, 43, 86–89, 122, 167–168
  and prudent judgment, 125–126
Compliance, 150–151
Compromise, 14–17, 64–65, 166, 172–173, 180, passim

definition and explanation, 8–9, 62–63, 63–65, 75, n. 1, 165
  and integrity, 8–9, 82–83
  justifications for, 23–24, 60–62, 70–72, 84–86, 124–128, 132–136, 163–169, passim.
  limits of, 68–69, 146–148, 152–155, 156–158, 159–160, 165, 187–188
  moral ambiguity of, 8–9, 62
  relation to liberal democracy, 2–3, 9–10, 79–84, 109–111
  role in politics, 21, 46–49, 110–111, 163–165
  standards to evaluate, 139–141, 167–170
  of tyrants and totalitarians, 108–109
Concrete effects, focus of prudent judgments, 120–122, 170–171
Conflict, 45
Conflict Resolution, 93–94, 156
  builds on rituals and civility, 47–49, 112–113
Conscientiousness, 80, 121
Consensus, 180
Consequences, 39
  crux of political morality, 53–54
Consequentialist ethics, 180–181
Conservatism, 13–16
  critique of principles and moralism, 16–18, 92–93
  attitude towards compromise, 17–18, 156
Consistency, 96–97
Constitution (United States), 10, 13
Constitutionalism, 90–91, 157–158, 178
Context, as source of justification, 93–94, 168
Conversation, as metaphor of politics, 16–18
Cooperation, 83–84
Cooption, 145
Core values, 123

Coresponsibility, 35–36, 168–169
  justification implicates citizens in, 45, 59
Convictions, 62, 121–122. *See also* commitments
Corcoran, Thomas, 3
Craft selfishness, 150
Credibility, 151–153, 155
Crick, Bernard, *In Defense of Politics,* 90, 101, 115–116
Cromwell, Oliver, 21–22, 31, n. 9
Crucial moment, 129–130
Crusaders, 1–3, 18
Customs, 14–16
Cycles, of retaliation, 109–111, 173

Deceit, 102–103
Dehumanize, 22–23, 91–93, 105
Deliberation, 122–123
Democratic party, 65–66, 157
  compromises of liberal wing, 128–129, 183–187
  Southern members, 144, 158, 184–187
Devil's bargains, 10, 64, 128–129, 176
Devotion to a cause, 171
Dialectic of violence, 105–106
Dialogue, 51
Dictatorship, 15
Dignity, 37, 127
  critique of constituted self, 95–96
  justification to compromise, 43–44, 59, 81–82, 85–86, 164
  limits of, 55–56, n. 2
Dirksen, Everett, 185–186
Discretion, vested in office and roles, 39–40
Disinterestedness, 26–28, 41
Disraeli, Benjamin, Prime Minister, 143
Domenici, Peter, Senator, 113–114
Domesticating violence, 101–103, 174
Domination, 166, 181
Domino theory, 151

Douglas, Stephen, 13, 91, 112
Douglass, Frederick, 19
Durability, aspect of good compromise, 66, 131–132
Duty, 26–27

Earning, as moral justification, 86–87
Economic rationality, 60–63
Effectiveness imperative, 53
  basis of prudence, 120–121
  drives political morality, 41–43
Effectiveness, 141
Efficiency, 62
Eichmann, Adolph, 38
1877, Compromise of, 11, 143–144
Eisenhower, Dwight, President,
  attitude on civil rights, 16, 104, 172, 184–185
  policy towards Joseph McCarthy, 154–156
Embodied self, critique of, 95–96
Eminent domain, 87
Empathy, insufficient for prudence, 97
Empower, 72, 126
  justification for compromise, 83–84
Enemies, 22, 76, n. 6, 103–104
  effect on compromise, 67–68, 154–155
  compared to opponents, 22–23
Enforcement, in a compromise, 133–134, 171, 173
Environment
  compromises in the movement, 45–46
  example of complex compromises, 125, 132
Equal political resources, 157
Equal respect, 157
"Ethic of responsibility", 73–74
"Ethic of ultimate ends", 73–74
Ethics, and morality, 55, n. 1
Ethos, democratic, 83–84, 90–91
Euro-communism, 115

Examination of conscience, 169
Exchange relation, compared to compromise, 59–63
Excuses, 35, 42, 72
Exemplary ideals, 62
Exonerate, 38, 42–43
Experience, source of political evaluation, 49–50, 125, 178
External assessments, of compromise, 177, 167–168
Extremism, 2, 158–159

Fairness, 114–115, 179
Falwell, Jerry, 115
Families of justification, 52–54, 168
Fanatics, 114
Federalist party, 65–66
Federalism, 153–154
Fessenden, William Pitt, Senator, 7, 12–13
Fetus, status of, 87–88, 150
Fifteenth Amendment, 13
Force, 102–103
Foresight, 130–131
Formal equality, 178
Formal liberty, 157
Foundings, and compromise, 48
Framework for judgment, maxims, 169
Francis of Assisi, Saint, 19
Free choice, 46
Free riders, 129
Freedmen's Bureau, 10–14
Frick, Henry Clay, 39
Fugitive Slave Law, 135–136
Fulbright, William, 16
Fundamental political choice, 52–54
Future generations, 25, 176

Game Theory, 75, n. 2, 110–111
    limits to understand compromise, 60–62
Garrison, William Lloyd, 10, 27
    agitation as a technique, 20–21

Ghandi, 96
Gladstone, William, 124
Goals, in politics, 41–42, 63–64
Gompers, Samuel, 149
Good compromises, standards, 167, 187
Good faith, 173
Good, moral status of, 93–94
Good reasons, in politics, 24–25, 43–44, 63
Grant, Ulysses S., 11
Grasp of war theory, 11–14
Grassroots levels, 150
Groupthink, 147–148
Guelphs and Ghibbilines, 110
Guilt, and moral commitment, 9, 72–73
Gut intuitions, 97

Half a loaf, 149, 152, 185
Harm, 73–74
    compared to wrong, 180–181
    justification to act, 43
Hate, 105–106
Hayes, Rutherford B., President, 144
Heroes, 102, 105
High Noon, 9
Higher causes, 23
History, central to prudence, 174
Historical genealogies, 50–51
Honesty, 171
Humanity, as justification, 27–28, 38, 92–97
Humiliate, 110–112
Humility, 80
Hypocrisy, 97
Hythloday, Raphael, 141–142

Ideals, 5, 23–25, 32, n. 13, 145
    roles in politics, 94–97
    underdetermined, 122. *See also* principles
Iliad, 105
    role of speaking in politics, 24–25, 31–32, n. 12

The Iliad or the Poem of Force (Simone Weil), 104–105
Imbedded morality, 94–95
Immaturity, 142
Impartiality, 95–96
Imperfectly shared terms, 46–48, 57, n. 10
Imperious, characteristic of principles, 27
Implementation, 153–154, 165
Incompetence, 119
Incremental change, 143, 149, 152–154
Indeterminacy, of principles, 28. *See also* underdetermination
Indifferents, 36, 46–47
Indifference, moral, 158
Indirect approach, to goals, 141–142
Indispensable person, 147
Ineptitude, 22, 42
Inequality, effect on compromise, 78–79
Innovation, of opponents, 168–169
Inquisition, 134
Instability of compromise, 64–65
Institutional justifications, 90
Integrated solutions, 69–70, 128
Integrity (moral), 8–9, 24–25, 41–42, 80–81, 108, 140–142, 170
  compromise builds upon, 80–84, 140–142, 146–148, 165–166, 169, 188, n. 4
  moral ecology of, 82–83, 157–158
  promising depends upon, 35–37, 40–41
  relation to commitments, 62–64, 123
  responsibility for consequences, 40–41
  threatened by compromise, 141–146, 151–152, 158
Intensity of commitment, 149
Intentions, 53–54, 67–68
Interests, 71–72, 132–133

Internal evaluation, of compromise, 177

Jim Crow Laws, 175
Johnson, Andrew, President, 11–13
Johnson, Lyndon B., President, 16, 106, 109, 130
  attitude toward compromise, 127, 152, 154
  and civil rights, 127, 129, 183–187
  exemplar of good compromise, 184–187
Just repression, 150
Justification, 21–23, 72–73, 128–129, 132–135, 157
  central to free politics, 24–25, 81–82, 166–167, 192–194
  citizens responsible for terms, 51–53
  in politics, 36, 44–49, 124–125
  needs acceptance, 42–44, 54–55
  within a context of meaning or accomplishment, 16–17, 43–47

Kennedy, Edward, Senator, 115
Kennedy, John, President, 19, 130, 172, 185
Khomeini, Ayatollah, 21
King, Martin Luther, 20, 45–46, 96, 186
Kuflik, Arthur, 98, n. 1, 188, n. 4

La Follette, Robert, 149
Law of emulation, 105–106
Legitimate force, 104
Legitimacy, 49–51, 126, 148
  compromise influences, 168, 177
  need to gain for compromises, 49, 64–65, 131–133
  relation to symbols and rituals, 47–49
Lenin, V. I., 23–24, 114, 149–150
Leverage trap, 152
Liberal and democratic life, 25–26, 76, n. 4

criteria to evaluate compromise,
119–120, 140–141, 166
depends upon compromise, 79–80,
130, 165–167, 169–170
needs accountability, 51–52
need to domesticate coercion, 74,
102–104, 115–116
liberal democracy, 9, 19–22, 103,
105–107, 168
criteria to evaluate compromise,
52–53
foundations of, 178–179
depends upon free justification,
44–46
tensions within, 48–49, 177–178
Lincoln, Abraham, 14, 91, 104, 109,
127–128, 135–136
masterful inactivity, 130—131
Lincoln-Douglas debates, 112
Listening to others, 82–84, 164–165
Literacy tests, 172
Lobbyists, 153, 156–157
Logroll, 128
Long, Russell, Senator, 113–114

McCarthy, Joseph, Senator, 154–156
McGovern, George, Senator, 127
McNaughton, John, 154
McPherson, Harry, 16–17
Machiavelli, Niccolo, 51, 110, 130–
131
idea of political morality, 7–8, 22,
39–40
Man for All Seasons (Robert Bolt),
40
Manipulation, 36, 44–45, 52, 75, n. 2
Map, metaphor of political morality,
191–192
Marshall, George, 155
Martyr runs, 111
Martyrs, 18–20, 142
Mass bombing of cities, 134
"Masterful inactivity", 130–131
Maxims of Action, 192

of good compromising, 170–183
moral status of, 168–170, 172, 188,
n. 2
Means to an end, 8–9, 41–42, 71–72
Meat Packing Act of 1906, 135
Merleau-Ponty, Maurice, 119–120
Micro-economics, 60–62
Militancy, 159, 179, 183
Minimum abuse imperative, 133–134,
176–177
Minorities in politics, 178, 181
Missouri Compromise, 65–66
Mobilize, 44–46
Moderates, 66, 124, 145, 156, 159,
185–186
relation to agitation, 20–21, 45–46
Momentum, 125
Morality, as opposed to ethics, 55,
n. 1
Moral
ascendancy, 150
claims, 13–15
complexity, 9, 43, 86–89, 122, 125–
128, 167–168
exemplars, 122–123, 137, n. 5
imperialism, 91–93
narcissism, 121–122
pluralism, 16
purity, 42
self-discipline, 103–104
suasion, 41
theory, 91–93
Moral point of view, 26–28, 95–97
Moralism, 15–16, 19–23
Moral Majority, 2, 114–115
More, Saint Thomas, 20, 40, 141–
142, 151
Morley, John, 3, 122, 96–97, 144–
145, 158
Moses, Robert, 96–97, 142–143, 147
Motivate, 92–93
Multiple audiences, and justification,
45–48
Mutual gain, 128

Mutual respect, 83–84
Murder, 46

National security, 38
Nazi party, 85, 115, 146
Necessity, 80
Negotiate, 39, 69–70, 145–146
"Nice" tactics, in game theory, 110–111
Nonlinear, political morality, 124–125. *See also* oblique
North, United States, 66, 126

Oakeshott, Michael, 14–16, 18, 30, nn. 3, 4, 5
Oath, 40. *See also* promise
Obedience, 52
Obstinacy of reality, 42–44, 103, 141
Obligations, 25–26, 37–39, 84–86, 96
    from promises, 36, 40–43, 66–68
Oblique, political morality, 130, 165
Obstacles, to action, 126. *See also* effectiveness imperative
Office, and personal responsibility, 38–40
Olson, Mancur, 129
Openness, 177
    aspect of prudence, 53–54, 134–136
    justifications for compromise, 175–176
    role in politics, 45–47
Oppenheimer, Robert, 155
Oppression, 17–18, 104, 166
Opponents, 48–49, 82, 101–103, 142, 152–153, 172–173
    absolutists and, 22–23
    compared to enemies, 67–71
    compromise with, 36, 84, 45–47, 52–53, 130
Optimism, 144–145
Ordering, of principles, 32–33, n. 14, 86–87
Organized Groups, 156–157

Paradox of compromise, 140–141
Pareto limits, 61
Parliament (English), 145
Participation, 72, 126–127, 153–154, 177–178
Passion, 75, 124, 130, 182–183
Patroklos, 24
Peace, 101–104
Performance, standard to evaluation promises, 67–68
Periander, 108
Persuasion, 63–64, 71–72, 84–85
    and community of meaning, 41, 93–95, 150–151
    and justification of liberal democracy, 42–44, 187
Plato, 7, 107–109
Pluralism
    in political justification, 24–25, 54–55, 91, 93–94
    moral, 32–33, n. 14, 165–166
Pluralist democracy, 157–158
Polarization, 2, 15, 52, 63, 124, 159, 185–186
Political
    actors, 59–60, 166–168
    agenda, 19–20
    peace, 102–103
    realities, 164
    success, 51–52, 131–133
"Political schizoid", 21, 31, n. 7
Political morality, 37–43, 191
    consequentialist, 51–52, 53–55, 165, 167
    nonlinear and oblique, 37, 124–125, 130, 165
    and personal morality, 37–41, 56, n. 4, 147–148
Politics,
    based on justifications and the word, 24–25, 36
    family of justifications, 6, 101–104
Popular sovereignty, 91
Possibilities
    of a culture, 123–124

of justice, 194
of politics, 103
Postures, political, 173–174
Potter, David M., 112
Power, 157, 164
  acquisition as a justification, 53–
    54, 63–64, 122, 127–128, 167,
    174–175
  as others, 43, 126, 156–157
  temptations of, 142–144, 151–152
Power base, role in compromises,
    127–128, 140, 147–150
Precedent, 135, 151
Preclearance, 153–154
Preference, 65, 95
Prejudice, 97–98
Primary goods, 84–85
Principles, 7–8, 11–13, 26–28, 71–72
  characteristics of, 25–28
  critique of, 15–16, 92–93
  justify compromise, 80–86
  role in political morality, 5–6, 18,
    26–29, 94–97
Privileged knowledge, 193
Proabortion, 46, 149
Process, 71–72, 76, n. 10, 157–158
Promises, 123
  conditions of, 23, 67–69
  moral status, 56, n. 6, 62–63, 82–
    83
  role in compromise, 8, 35–36, 40–
    42, 62–63, 156, 172
Property rights, 86–87, 157
Prophets, 18–23, 164
Protest, 148–149
Provocability; 173
Prudence, 131
  as a family of justifications, 6, 53–
    54, 119–131, 136, n. 1
  difference from principles, 120–122
Public persona, 95–96
Public officials, 143, 169, 181–183
  special permissions of, 38–40
Public opinion, 130

Public rituals, 164
Punishment, 103
Purity, moral, 23, 73, 141–142
Purposes of politics, 164–165
Purposeful ambiguity, 135

Radicals, 145
Rationalism, 15–16, 18
Rationalize, 146–147, 180
Rawls, John, 32–33, n. 14, 94, 114,
    157
Reagan, Ronald, President, 23, 156,
    158
Reactionaries, 161, n. 5
Realism, 51, 56, n. 7, 92
Reffutable, 168–170
Reciprocity, 66–67
Reconstruction, post-Civil War, 10–
    14, 104, 150
Redemption (1877), 144
Redistribute, 86
Reflective equilibrium, 32, n. 14
Reflection (moral), 123
  impartial and disinterested, 5, 37–
    38
  as moral discipline, 26–28, 94–97.
    See also moral point of view,
    principles
Reform, 18
Regime values, 24
Republican party, 10, 135–136, 144–
    155, 153–155, 184–187
  Radical wing, 10–13, 158
  tensions within, 11–13, 128, 150
Resources, political, 70, 124, 129–131
Respect, 82–84, 113–114
Responsibility, 61–62, 103, 192–194
  entailed by integrity, 37–39
  includes all consequences, 40–43,
    63, 181–182
  personal for actions, 8–9, 38–40,
    65–66
Revolutionary politics, 50
Revolutionary War (United States),
    104

Rhetoric, 28–29, 176
Right, as opposed to good, 93–94
Rituals, 150–151, 175
    contribute to civility and legiti-
        macy, 46–48, 103, 112–113, 176
    reason to compromise, 63–64, 131–
        132
Roles, and responsibility, 38–40
Roosevelt, Franklin, President, 21
Roosevelt, Theodore, President, 135
Rorty, Richard, 57, n. 15
Rostenkowski, Daniel, 169
Routinize actions, 153
Rules of the game, 145, 172
Russell, Richard, 184

Saints, in politics, 19, 102, 132
Saviors, in politics, 103–104
Savonarola, 22, 31, n. 9
Second-order reflection, 60–61, 94–
    96
Secret intentions, 141–142
Security, 25, 101–104
Segregation, 16, 126–127, 151–152,
    172
Self-image of groups, 150
Self, theories of and politics, 93–97
Self-deception, 3, 51, 96–97, 140–
    141, 145–147, 166, 170
Self-defense, 68, 171, 174–175, 183
Self-esteem, 146, 170
Self-interest, 67–69, 132–133, 170
Self-limiting actions, 80–84, 90, 171,
    181
Self-respect, 80–83
Self-worth, 142
Selfishness, 142
Selma, Alabama, 127–128, 130
Seward, William, 127–128, 130
Shape, 65, 121–123
    give concrete form to goals, 122–
        126
Shared
    terms, 53
    understandings, 28–29

Shoulder rubbing effect, 148
Single-issue groups, 117, n. 9, 159
Skills, political, 83–84, 140–141, 169
Slavery, 13, 91, 181
Smith, T. V., The Ethics of Compro-
    mise, 80, 116
Social practices, 131–132
Social security, 113
    compromise of 1983, 22, 110–111,
        133
Socialize, 117, 114
South (United States), 126, 144
Southern Baptists, 45
Southern Christian Leadership Con-
    ference, 126–127
Sorcerer's Apprentice effect, 179
Special permissions, of office, 38–41
Speaking, as essence of free politics,
    81–82
Spiral, of violence, 105–106, 109–111
Stalin, Joseph, 21
States' rights, 11–12, 85
Stevens, Thaddeus, 10, 12–13
Stockman, David, 113, 156–157
Subhuman, 81
Sumner, Charles, 7, 10, 11
Sunken investment trap, 152
Symbols, 19, 64, 130–132, 153, 157,
    175–178
    persuasion depends upon, 46–48,
        150–151
Sympathy, 121

Tax Cuts of 1981, 152–153, 156–157
Taxation, 132
Temptations of power, 146–149
Tenacity, 140–141
Terrorism, 50, 73–74, 104–105
Mother Theresa, 19
Thrasybulus, 108
Threats, in politics, 67–68
Timing, as justification, 129–130
"Tit for tat", 111–112
Toleration, 158

Totalitarianism, 93, 102–103, 108–109
Torture, 134
Trade-off, 9
Tragedy, in politics, 74, 77, n. 11
Transform, terms of justification, 50–51, 123, 132
Traps, of compromising
  effectiveness, 151–152
  leverage, 152
  tar baby, 152–153
Trimming, as a way of life, 144–145
Trumps, in moral argument, 26–27
Trust, 41–42, 67–70, 107, 113, 151, 174
Truthseeking, aspect of prudence, 53–54, 122, 125, 134–135
Truth, Sojourner, 19
Tyranny, 90, 103–104, 107–109

Unanticipated consequences, 134–135
Unanticipated wrongs, 174, 181
Unconditional surrender, 112
Underdetermination, of principles and ideals, 48–49, 122–123, 132–133
Union (United States), 66, 91, 135–136
Unionists, 10, 90–91
Unions (labor), 129, 145
United States Information Agency, 155–156
Universality, 92, 95–97
Urgency, moral, 156
Utility, 60–63
Utilitarianism, 73, 75, n. 2, 86, 165, 188, n. 5

limits on justifying compromise, 60–64, 69
Utopian moral theory, 136, n. 4

Veil of ignorance, 97, 99, n. 9
Vidal, Gore, *Lincoln: a Novel*, 104, 109
Vietnam War, 151, 154–156
Violence, 41, 50, 74–75, 106–107, 126–127, 174, 179–180. *See also* coercion
Voluntary compliance, 153–154
Voting, 61–62, 75, n. 2
Voting Rights Act of 1965, 153–154, 172, 186

Wade, Benjamin, Senator, 11
Walzer, Michael, 77, n. 11, 98, n. 5
Warrants, for coercion, 95
Weber, Max, 23, 31, n. 9, 73–75, 77, n. 11
Welfare programs, 132
Weil, Simone, 104–105
Whig party (American), 66, 90–91, 127–128, 149, 156
White primaries, 172
Williams, Bernard, 98, n. 5
Wills, Garry, 30–31, n. 6
Wilson, Henry, 13
Win/win, outcomes in game theory, 111–112
Witness bearers, 19–21
World War II, 112
Wrong, address as justification to act, 433, 72–74, 181

Zero sum game, 69
Zealotry, 3, 19–23